INDIAN KITCHENS

TREASURED FAMILY
RECIPES FROM
ACROSS THE LAND

ROOPA GULATI

INTERLINK BOOKS
AN IMPRINT OF INTERLINK PUBLISHING GROUP, INC.
NORTHAMPTON, MASSACHUSETTS

FOR MY FATHER, BALDEV SETHI, WHO DEDICATED MUCH OF HIS LIFE TO THE BRITISH NHS AS AN OPHTHALMIC SURGEON.

First published in 2025 by

Interlink Books
an imprint of Interlink Publishing Group, Inc.
46 Crosby Street
Northampton, MA 01002
www.interlinkbooks.com

Published simultaneously in Great Britain by Bloomsbury Publishing Plc.

Text © Roopa Gulati, 2025
Recipe photography © Yuki Sugiura, 2025
Indian photography © Roopa Gulati, 2025

All rights reserved. No part of this publication may be reproduced or transmitted in any form or by any means, electronic or mechanical, including photocopying, recording, or any information storage or retrieval system, without prior permission in writing from the publishers

Library of Congress Cataloguing-in-Publication data available

ISBN 978-1-62371-651-6

10 9 8 7 6 5 4 3 2 1

MIX
Paper | Supporting responsible forestry
FSC® C004800

Editor: Rowan Yapp
Project Editor: Emily North
American Edition Editor: Leyla Moushabeck
Designer: Sarah Greeno
Photographer: Yuki Sugiura
Food Stylist: Valerie Berry
Prop Stylist: Jennifer Kay
Proofreaders: Susan Low, Jennifer McKenna
Indexer: Hilary Bird

Printed in Dubai by Oriental Press Ltd.

To find out more about our authors and books visit www.interlinkbooks.com and sign up for our newsletter

CONTENTS

INTRODUCTION
6

SMALL PLATES
24

LARGE PLATES
94

VEGETABLE SIDES
214

242
DALS & PULSES

276
ACCOMPANIMENTS

290
SWEETS

314
INDEX

INDIAN KITCHENS

TREASURED FAMILY RECIPES
FROM ACROSS THE LAND

I've written this book many times in my head, and although the content has been chopped and changed over the decades, its focus has remained constant. This is a book about the talents of India's home cooks, who, without fanfare, put meals on plates and keep cultural traditions alive and communities together. They are my friends, colleagues, neighbors and relatives; they are the people I've cooked with, shared meals with and learned from. They are also people I've met while traveling—drivers, home caterers in urban kitchens, and mothers cooking for their extended family on an open fire. And, alongside their recipes, I've shared my own classic recipes, as well as modern interpretations inspired by my own background.

I grew up in Cumbria, England, the daughter of Punjabi immigrants, who settled in the village of Dalston, on the outskirts of Carlisle, in the mid 1960s. Ours was the first Indian family in the area, and for many years the only one—so there is such a thing as Cumbrian Indian, and I am an early claimant to the title. Mom wore her Indianness with pride. I remember her tightly lidded spice box crammed with pods, sticks and seeds—the seasoning kit for her curries and biryanis.

If anyone thought her billowing silk saris, the bindi on her forehead (imprinted with Elizabeth Arden lipstick) and her cooking were, well, a bit unusual, no one actually said so. It didn't take long for talk of her fragrant masalas and perfectly round chapatis to spread, and for mom to host informal cooking demonstrations for neighbors and friends. I can vouch that British Herdwick lamb, reared on the Lake District fells, really does make for an outstanding biryani. Although flamboyant and creative with daily Indian meals, she remained faithful to traditional Cumbrian recipes too—the wildest spice ever to make it into her shepherd's pie was a snuff's worth of white pepper, ready ground, from the local corner store. Fusion wasn't on the menu—it was the late 1960s.

Mom became intrigued and excited by British baking, and with the help of our neighbors, Avril and Joan, she soon got the hang of rubbing fat into flour for scones and making a Victoria sponge. We both spent weekends cooking for the family and soon I was feather-icing cakes, whisking meringues and blind baking flans, with only an occasional cremation and curdled custard to dent my enthusiasm. Having conquered northern English comfort food, I left Cumbria in 1981 for London at eighteen years old, to complete a diploma in French cookery at Le Cordon Bleu. Most students went on to cook directors' lunches in London before marrying and settling down to host elegant dinner parties. My kitchen tools went straight into wooden crates, ready for shipping to a new home in Delhi.

I lived in India for close to two decades and was a chef at the Taj Mahal Hotel in New Delhi for five of those years. During my time, I worked with and learned from Maharajahs and their cooks, and world-class chefs. But it was the regular kitchen hands, drawn from all over India, who introduced me to India's culinary diversity, often through simple staples served in the staff cafeteria. I remember the warmth of steamy South Indian *rasam*—peppery lentil broth—on a chilly January morning, and breakfasts of Mumbai-style *vada pav*—fried potato dumplings served in burger buns with fresh cilantro and mint relish. I was soon invited to my colleagues' homes, where I met their families and friends, and learned from and cooked with aunties, grandmas, ayahs and home helpers. I also bartered my Cordon Bleu recipes for the lowdown on smoking paneer and making curries that glistened like consommé. For me, these were the dishes that defined and distinguished India's diverse communities.

My intention in this book isn't simply to share recipes, but to give some insight into the daily lives and kitchen routines of twelve talented home cooks. These contributors are drawn from different communities, and each has a distinctive cooking style reflective of India's varied cultures. They have all shared a much-loved family recipe, which I've recorded so that readers can recreate the flavors of regional India in their own home kitchens. In writing this book, I spent six weeks traveling across India, chatting with families, visiting their local markets and watching cooks pound masalas and prepare meals.

I discovered that, although regional cuisines have distinct characteristics, what brings people, places and good food together is a generosity of spirit. I've been in homes when several guests have arrived unannounced for lunch and the host didn't miss a beat in pulling up extra chairs around the table, or putting more steel thalis on the floor. When I lived in India, it was normal for us to hold back a portion of dal and rice just in case an extra diner dropped by—as they often did.

The handing down of recipes remains very much an oral tradition. Like my own mother, the twelve contributors to this book never referred to written notes while making their dishes. Simmering meat masalas were assessed for readiness with an appraising eye on the pot and not the clock, and spices sizzled in hot oil until they smelled just-so. I'm reminded of my mother's vague directions to "cook the curry until it is done" or to "use the normal masala when frying fish." In compiling this book, I've tried to provide less enigmatic directions, and developed recipes for those curious home cooks who would like a gentle steer and helping hand in making their own Indian dishes.

▶

In my interviews, I asked the home cooks about the popularity of international fast-food brands in India, and whether they were concerned about their own culinary heritage being overshadowed. They were dismissive: "A paneer pizza is hardly going to outshine the likes of our snacks and kebabs!" I also had versions of "everyone wants to return home when they miss the comforting hug of my dal and chawal [rice]". They are right. Although global burger and fried-chicken outlets are popular in airports and cities, the largest lines are for Desi Indian choices. One consequence of Covid and lockdowns has been an increase in food delivery businesses, and in larger towns and cities, customers are now ordering affordable, top-quality regional meals, made by cooks in their own home kitchens. The variety of menus is dazzling and outdoes most Western fast-food choices.

Cooking styles reflect the landscape and cultural beliefs of communities, and dishes retain their distinctive nature, often because they are rooted in the region. And yet, even within the same household, two cooks will make dal with similar ingredients but personalize their own offering with contrasting spices and finishing flourishes. Both dals will be authentic to the area—but Indian home cooking isn't shaped by formulaic recipes. Its attraction is in difference and diversity. In this book, I hope to give voice to those little-known home cooks who live in hamlets, bustling cities, coastal villages and small towns.

It has been a long time since an in-depth exploration of regional India was the focus of a cookbook. While traveling, I discovered that there's little risk of the country's dishes being reduced to a homogenized commodity—at least not in home kitchens. I love how the people I talked to, whether in Mumbai or Delhi, passionately believed that their community's cooking led the way when it came to rating the best Indian dishes.

As I write, on a grey and wintry morning in England, I know I can bring sunshine and warmth into my kitchen with a simple dal for lunch. All the recipes in this book have a supporting cast of associated memories. In the hills of Coorg, the aroma of pork simmering in dark, glossy, vinegary masala is as unforgettable as my three-hour taxi ride in darkness back to the plains. Windscreen wipers swishing furiously against sheets of rain, the driver braked as the headlights picked out a fat yellow snake slithering across the wet road. I wanted for nothing while crossing the Arabian Sea in a ferry at dawn—the warm breeze was on my face and, for a couple of rupees, I feasted on a fabulous green chile-laden *vada pav*. In Old Delhi, I visited a 200-year-old *haveli* (a spacious townhouse with an open courtyard) and watched the cook take the lid off a pan of red chile "mutton" curry, while the call to prayer from the Jama Masjid mosque next door reverberated around the kitchen.

▶ I've been welcomed into the kitchens of Parsi, Rajasthani, Bengali, Jewish and Kashmiri contributors and introduced to the nuances of Tamil-Franco cooking in Pondicherry. I stayed at a homestay in Kerala where fabulous meals were seasoned with spices harvested from the host's tropical garden. Then there were the bright lights and crowded markets of Mumbai; a memorable visit to rural Gujarat; and the warmest of welcomes extended by my cousin's family in North Delhi. Each of the home cooks I met shared extraordinary stories from their everyday lives.

India isn't a closed book—it absorbs influences from global kitchens and has done so for centuries. Alongside indigenous recipes, there are imports from Central Asia, the Middle East and Southeast Asia. Other nations bring a dish to the table too, including Britain, Portugal, France and China. The French governed Pondicherry for 280 years and left an indelible mark on its cooking style. There isn't really any such thing as imported dishes from abroad—somewhere along the line, dishes are naturalized and absorbed into the Indian recipe repertoire. In this book I'll recognize these influences and give *moules marinère* a South Indian flourish, fry Goan-style chorizo with chile-flecked onions, and fill puff pastry patties with Punjabi-style paneer. I've also given a nod to the changing tastes and lifestyles of modern India as well as its historical past.

Some Indian ingredients aren't easily available over here, so I've used alternatives that will work well. I've used milder Kashmiri chiles instead of specialist varieties, and although this impacts on the fiery strength of finished dishes, it doesn't detract from the overall character. Full-fat Greek yogurt has been used instead of the *dhai* made daily in Indian kitchens, because it has a high fat content and is less likely to split on cooking. Lentils, dried beans and legumes bought in the West take longer to cook than Indian varieties, and I've made an allowance for this in the methods. The use of "mutton" in Indian kitchens can be confusing, especially as it usually refers to goat meat. I've used lamb for my recipes, although goat would work equally well. You can buy all the ingredients used in this book in supermarkets, South Asian stores and online stockists. Whole spices will keep for 6–9 months in tightly lidded jars at room temperature. However, once they are ground, they will lose aroma and flavor within a few weeks. To retain freshness, it's a good idea to seal any extra powdered spices in bags and store them in the freezer. The exception to this is turmeric and chile powder, which remain good for 3–5 months in an airtight jar.

This book promises to guide both kitchen novices and practiced hands into making their own masalas and fragrant spice blends. Indian food doesn't need to be complex, and the simplest of dishes are often the most memorable.

INTRODUCTION

THE SIX REGIONS

I have featured recipes from six roughly designated geographical regions: the Himalayan Belt, Northwest India, Northeast India, Central India, West India and South India. It's not a definitive guide to the country's kitchen heritage—India is too large and diverse for this book to do justice to such a rich tapestry of culinary tradition. As you read these recipes, you'll become familiar with those much-loved spice blends and seasonings favored by home cooks living in different states. Some of these dishes will have their origins in the Himalayan foothills, the plains of Punjab, or perhaps the coastal kitchens of Cochin. For me, the best way to get to know India's various communities is through its diverse tastes, preferences and recipes. I hope you enjoy bringing a little bit of regional India into your own home kitchen as you cook.

HIMALAYAN BELT
HIMACHAL PRADESH, KASHMIR

The abundance of fresh fruit, mushrooms and seasonal vegetables grown in the Himalayan foothills contrasts sharply with often frugal pickings from a harsh and high-altitude terrain. Food that lasts is very important here—spiced pickles and preserves go a long away in helping to perk up meals during the cold winter months. There's an emphasis on wholesome pulses paired with robust flavors, such as asafoetida and dried ginger, and in some remote areas, chiles are elevated to a main ingredient. In Kashmir, Mughal-inspired dishes are influenced by the cooking traditions of Central Asia and include sophisticated rice dishes, fragrant with saffron and sweet cardamom, and slow-cooked lamb ribs simmered in milk, spiced with fennel seeds.

NORTHWEST INDIA
DELHI, PUNJAB, HARYANA

Often referred to as the granary of India, Punjab's fertile farmland provides generously for its people. In addition to breads, the state is famed for its dairy produce, meat and poultry, and earthy masalas. Punjabi cooking is known for its simplicity and big, bold flavors—expect plenty of smoky, grilled kebabs and hearty curries cooked in ghee. In Delhi, there are other communities too, such as the Baniyas, who will season their vegetarian dishes with tart spices such as mango powder, and the Kayasths, whose recipes combine Muslim and Hindu cooking styles.

NORTHEAST INDIA
WEST BENGAL, BIHAR, NAGALAND, ASSAM

Mustard oil is the preferred cooking medium in this part of India. In the higher reaches of the Northeast, basic spices are used, but it's usually herbs and hot, often smoked chiles that take center stage. Mustard seeds are a key seasoning in West Bengal—it's a spice that works especially well with fish and seafood preparations. For religious reasons, many Hindus here don't cook with onions and garlic, preferring the distinctive nature of nutty-tasting poppy seed paste, popped mustard seeds, ginger and *panch phoran* (a blend of five whole spices; see page 20). Expect a spectrum of flavors across the region, ranging from sweet and mild to the mouth-numbingly fiery.

▸ CENTRAL INDIA
MADHYA PRADESH, RAJASTHAN, UTTAR PRADESH

Influenced by the cooking styles of neighboring Rajasthan, Gujarat, Uttar Pradesh and Maharashtra, home cooks in Madhya Pradesh transform simple staples with the creative use of spices. A trio of nigella, fenugreek and fennel seeds, when dropped into oil, lends a pickled flavor to masalas, while the pungency of asafoetida is matched with turmeric and fried chiles in whipped yogurty masalas. In Bhopal and Lucknow, a regal culinary heritage showcases often complex masalas; in Rajasthan, dishes from palace kitchens are acclaimed for their richness and chile-laden masalas. Many of the Marwari community are settled here and follow a vegetarian diet, often excluding eggs, onion or garlic.

WEST INDIA
GOA, MAHARASHTRA, GUJARAT

The use of spices in Western India reflects the varied landscape and culture of its people. The desert-like landscapes of parts of Gujarat contrast with the tropical coastline of Maharashtra and Goa and the cooking styles are as distinctive. Savory dishes in Gujarat are characterized by sweet-sour flavors underpinned by astringent spices and jaggery—but along the Konkan coastline, hot-and-sour fish and seafood curries, softened by creamy coconut milk and often cooked with fruit such as green mangoes, are famed. Goa is well known for its garlicky Indo-Portuguese repertoire of dishes, inspired by its history.

SOUTH INDIA
KERALA, TAMIL NADU, ANDHRA PRADESH, KARNATAKA

Rice, in all its guises, is the staple here and curries are likely to be seasoned with cardamom, cinnamon and black peppercorns grown in Kerala. Coconuts provide a cooling contrast to robustly spiced dishes, while in Andhra Pradesh, masalas deliver a fiery kick from locally grown red chiles. No home is without a bunch of citrussy curry leaves, to be crackled into hot oil. Hyderabad is famed for its biryanis, with many dishes traced to Persian heritage. Familiar, everyday food is as memorable: simple dals sharpened with tamarind, thorans similar to stir-fries and coconutty fish masalas. Travel into the hilly region of Coorg and taste the sharpness of homemade fermented vinegar, which lends a tang to *pandi* pork curry, seasoned with a peppery blend of spices.

Left: Chandni Chowk, the bazaar area of Old Delhi.

This page: Deogarh, Rajasthan. Waiting for henna (*mehndi*) to dry on their hands and reveal its auburn design.

This page: Dabasang, Gujarat. Sonaben, the Shah family's farm manager.

Right: Keralan backwaters. Driving to the duck farm in Kadamakkudy.

Left: Deogarh, Rajasthan. Village shop, getting ready for the winter festive season.

This page: Mumbai. Sunrise, as seen from my ferry as it draws away from Bhaucha Dhakka ferry terminal on the Arabian Sea. I'm on my way to Mandwa Jetty, Alibag.

GHEE Makes 7 oz (190 g)

Ghee has a lovely buttery flavor and, like clarified butter, can be heated to a high temperature without burning. In Indian homes, it's traditionally made with cream skimmed from the top of boiled milk, which is then churned into butter and cooked over a gentle heat until golden. The butter becomes ghee after it's strained and any sediment is removed.

---

2 sticks plus 2 tbsp (250 g) unsalted butter

Heat the butter in a small, sturdy saucepan and cook it on low heat, without stirring, for 15-20 minutes, until the milk solids start to brown and the butter is golden. Turn the heat off and leave the pan undisturbed for a few minutes.

Line a metal sieve with cheesecloth or strong paper towels and place it over a bowl. Pour over the melted butter, taking care to leave the browned milk solids in the pan. Leave the ghee for a few minutes to drip into the bowl, then pour it into a jar. Because ghee has no moisture or milk solids, it will keep at room temperature for 2-3 months without spoiling.

BOILED BASMATI RICE Serves 4

There are many varieties of rice grown across regional India—my favorite is basmati, which is famed for its long, slender grain and delicate aroma and flavor.

1½ cups (300 g) basmati rice

Wash the rice in a sieve under cold running water until the water runs clear. Put it in a bowl, cover with water and leave it to soak for 20-30 minutes. Drain the rice, transfer it to a Dutch oven or pot and cover with fresh water that comes ¾ in (2 cm) above the rice.

Place the uncovered pot over medium heat and bring the water to a boil. Turn the heat very low and cover the pot with foil and a tight-fitting lid.

Simmer the rice for about 10 minutes, then lift the lid and check that the grains are tender and have absorbed all the water. Add a little more water if the rice needs it. Turn the heat off and leave the pot undisturbed for 10 minutes. Lightly fluff the grains with a fork before serving.

GARAM MASALA Makes 3½ oz (100 g)

Many households will have their own variation of this intensely aromatic spice blend. I've been using this blend of spices, favored across North India, for over 40 years—it's a great all-rounder. Warming, aromatic and full-bodied, there's no comparison between this version and store-bought varieties.

---

seeds from about 1½ oz (50 g) brown cardamom pods (enough to provide 1 oz/25 g seeds)

1 oz (25 g) cinnamon stick, in pieces

¼ cup (25 g) black peppercorns

1½ tbsp royal cumin seeds (*shai jeera*) or caraway seeds, or 2½ tbsp regular cumin seeds

2 large blades of mace

1 tsp cloves

¼ whole nutmeg

Tip all the spices into an electric grinder and process until finely ground. (You can alternatively use a mortar and pestle for this.)

Sift the spices and store them in a tightly lidded jar. The garam masala will keep well for about 2 months. If you're not likely to use it all up in that time, you can freeze the spice blend in an airtight freezer-proof container for 6–8 months.

CHAAT MASALA Makes 2½ oz (75 g)

Popular across Northern and Central India, this tart and fruity spice blend is often sprinkled over fried street food snacks, fruit salads and smoky kebabs.

---

1 tbsp cumin seeds

1 tbsp black peppercorns

½ tsp carom seeds (*ajwain*)

1½ tbsp dried mint leaves

small pinch ground asafoetida (*heeng*)

¾ tbsp ground black salt

1 tsp sea salt

3 tbsp mango powder (*amchoor*)

1 tsp ground ginger

½ tsp grated nutmeg

½ tsp Kashmiri chile powder

Roast the cumin, peppercorns and carom seeds in a dry pan on medium heat, stirring all the time, for about 1 minute, until the spices are fragrant. Take the pan off the heat and stir in the dried mint and asafoetida. Grind everything to a powder in an electric grinder or pound in a mortar with a pestle. Then, add the black salt and sea salt, mango powder, ground ginger, nutmeg and chile powder.

Store the chaat masala in an airtight jar. It'll keep at room temperature for 2–3 months or for 6 months in an airtight freezer-proof container in the freezer.

PANCH PHORAN Makes 1½ oz (40 g)

This whole spice mix is a Bengali and Bangladeshi specialty. The aromatics are released when a small quantity is fried in oil at the start or end of cooking (as little as one teaspoon in a dish to serve four people). The heat releases sweet, astringent and pungent flavors and provides distinctive seasoning for chutneys, dals and a range of masalas. It's sold ready mixed in South Asian shops and online stockists.

1⅔ tbsp cumin seeds

1 tbsp brown mustard seeds

1⅔ tbsp fennel seeds

1½ tsp nigella seeds

heaped 1 tsp fenugreek seeds

Combine the raw spices in a small bowl, then transfer them to a lidded jar to store at room temperature. The mixture will keep fresh for 6–8 months.

PANEER Makes about 8½ oz (240 g)

Homemade paneer has a softer, creamier texture and fresher flavor than store-bought varieties. Making your own is a good way to use up milk close to its sell-by date. You'll get a better yield when it's made from slightly sour milk.

½ gallon (2 liters) whole milk that's close to its sell-by date

juice of 1 lemon

1 tsp salt

Pour the milk into a large pot and place it on low heat. Bring to a simmer, stirring occasionally—this should take about 30 minutes.

Once it begins to bubble and rise up the pan, add 2 tablespoons of the lemon juice and the salt—the milk will soon begin to separate. Add another tablespoon of lemon juice and continue simmering until the mixture separates into solid curds and liquid whey. The amount of lemon juice you need will depend on the milk's freshness.

Line a sieve with a double layer of cheesecloth and place it over a bowl. Pour the cheese mixture into the sieve and leave the whey to drain. After about 10 minutes, draw the cloth around the paneer and gently squeeze out any excess liquid.

Transfer the cloth-wrapped cheese to a tray and pat it out until it is about ¾ in (2 cm) thick. Cover it with a slightly smaller tray and a couple of weighty cans and leave it for at least 2–3 hours, or overnight, if you can, in the fridge. Unwrap the paneer and keep it chilled and submerged in cold water if you are not using it straight away—it keeps like this for 2–3 days.

TAMARIND PULP   Makes 6–8 tablespoons

The tartness of tamarind is used in masalas and chutneys across South Asia. The fresh fruit is available in pods and comes in two varieties—sweet and sour. It's the sour variety that is used in Indian cooking. Although tamarind concentrate may be convenient, it often has a metallic aftertaste and doesn't match the quality of pulp extracted at home. Look for wet, seedless tamarind blocks, sold in packages, rather than the unyielding dried slabs. The blocks will keep for at least a year at room temperature.

---

7 oz (200 g) wet, seedless tamarind block

boiling water

Break up the tamarind with your hands and put it in a heatproof bowl. Pour over enough boiling water to cover the tamarind by a depth of 1 in (3 cm) and soak it for 15–20 minutes, until softened. Leave to one side to cool.

Push the tamarind pulp through a metal sieve and discard any fibers. Sometimes a fine-meshed sieve can become clogged with the pulp—it's best to use a coarse sieve or a conical strainer, or even a colander will do.

Add a little more water if the tamarind is too thick to easily pass through the sieve. Aim for a consistency similar to a cake batter. This pulp freezes well—spoon small quantities into large ice-cube trays, put the trays in the freezer and leave the pulp until solid. Then pop the frozen pulp cubes out of the trays and store them in a sealed bag in the freezer to use as needed.

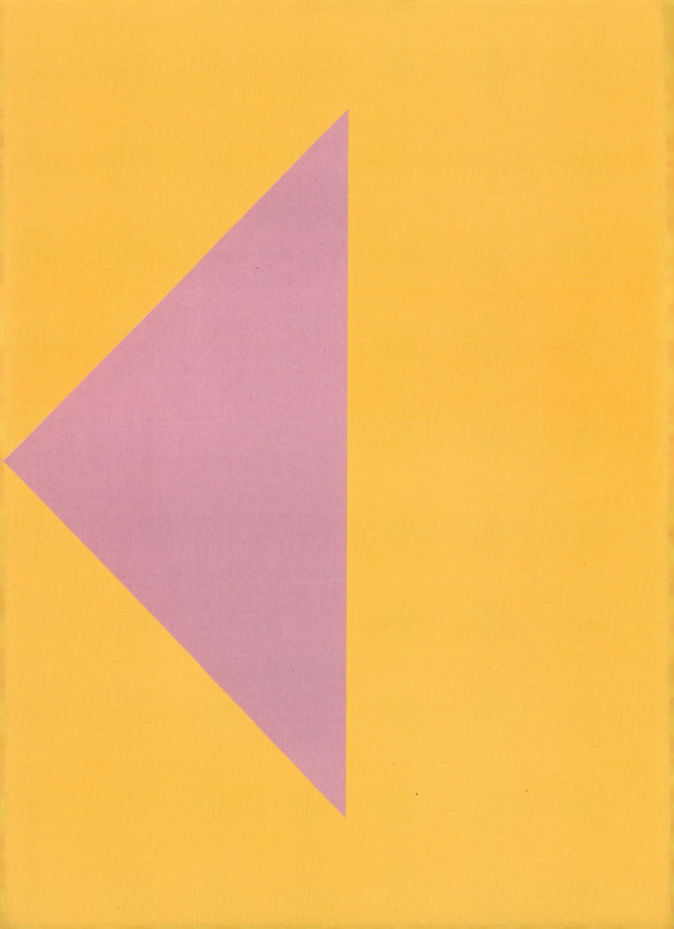

SMALL PLATES

ROAST BABY CARROTS WITH RAISIN & LIME RELISH Serves 4

My mother, although flamboyant with her Indian spice box, tended to stick with salt and a shake of pre-ground white pepper when cooking English dishes in the 1970s. Had she been around today, I think she would have approved of this Indo-British culinary combination of homegrown carrots cloaked in chile and turmeric oil, partnered with a Punjabi raisin relish. Serve it without crème fraîche if you prefer to keep the recipe dairy-free.

FOR THE RAISIN & LIME RELISH

⅓ cup (50 g) raisins

1 tsp honey

2 tbsp coarsely chopped mint leaves

½ red chile, deseeded and finely chopped

½ tsp roasted and ground cumin seeds

juice of ½ lime

FOR THE CARROTS

1 lb (500 g) baby carrots

4 tbsp extra virgin olive oil

½ tsp red chile flakes

¼ tsp ground turmeric

¼ tsp coarsely ground black peppercorns, plus extra to season

sea salt

1 tbsp chopped mint leaves, to serve

FOR THE CUMIN CRÈME FRAÎCHE

2 tbsp crème fraîche

1 tsp extra virgin olive oil

½ tsp roasted and ground cumin seeds

½ red chile, deseeded and finely chopped

Make the relish. Soak the raisins in boiling water for 30 minutes, then drain, finely chop and transfer them to a small bowl. Stir in the honey, mint, red chile and cumin. Add enough lime juice to sharpen—aim for a balance of sweet-sour flavors. Leave to one side while you prepare the carrots.

Preheat the oven to 425°F (220°C). Line a roasting pan with foil, add the carrots and spread them out in a single layer. Whisk the oil with the chile flakes, turmeric and black pepper and season with salt. Using your hands, mix this with the carrots (I like to wear disposable gloves, so that the turmeric doesn't stain my fingers). Put the pan in the oven and roast the carrots for 10 minutes, then flip them over with a spatula and cook for a further 10 minutes—until they are just tender but still have bite.

Meanwhile, make the cumin crème fraîche. Mix the crème fraîche with the olive oil, cumin and red chile, and season with salt and black pepper.

Transfer the carrots to a serving plate and drizzle with 2 tablespoons of the chile and turmeric oil left behind in the roasting pan. Spoon over the raisin relish, dot with teaspoonfuls of the flavored crème fraîche and scatter with mint leaves before serving.

NORTHWEST INDIA — **SMALL PLATES**

CORN BHAJIAS Serves 4

Whenever I think of these *bhajias*, I imagine myself in Jaipur, sitting on a veranda under a slow-whirring ceiling fan. The clouds are darkening, and the monsoon rain will soon fall, banishing the searing summer heat—if only for a few precious hours. It's in this short period that appetites will be restored and kitchen activity resumed. These simple fried snacks will forever remind me of rainy days—even if I make them when the sun is shining. I love the balance of chile heat, citrussy coriander and sharp ginger bite, all of which provide a strong supporting cast for the sweetness of corn. Serve these *bhajias* with tomato ketchup if you don't have tomato-chile sauce on hand. They're also good with fresh cilantro & mint relish (see page 284).

½ cup (50 g) chickpea (gram) flour, plus 1-2 tbsp extra if needed

2¾ tbsp rice flour

1 tbsp cornstarch

1 tsp roasted and ground cumin seeds

½ tsp ground turmeric

¾ tsp coarsely ground black peppercorns

5 ears of fresh corns, kernels coarsely grated

1 large red onion, diced

3 green chiles, deseeded and finely chopped

¾ oz (20 g) ginger root, peeled and finely grated

1 small handful of cilantro, leaves and stems chopped

about 2 cups (500 ml) sunflower oil, for deep-frying

salt

TO SERVE

Tomato-chile sauce (see page 283), warmed

Sift the chickpea flour, rice flour and cornstarch into a bowl and whisk in the ground cumin, turmeric and black pepper and season generously with salt.

Stir in the grated corn, onion, chiles, ginger and cilantro. Add 3-4 tablespoons of cold water or enough to make a thick batter. Aim for a soft dropping consistency, similar to mashed potatoes.

To deep-fry, fill a karahi or wok no more than two-thirds full with oil. The oil is ready for frying when it reaches 350°F (180°C) on a food thermometer, or when a cube of bread dropped into the oil browns in 30 seconds. Drop a tester teaspoonful of batter into the oil—if it's too slack, the *bhajia* will lose its shape and you'll need to thicken the batter with 1-2 tablespoons of chickpea flour.

Fry heaped teaspoonfuls of batter in the oil for 3-4 minutes on medium heat, turning them often so that they are evenly colored. It's best to do this in batches so that the pan isn't overcrowded. Drain the *bhajias* on paper towels, sprinkle with salt and serve with warm tomato-chile sauce.

GINGER-SPICED GREENS Serves 4-6

I lived in Delhi for many years, and a version of this dish, known as *saag*, was a lunchtime staple during winter. *Saag* is made with a variety of leaves, which include fenugreek and spinach, each one lending bitter, sweet, mellow or pungent flavors to the finished dish. Traditionally, these greens are simmered for hours, then mashed and finished with softened onions cooked in ghee, with ginger, garlic, green chiles and cumin. I've simplified and updated this recipe here, used leaves that are widely available, and shortened the method. I haven't skimped on the indulgence, though—this is a recipe that demands generous amounts of butter, both in the *saag* and for skidding across hot cornmeal flatbreads.

---

2 bunches fenugreek (about 10½ oz/300 g); or 2½ oz (75 g) frozen fenugreek leaves, defrosted

5½ oz (150 g) kale, large stems removed and leaves thickly shredded

12 cups (350 g) baby spinach leaves

1 cup (250 ml) hot water

FOR FINISHING

¼ cup (50 g) ghee (see page 18), or 5 tbsp sunflower oil

1 tsp cumin seeds

1 onion, diced

¾ oz (20 g) ginger root, peeled and finely chopped

4 large garlic cloves, finely chopped

2 green chiles, deseeded and finely chopped

2 tsp fine cornmeal

sea salt

TO SERVE

3 tbsp unsalted butter

1 red onion, finely sliced

cornmeal flatbreads (see page 278)

If using fresh fenugreek, pick the leaves off the stems—you should have about 5½ oz (150 g) of leaves. Wash them in a colander and then roughly chop—you can use a food processor for this, if you like. If you are using defrosted fenugreek, most of the stems will already have been removed—squeeze any extra water from the leaves with your hands.

Heat a large, sturdy Dutch oven or pot on high heat. Add the fresh or defrosted fenugreek leaves, and cook for 3-4 minutes without oil until they have softened and the moisture has evaporated. Add the prepared kale to the pot and continue cooking for 5-7 minutes, stirring often.

Stir in the spinach (you may need to do this in two batches), and cook for about 1 minute, until the leaves start to wilt and lose their volume. Tip the leaves into a colander placed over a bowl so that the excess liquid can drain away.

Put half the softened greens in a blender with half the hot water and blend until smooth. Add the remainder of the greens, pour in the remaining hot water and process again. Leave to one side.

To finish, heat the ghee or oil in a karahi or wok on medium-high heat. Add the cumin seeds and sizzle for about 30 seconds, until they release a nutty aroma. Turn down the heat to medium, add the onion and fry for 12-15 minutes, stirring often, until they are a deep golden brown.

Stir in the ginger, garlic and green chiles and continue cooking for 2 minutes. Then, add the puréed leaves and sprinkle over the cornmeal. Season with salt and cook, stirring all the time, for about 5 minutes, until lightly thickened and piping hot. Divide the greens among 6 small bowls and top each with a generous teaspoon of butter and a few red onion slices. Serve with cornmeal flatbreads (*makki ki roti*).

STUFFED EGGS WITH TOMATO & POPPED MUSTARD SEEDS

Serves 4–6

Filled with garlicky tomato masala and finished with a flurry of popped mustard seeds and chile flakes, these eggs make for a brilliant light lunch, especially when teamed with a green salad and crusty bread. And a glass of chilled white wine.

---

3 ripe tomatoes

2 tbsp sunflower oil

1 onion, finely chopped

2 large garlic cloves, crushed

¾ oz (20 g) ginger root, peeled and finely grated

½ tsp ground turmeric

½ tsp Kashmiri chile powder

½ tsp roasted and ground cumin seeds

1 tsp tomato paste

1 tbsp white wine vinegar

1 tsp sugar

6 eggs, hard-boiled and shelled

sea salt

TO FINISH

2 tbsp sunflower oil

¾ tsp brown mustard seeds

½ tsp red chile flakes

1 lime, for squeezing

2 tbsp chopped cilantro

sea-salt flakes

Bring a pot of water to a boil, then turn off the heat and plunge in the tomatoes. After about 30 seconds, scoop them out of the water and transfer them to a bowl filled with cold water. Once they are cool enough to handle, peel off the skins and roughly chop the flesh (including the seeds) and leave to one side.

Heat the oil in a karahi or wok on medium heat, add the onion and fry for 7–10 minutes, until golden. Stir in the garlic and ginger and cook for a further 1 minute.

Add the tomatoes, turmeric, chile powder, cumin, tomato paste, vinegar and sugar, and season with salt. Cook, uncovered, on medium heat, until the tomatoes have thickened and beads of oil appear around the side of the pan (about 5 minutes) then leave to cool.

Make a vertical slit along the length of each egg—not quite all the way through. Using a teaspoon, fill the incision with a generous spoonful of tomato masala and arrange the eggs on a heatproof plate. I like to secure them with a teaspoon of the tomato masala to stop them sliding around.

To finish, heat the oil in a small frying pan on medium-high heat. Add the mustard seeds and sizzle for about 30 seconds, until the popping stops and then stir in the chile flakes. Turn off the heat and swirl the spices around for a few seconds. Pour the hot oil over the eggs. Squeeze over the lime, sprinkle with chopped cilantro and season with sea-salt flakes. Serve warm or at room temperature.

EGGPLANT PAKORAS WITH ONION & TAMARIND RELISH

Serves 4–6

So much Indian cooking is about ad-libbing and although I've used eggplants for this snack, you can swap them with sliced onions, blanched cauliflower florets or thinly sliced potatoes. I love the accompanying relish for its combination of sweet-sour and herby flavors. If you can, do make your own tamarind pulp—I make a big batch every couple of months and freeze it in small foil containers. It's worth the effort—the resulting flavor is miles better than store-bought pastes.

FOR THE RELISH

1 red onion, diced

3 tbsp chopped cilantro leaves

2 tbsp chopped mint leaves

1 green chile, deseeded and finely chopped

1 tbsp tamarind pulp (see page 21)

1 tbsp jaggery or light brown sugar

FOR THE PAKORAS

scant 1 cup (75 g) chickpea (gram) flour

½ cup (75 g) rice flour

½ tsp ground turmeric

½ tsp Kashmiri chile powder

1 tsp roasted and ground cumin seeds

1 tsp sea salt

¾ oz (20 g) ginger root, peeled and finely grated

about 2 cups (500 ml) sunflower oil, for deep-frying

1 eggplant (about 10½ oz/300 g), sliced into ¼ in (5 mm) thick rounds

1 tsp store-bought or homemade *chaat masala* (see page 19)

sea-salt flakes, for sprinkling

Mix the onion with the cilantro, mint, green chile, tamarind, jaggery and salt to season. Aim for a sweet-sour flavor—you might need to add a little more tamarind or jaggery to get the balance right. Leave to one side.

Sift the chickpea flour and rice flour into a bowl and whisk in the turmeric, chile powder, cumin, salt and ginger. Pour in 1⅛–1¼ cups (275–300 ml) of cold water, or enough to make a slack batter—aim for the consistency of heavy cream and whisk until smooth.

To deep-fry, fill a wok or karahi no more than two-thirds full with oil. The oil is ready for frying when it reaches 350°F (180°C) on a food thermometer, or when a cube of bread dropped into the oil browns in 30 seconds.

Dip the eggplant slices in the batter and fry them in batches for 2–3 minutes on each side, until golden all over, turning them with a spatula once or twice during cooking. Drain the pakoras on paper towels, sprinkle with *chaat masala* and sea-salt flakes and serve straight away with the onion and tamarind relish. It also works well when served with creamy yogurt sprinkled with crisp-fried chickpea flour batter "scrapings" from the pan.

COMMUNITY ROOTS
NORTH WEST

SHAMA CHADHA, DELHI

"Roopa," said Shama, "You know we're in the in the middle of Navaratri, so lunch won't be the same as usual." Having lived in India for many years, I was well aware of what she meant.

Navaratri takes place towards the end of summer. It's a time for religious reflection, offering prayers to goddess Durga, and celebrating the victory of good over evil. For many, it's also about the gathering of families and friends, dressing in bright colors and often dancing through the night. Although the duration and interpretation vary across regions, Navaratri usually extends for nine days and nights. Shama follows a restricted diet and many devotees eat only fruit and yogurt during this time.

Shama is married to my cousin Rajiv, and they live in West Delhi with my dad's younger sister, Pami Aunty, and her husband, Virender. Although they're only a few miles from where I'm staying, the drive takes over an hour because of heavy traffic. It's a relief when the taxi leaves the main road for quieter residential streets. We pass elderly ladies in salwar suits and sneakers walking briskly in neighborhood parks; there's a group of schoolgirls waiting at the bus stop, and a vegetable vendor pushing his wooden cart shouting out a list of today's specials.

Meeting the Chadha family is an emotional reunion. My dad died five months earlier, at 94 years old, and this is my first visit to India in four years. I sink into one of their comfortable sofas and, through the tears, we reminisce about dad, swap stories and I tell them how much he loved Shama's cooking.

I've asked Shama to recreate one of dad's favorite side dishes, fried *arvi*. It's a starchy root, also known as colocasia. But all I had to go on was a hazy description, based on what his mom had cooked more than eight decades earlier. He'd enjoy it lightly spiced, straight from the pan and squashed into a sandwich, the hot *arvi* melting the butter on the soft white bread. It probably boasted the same appeal as a comforting chip butty.

But first, lunch. Shama has cooked an impressive spread of Navaratri dishes alongside regular vegetarian ones. I join her in the kitchen with my cousin Ashi, where soft lentil dumplings, cloaked with yogurt, have been dusted with cumin and chile powder.

She turns her attention to the parathas. As wheat and rice are off limits during Navaratri, she has kneaded a dough made from water chestnut flour, mixed with grated pumpkin, shredded spinach, mashed potatoes, green chiles and coriander. I watch as she rolls it out and cooks the first paratha on the *tawa*, drizzling homemade ghee around the edges. It then slides onto a plate, and

A street vendor selling hot and smoky sweet potatoes, seasoned with sweet and sour spices, and sharpened with lemon juice.

▶ she dollops freshly churned white butter in the middle. The bread, with its soft texture and earthy, sweet taste, contrasts very well with the piquancy of green chiles.

Lunch hasn't even been served yet, but I'm already off the starting block. I want to stay in the kitchen and catch up on family news, flip parathas and sizzle vegetables in a karahi with a big spoon, but I'm ushered out to join the family already seated around the dining table.

Highlights from the feast include *sabudana khichdi*—fried, glistening pearls of tapioca, sharpened with lime and green chiles—and *Rawalpindi cholay*—chickpeas made without onions, garlic and tomatoes, but run through with ginger, fenugreek leaves and pounded pomegranate seeds. Shama takes the lid off a jar of homemade black lime pickle—it's a Punjabi specialty and this batch has been maturing for seven years. A piece of lime, cloaked in cardamom-scented masala, is scooped onto my plate—the fruit has turned jet black with age, is as soft as marzipan, and has a sweet, smoky and almost liquorice flavor. I love it.

Desserts are showstoppers. Butterscotch-like kulfi, *malpua*—shallow-fried pancakes steeped in rose and saffron syrup—and *rabri*, which resembles softly set clotted cream, and is made from reduced and sweetened cardamom milk. Then there are homemade *mithai*, dairy-based sweets, many with a soft, crumbly texture and caramelly flavor.

Shama takes home-catering orders for her *mithai*. She wryly recalls arranging for a delivery of 20 liters (5 gallons) of milk from the local dairy when her first order came in for 60 kg (130 lb) of fudgy *barfi*. Using every pot in the kitchen, the milk was boiled down to a creamy solid—saffron soaked, nuts chopped, ghee made and sugar weighed. Her fabulous sweets have since resulted in a loyal neighborhood fan following.

I ask if she employs helpers in the kitchen and she laughs and says not a chance—"This is my space and I'm not going to share it with anyone." Many families in her locality have live-in or part-time cooks and, initially, there was some bewilderment at her approach. I understand why she's so comfortable in this space though—the kitchen is her kingdom.

After lunch, dishes are cleared and the two of us head upstairs and sit in her air-conditioned bedroom. I ask about her routine. Once a week, just before 7am, Rajiv visits the *sabzi mandi*, a 5-minute drive from home. It's a lively, bustling fruit and vegetable market, and he fills the trunk with a week's worth of produce. The smaller markets located in residential areas are just as chaotic and crowded. Even after having left Delhi two decades ago, my local fruit and vegetable market remains a vibrant community hub today. Alongside the established stallholders are vendors pushing carts piled high with fruit, "aunties" sitting on the ground selling just limes and chiles, and street hawkers peddling everything from samosas to marigolds to cotton candy to plastic toys. After filling my shopping bag, I'd treat myself to a potato tikki, or sweet potato chaat steeped in lime juice and seasoned with chile and mango powder. And there are always hot, syrupy *jalebis* to finish.

▶ Back at home, Shama preps a few basics. She'll pressure cook tomatoes with Kashmiri chile powder and freeze the sieved pulp in small boxes. Onions will be puréed in the blender and fried in batches with garlic for the freezer too. This way, she tells me, it'll be quicker to rustle up meals for unexpected guests. Spices are bought whole so there's no chance of impurities being mixed in on the sly. They're pounded at home—dried strips of mango are ground into *amchoor*, and finger lengths of turmeric root and Kashmiri chiles treated in the same way.

When we return downstairs, Shama opens a kitchen cabinet and prises the lid off a weighty stainless-steel can, to reveal 4½ lb (2 kg) of golden homemade ghee. Every day, a quart of milk is boiled, and after the cream has risen to the top, it's collected and mixed with a little yogurt, which helps it thicken. After a couple of days, this cream is blended in a blender until it separates into butter and liquid whey. The whey isn't wasted, but whipped with roasted cumin, mint and black salt and served as a quencher. To make ghee, she cooks the butter on low heat until the milk solids start to darken. It's then strained, and any crunchy bits left in the sieve are repurposed. Perhaps the buttery crumbs will be mixed with spiced crumbled paneer or transformed into a creamy sweetmeat.

We return to the *arvi*. Shama has already boiled and peeled it and, after thick slicing, it will be fried in hot oil. This is a typical dish made during Navaratri, and although it's a simple recipe, she intuitively knows how to extract maximum flavor and aroma from her seasonings. I watch as she decants the oil, leaving a shallow pool in the bottom of the karahi. With the heat turned off, she adds a spoonful of home-ground coriander seeds, mango powder and ground chiles. The spices are gently warmed over very low heat until they are hot enough to release their fragrance without scorching and turning bitter. Next, carom seeds (*ajwain*), which taste a bit like dried thyme, are rubbed between her palms, where they fall into the oil and release their distinctive astringency. Gold-hued *arvi* is returned to the pan along with chopped green chiles, and coated in the fruity, tartly seasoned oil. I ask if she has any sliced white bread—this sandwich is for dad, and I know right away that he would have approved. She looks at me quizzically—is this the recipe you were after? It's such a basic staple!

1. Pink-fleshed guavas are commonplace in Delhi's street markets.

2. Deep-fried *jalebis* for the sweet-toothed.

3. Time for a chat while tying bunches of cilantro in readiness for the evening market.

4. Selling auspicious dreams of prosperity and wisdom at Diwali.

5. Marigold flowers for a prayer offering.

6. Indian lemons are similar to limes in flavor, and are often sold alongside green chiles. They are often strung from doorways to ward off evil spirits.

1. My cousin's wife, Shama.

2. Colocasia, also known as *arvi*.

3. Sharp and citrussy green chiles, grown in Delhi.

SWEET POTATOES WITH MANGO POWDER & GREEN CHILES

Serves 4

SHAMA CHADHA

Shama, my cousin's wife, makes this dish with colocasia, a starchy root vegetable, which is also known as taro root, or *arvi* in Hindi. It's denser in texture than regular potatoes and has a neutral flavor, similar in taste to yam. Sweet potatoes and *arvi* will work equally well with the thyme-like spicing of carom seeds and fruity mango powder. I've written instructions for cooking with both below.

- 1 lb 5 oz (600 g) sweet potatoes, peeled and cut into 1½ in (4 cm) cubes
- 2 cups (500 ml) sunflower oil, for deep-frying
- 1 tsp ground coriander
- 2 tsp mango powder (*amchoor*)
- 1 tsp Kashmiri chile powder
- ¾ tsp carom seeds (*ajwain*), or ½ tsp dried thyme
- 2 green chiles, deseeded and chopped
- 2 tbsp chopped cilantro
- sea salt

Bring a large pot of salted water to a boil, add the prepared potatoes and simmer, half-covered, until tender. Drain in a colander and leave to cool on a wire rack.

To deep-fry, fill a wok or karahi no more than two-thirds full with oil. The oil is ready for frying when it reaches 350°F (180°C) on a food thermometer, or when a cube of bread dropped into the oil browns in 30 seconds. Fry the potatoes in batches for 4–5 minutes, until they are colored at the edges, turning them regularly with a spatula. Set each batch aside to drain on paper towels while you fry the remainder.

Carefully transfer 3–4 tablespoons of the hot oil to a frying pan. There should be enough to thinly cover the base of the pan by ⅛ in (3 mm). Without turning on the heat, add the ground coriander, mango powder, chile powder and salt to season.

Turn the heat on low and cook the spices for 30 seconds, stirring all the time. Roughly crush the carom seeds, if using, between the palms of your hands and add these or the thyme to the pan. Increase the heat to medium, stir in the sweet potatoes and chopped green chiles and cook for 3–4 minutes, stirring often, until warmed through. Scatter with the chopped cilantro before serving.

TARO ROOT (COLOCASIA) WITH MANGO POWDER & GREEN CHILES

Bring a large pot of salted water to a boil, add 1 lb 5 oz (600 g) washed and unpeeled colocasia and simmer, half-covered, until tender—this should take about 15 minutes.

Drain the colocasia in a colander. When cool enough to handle, peel off the skin with a sharp knife and cut the starchy flesh into ½ in (1 cm) thick slices. Fry and cook the slices in the same way as for the sweet potatoes.

PANEER MASALA PUFFS
Serves 4–6

This recipe is a tribute to the legendary range of puff-pastry patties sold by Wengers, a well-known Delhi bakery that has been in business since the 1920s, and still going strong today. I made these mini puffs for a recent Diwali celebration and served them with drinks—you could make them larger if you prefer. Store-bought paneer works well in this recipe.

---

2 large tomatoes

3 tbsp sunflower oil

¾ tsp cumin seeds

1 onion, diced

2 large garlic cloves, crushed

½ oz (15 g) ginger root, peeled and finely grated

¼ tsp ground turmeric

½ tsp Kashmiri chile powder

½ tsp garam masala (see page 19)

1 green chile, deseeded and finely chopped

9 oz (250 g) store-bought or homemade paneer (see page 20), diced into about ½ in (1 cm) cubes

2 tbsp chopped cilantro leaves

about 14 oz (400 g) all-butter puff pastry

1 egg, lightly beaten with a pinch of salt

tomato-chile sauce (see page 283), to serve

Bring a pot of water to a boil and then turn off the heat and plunge in the tomatoes. After about 30 seconds, take them out of the water and transfer to a bowl of cold water. Once they are cool enough to handle, peel the skins, roughly chop the flesh (including the seeds), then leave to one side.

Heat the oil in a wok or karahi on medium-high heat, add the cumin seeds and sizzle for about 30 seconds, until fragrant. Turn down the heat to medium, add the onion and fry for 8–10 minutes, until golden.

Stir in the garlic and ginger and cook for 1 minute, then add the turmeric, chile powder, garam masala, tomatoes and green chile. Cook the masala for 5–7 minutes, until thickened and beads of oil appear around the edge of the pan. Turn off the heat and leave to cool.

Put the diced paneer in a bowl, cover with boiling water and leave the cubes to soften for 10 minutes. Discard the soaking water and mix the paneer with the chopped cilantro and the tomato masala.

On a floured surface, roll out the pastry to a large square about ⅛ in (3 mm) thick, then cut it into 24 equally sized squares (they will be about 3 x 3 in/8 x 8 cm).

Place 1 tablespoon of filling into one half of each square. One by one, brush the pastry edges of each square with water and fold the unfilled half of pastry over the filling to make a rectangular package. Seal the edges with the prongs of a fork and transfer the puffs to baking sheets lined with parchment paper. Chill for at least 30 minutes—longer if you have the time.

Preheat the oven to 410°F (210°C). Brush the puffs with the salted beaten egg and bake for 15–20 minutes, until risen and golden in color. I like to glaze the puffs for a second time halfway through cooking for a deeper color. Serve the puffs warm with tomato-chile sauce.

POTATOES WITH MANGO POWDER
Serves 4

Amchoor (mango powder) imparts a deliciously fruity tang to masalas, fried snacks, meaty grills and salads. If you have never tasted mango powder, now's the time to pick some up from a supermarket, South Asian grocery store, or online stockist. For this dish, I've combined *amchoor* with sharp-tasting green chiles, crisp-fried ginger and warming spices, which lightly coat the potatoes as they cook. Serve this dish straight-up as a snack, or as a side dish with dal and chapatis.

¼ cup (50 g) ghee (see page 18), or 5 tbsp sunflower oil

1½ tsp cumin seeds

1½ oz (40 g) ginger root, peeled and cut into very thin matchsticks

½ tsp ground turmeric

½ tsp cracked black peppercorns

¾ tsp Kashmiri chile powder

1 lb 10 oz (750 g) new potatoes, boiled and halved

2 tsp mango powder (*amchoor*)

2 green chiles, deseeded and finely chopped

sea salt

Heat the ghee or oil in a karahi or wok on medium heat. Add the cumin seeds and fry for about 30 seconds, until they release a nutty aroma.

Add the ginger, and after a few seconds, the turmeric, pepper and chile powder. Swirl everything around for a few seconds then tumble in the boiled new potatoes and season with salt.

Fry the potatoes on medium heat for 5–10 minutes, until they start to deepen in color, then add the mango powder and green chiles. Continue cooking for 1–2 minutes, stirring all the time, until the mango powder evenly coats the potatoes.

GRILLED PANEER, MARINATED IN SAFFRON & ALMOND YOGURT

Serves 6

This recipe is redolent of offerings from royal palace kitchens. Although meat dishes are the mainstay of regal menus, many masalas can be adapted like this one for vegetarians, too. Paneer, with its neutral flavor and soft texture, is a good base for yogurty marinations and the addition of ground almonds and auburn-hued saffron lend richness and a celebratory feel to the finished dish. I'd serve these skewers straight from the oven and accompany them with flatbreads and plenty of chilled beer.

¼ tsp saffron strands

1 lb (500 g) store-bought or firm homemade paneer (see page 20), cut into 1½ in (4 cm) chunks, about ½ in (1 cm) thick

juice of 2 limes, plus extra lime wedges to serve

2 tsp Kashmiri chile powder

1½ tsp roasted and ground cumin seeds

sea salt

FOR THE SPICED YOGURT

1 cup (250 ml) strained full-fat Greek yogurt

3 brown cardamom pods

8 green cardamom pods

1 tsp sugar

3 garlic cloves, crushed

1 oz (30 g) ginger root, peeled and finely grated

2 green chiles, deseeded and finely chopped

½ cup (50 g) ground almonds

3 tbsp melted unsalted butter or ghee (see page 18)

Soak the saffron in 2 tablespoons of hot water, bruising the strands with the back of a teaspoon to release their flavor and color. Leave to one side for at least 1 hour.

If you are using store-bought paneer, soak the cubes in boiling water for 10 minutes and then discard the water. Mix the paneer with the lime juice, chile powder and cumin and season with salt. Leave to one side for 20 minutes.

Meanwhile, if you are using bamboo skewers, soak the sticks in water to help stop them burning under the broiler.

Make the spiced yogurt. Put the strained yogurt in a mixing bowl. Split the brown and green cardamom pods and remove the seeds with the point of a sharp knife. Put the seeds and sugar in a mortar and pound to a powder with a pestle. Tip the powder into the bowl with the yogurt and mix together. Stir in the garlic, ginger, green chiles, ground almonds and saffron and its soaking liquid, and season with salt. Carefully fold in the paneer and its spiced lime-juice marinade.

Heat the broiler to its hottest setting and line a broiler pan with foil. Thread the paneer onto skewers, leaving a ½ in (1 cm) gap between each piece. Cook the skewers under the broiler for 4–5 minutes on each side, or until the paneer is charred around the edges. Brush with melted butter or ghee and serve straight away with lime wedges on the side.

SEMOLINA PANCAKES WITH RED PEPPER, TOMATO & RED ONION

Serves 4

Spongy in texture, these vegetable-topped pancakes, called *uttapam*, are thicker than crêpe-like *dosas* and are a popular breakfast dish in Tamil Nadu. Although they're usually made with a ground rice and lentil batter, this version works well and doesn't need fermenting like regular *dosa* batter. I like to make mini *uttapam*, but you could make them any size and vary the topping ingredients, too.

FOR THE TOPPING

1 red onion, diced

1 tomato, diced

1 red pepper, deseeded and diced

2 green chiles, deseeded and finely chopped

1 oz (25 g) ginger root, peeled and finely chopped

2 tbsp coarsely chopped cilantro leaves

FOR THE BATTER

1¼ cups (200 g) fine semolina

1 tsp sea salt

juice of ½ lemon

½ tsp baking soda

6–8 tbsp melted coconut oil or ghee (see page 18) or sunflower oil

coconut, cilantro & peanut chutney (see page 286), to serve

Mix the onion with the tomato, red pepper, green chiles, ginger and cilantro, and leave to one side.

Whisk the semolina and salt with 1½ cups (350 ml) warm water, or enough to make a smooth batter that resembles the consistency of heavy cream. Leave the batter in a warm place for 1–2 hours to soften the semolina, then stir in the lemon juice and baking soda.

Brush a griddle or sturdy frying pan with 1 tablespoon of the oil or melted ghee and heat it on medium heat. Pour a small ladleful of batter into the center and, using the ladle's rounded base, spread it out to a 3 in (8 cm) diameter circle, about ¼ in (5 mm) thick. Lightly press a tablespoon of the onion-tomato mixture onto the top and drizzle 1 teaspoon of oil or melted ghee around the edge. Cook for 3–4 minutes, until the base is golden.

Using a spatula, flip the *uttapam* over so that the topping now faces downwards. Fry for 2–3 minutes, until golden, then remove the *uttapam* from the pan and drain it on paper towels with the topping facing upwards. Repeat with the remaining batter, keeping the *uttapam* warm in a folded tea towel—you should get about 14 from this quantity. Serve warm, with coconut, cilantro & peanut chutney.

CORN-ON-THE-COB WITH BROWN BUTTER, CHILE & MANGO POWDER

Serves 4

Corn roasted over charcoal, with kernels charred at the edges, remind me of Delhi's monsoon season. I'd buy mine from a street hawker. Squatting on the pavement, under a black umbrella, she would fan the flames on her makeshift stove and roll the cobs this way and that until cooked just-so. Then she'd dip a cut lime in tart spices and rub it over the corn, leaving behind a sheen of juice and speckles of nutty-tasting cumin, black salt and red chile. I'm recreating these "street" flavors in this updated recipe, and although these cobs are cooked in the oven, they'd work well on the grill, too.

- 2 tsp Kashmiri chile powder
- 4 tsp mango powder (*amchoor*)
- 2 tsp ground ginger
- ¾ tsp garam masala (see page 19)
- 2 tsp roasted and ground cumin seeds
- 1 tbsp jaggery or light brown sugar
- 2 tsp sea-salt flakes
- 4 ears of fresh corn, without leaves and husk
- 7 tbsp (100 g) unsalted butter, melted
- 1 lime, for squeezing

Preheat the oven to 410°F (210°C) and line a roasting pan with foil or parchment paper. Mix the chile powder, mango powder, ginger, garam masala, cumin, jaggery and salt on a flat tray. Brush the cobs with plenty of melted butter and then roll each one in the spice mixture and transfer it to the roasting pan. Drizzle any leftover butter over the corn.

Bake for 20 minutes, turning the cobs halfway through cooking, until the butter has browned and the kernels are crisp at the edges. Squeeze over the lime and serve straight away.

POPADUMS WITH RED ONION, TOMATO & CHAAT MASALA

Serves 4

I associate this simple snack with old-fashioned Indian clubs, where an experienced bartender makes gimlets with precision, and the waiter brings crisp *masala papad* to the table. These popadums, topped with chopped tomatoes, red onions and bitingly sharp green chiles, should be served within minutes of assembly, otherwise they lose their magnificent crunch. Pre-fried popadums won't work for this recipe. You'll need to buy the uncooked variety from South Asian grocery stores—they're much cheaper than those sold in supermarkets and will keep for up to a year in an airtight box.

---

1 small red onion, diced

1 large tomato, diced

1 green chile, finely chopped

juice of 1 lime

1 tsp store-bought or homemade *chaat masala* (see page 19)

¾ tsp roasted and ground cumin seeds

¼ tsp Kashmiri chile powder

2 tbsp chopped cilantro

2 cups (500 ml) sunflower oil, for deep-frying

4-6 large uncooked popadums, plain or spiced (available from South Asian stores)

sea salt

For the topping, mix the red onion with the tomato, green chile, lime juice, *chaat masala*, cumin, chile powder and cilantro. Season with salt and leave to one side.

To deep-fry, fill a large wide, sturdy pan no more than two-thirds full with oil. The oil is ready for frying when it reaches 350°F (180°C) on a food thermometer, or when a cube of bread dropped into the oil browns in 30 seconds.

Cook the popadums one at a time, for 20-30 seconds each, without flipping them over—they will puff almost straight away. Drain each popadum on paper towels, scatter with some of the onion and tomato topping and break into large pieces. Serve straight away while they are still crisp.

LENTIL, GINGER & TAMARIND BROTH Serves 4

Hot and peppery, this broth—called *rasam* in South India—revels in big, bold flavors and is great as a pick-me-up at any time of the day. Use fresh curry leaves rather than dried for this recipe, even if it means ordering them online—their punchy, citrussy flavor is incomparable.

---

scant 1 cup (150 g) split pigeon peas (*toor dal*), rinsed

¼ tsp ground turmeric

1 tsp Kashmiri chile powder

½ tsp coarsely ground black peppercorns

1 tsp roasted and ground cumin seeds

1 oz (30 g) ginger root, peeled and finely grated

1 tbsp tamarind pulp (see page 21)

sea salt

FOR FINISHING

3 tbsp sunflower oil

1 tsp brown mustard seeds

¼ tsp fenugreek seeds

about 15 fresh curry leaves

Put the split pigeon peas in a bowl and soak them in hot water for 1 hour. Discard the water and transfer the peas to a pressure cooker. Cover with fresh water by about 1½ in (4 cm), and add the turmeric, chile powder, black pepper, ground cumin and ginger. Cook under pressure for 30 minutes, until the lentils are soft and have broken down. Alternatively, you can cook the peas in a pot with the spices and water for about 1 hour, until completely soft. Leave the dal to cool until lukewarm.

Using a blender or handheld immersion blender, process the dal with its cooking water until smooth. Whisk in enough hot water to thin the consistency so that it's broth-like.

Reheat the *rasam* and add the tamarind pulp to sharpen, then season with salt. Cover with a lid and keep warm while you fry the finishing spices.

Heat the oil in a small frying pan on medium-high heat. Add the mustard seeds and sizzle for 30 seconds, until the popping stops, then add the fenugreek seeds and curry leaves. Fry the spices for another 30 seconds, until the leaves release their aroma, and then tip everything into the *rasam* and stir to combine. Cover and leave for 10 minutes before reheating. Serve piping hot in soup bowls or mugs.

POTATO DUMPLINGS WITH PEANUT-GARLIC CRUMBS Serves 6–8

FOR THE POTATOES

4 starchy potatoes (such as Russets; about 12 oz/350 g)

1½ tbsp unsalted butter

½ tsp coarsely ground black peppercorns

2 tbsp sunflower oil

1 tsp brown mustard seeds

1 tbsp (about 15) fresh curry leaves

pinch of ground asafoetida (*heeng*; optional)

¾ tsp cumin seeds

¼ tsp fenugreek seeds

2 green chiles, deseeded and chopped

2 garlic cloves, crushed

¾ oz (20 g) ginger root, peeled and finely grated

2 tbsp chopped cilantro leaves

sea salt

I once made this famed Mumbai street snack, known as *vada pav*, as a vegetarian alternative to hamburgers and they went down a treat. Don't be put off by the lengthy method—you can make most of the different elements in advance. The potato mixture benefits from being assembled the day before, and the peanut crumbs will keep for 3–4 weeks in a jar. I would blend the herb relish on the same day though, so that it retains its fresh flavor and vibrant green color.

FOR THE BATTER

1¾ cups (150 g) chickpea (gram) flour

½ cup (75 g) rice flour

¼ tsp baking soda

¼ tsp ground turmeric

½ tsp Kashmiri chile powder

¼ tsp ground asafoetida (*heeng*; optional)

about 2 cups (500 ml) sunflower oil, for deep-frying

sea-salt flakes, for sprinkling

TO SERVE

12–14 soft white mini bread rolls

fresh cilantro & mint relish (see page 284)

peanut & coconut crumbs (see page 283)

Peel and halve the potatoes, or quarter them if large. Cook them until tender in simmering, salted water, then drain and mash them in a bowl with the butter, black pepper and salt to taste. Leave to one side.

Heat the oil in a small frying pan on medium-high heat and add the mustard seeds—they should sizzle straight away. Swirl them around for a few seconds until the popping stops, then add the curry leaves—they will splutter, so step back as they hit the oil. Lower the heat to medium and add the asafoetida, if using, followed by the cumin and fenugreek seeds. Swirl the spices around for about 30 seconds, until they release their aroma.

Add the green chiles, garlic and ginger and continue frying for about 2–3 minutes, stirring all the time, then mix everything with the potatoes, add the chopped cilantro and season with sea salt.

Using damp hands, shape the spiced potato mixture into 12–14 small balls, each about 1 in (3 cm) in diameter, and arrange them on a tray lined with parchment paper. Put the tray in the fridge for the balls to firm up while you make the batter.

Sift the chickpea flour, rice flour, baking soda, turmeric and chile powder into a mixing bowl. Add the asafoetida, if using. Season with salt and whisk in enough cold water to make a batter, which should be slightly thicker than the consistency of heavy cream. Leave to one side for 20 minutes.

To deep-fry, fill a karahi or wok no more than two-thirds full with oil. The oil is ready for frying when it reaches 350°F (180°C) on a food thermometer, or when a cube of bread dropped into the oil browns in 30 seconds. Whisk the batter and add a little extra water if it's too thick, then stir in 2 teaspoons of hot oil from the karahi or wok—this helps ensure a lighter batter.

Dip a few potato balls at a time into the batter and fry in batches for 5–7 minutes, turning them often, until golden all over. Drain the potato dumplings on paper towels and sprinkle with sea-salt flakes.

Split the bread rolls in half. Spread the lower portion of each roll with cilantro and mint relish and then sprinkle with a thick layer of peanut and coconut crumbs. Put the dumplings on top of the crumbs, cover with the top halves of each roll and serve.

BROWN SHRIMP WITH GINGER & MUSTARD

Serves 2

These salty-sweet shrimp are warmed in mustard and ginger butter and lightly spiced with nutmeg and chile. I like to heap them on thickly cut toast and then wait a few seconds for the buttery-fishy juices to soak into the bread. This is a Sunday sofa supper kind of treat—it's a good idea to keep a roll of paper towels handy for mopping buttery smudges.

---

juice of ½ lime

¾ tsp peeled and finely grated ginger root

1 tsp wholegrain mustard

1 green chile, deseeded and finely chopped

pinch of grated nutmeg

¼ tsp Kashmiri chile powder

3 tbsp unsalted butter

2½ oz (70 g) brown shrimp, cooked

1 tbsp chopped cilantro leaves

sea salt

2 slices of sourdough, char-grilled or toasted, to serve

Mix the lime juice with the ginger, mustard, green chile, nutmeg and chile powder, and season with sea salt.

Heat the butter in a frying pan on medium heat until it turns deep golden and releases a lovely, toasted aroma.

Add the spiced lime juice and swirl it around in the pan for a few seconds. Turn off the heat, stir in the shrimp and cilantro, then heap everything onto warm sourdough toast to serve.

FISH FRY Serves 4

This fried fish doesn't have a batter or crumb coating. Instead, nutty-tasting cumin, turmeric and warming chile are mixed with lime juice and rubbed over white fish fillets to great effect. My friend Yael Jhirad made this simple and delicious snack for me at her home in Alibag, a balmy coastal town about an hour's ferry ride from Mumbai, across the Arabian sea (see page 119). She used *rawas*—a local white fish, known colloquially as Indian salmon, even though it has nothing in common with the Atlantic variety that we're familiar with. Any firm-fleshed white fish will hold up well to this winning blend of spices, though.

---

2 tsp Kashmiri chile powder

1½ tsp ground turmeric

1 tsp roasted and ground cumin seeds

2 tsp fine sea salt

juice of 2 limes, plus extra wedges to serve

1 lb 10 oz (750 g) skinless hake fillets, cut into 5-6 pieces (each about 4 x 2½ in/10 x 6 cm)

4 tbsp melted coconut oil or sunflower oil

Mix the chile powder, turmeric, cumin, salt and lime juice together in a small bowl.

Put the fish on a tray and, using your fingers, rub the paste all over each piece so that the pieces are evenly coated—it's a good idea to wear disposable gloves for this. Leave to one side for 10 minutes.

Heat the oil in a frying pan on medium heat and cook the fish for 2-3 minutes on each side, until the spices darken and the flesh flakes easily. You might need a minute longer depending on the thickness of the fillets. Serve straight away with lime wedges for squeezing over.

KONKAN-STYLE SHRIMP WITH MANGO
Serves 3–4

The tart mango in this quick-to-make dish riffs nicely with the sweetness of shrimp and the crackle of peppery-tasting curry leaves. It's a recipe inspired by home cooks living close to the Konkan shoreline along the west coast of India. South Asian shops sell green mangoes but I've often made this dish with firm supermarket varieties too.

- 1 lb (500 g) raw, shelled, tail-on jumbo shrimp, deveined
- ½ tsp ground turmeric
- 1 tsp sea-salt flakes, plus extra to season
- 4 tbsp melted coconut oil or sunflower oil
- 1 tsp brown mustard seeds
- about 15 fresh curry leaves
- 2 star anise
- 1 large onion, thinly sliced
- ¾ oz (20 g) ginger root, peeled and finely grated
- 1 unripe mango, peeled, pitted and cut into ½ in (1 cm) wide strips
- 2 green chiles, deseeded and finely grated or shredded
- ½ tsp Kashmiri chile powder
- ½ tsp ground coriander
- ½ tsp roasted and ground cumin seeds
- ½ tsp garam masala (see page 19)
- juice of ½ lime
- 1 tbsp chopped cilantro leaves

Mix the shrimp with the turmeric and salt and leave to one side.

Heat the oil in a karahi or wok on medium-high heat and add the mustard seeds—they will splutter as they hit the oil, so stand back. Once the sizzling stops, add the curry leaves and star anise and swirl everything around for about 30 seconds, until the curry leaves release their citrussy aroma.

Turn down the heat to medium, stir in the onions and ginger and lightly season with salt. Fry for about 10 minutes, until the onions are golden.

Turn down the heat to low, and add the mango and green chiles. Cover the pan and cook for 3–4 minutes, until the mango has softened but still holds its shape.

Uncover, stir in the chile powder, coriander, cumin and garam masala and cook for about 30 seconds to release the flavor from the spices.

Add the shrimp and fry for 2–3 minutes, stirring all the time, until tender and opaque. Sharpen with the lime juice and add the chopped cilantro just before serving.

BATTERED AMRITSARI HADDOCK Serves 4

This Punjabi classic is traditionally made with river fish. I've taken the liberty of using haddock here although pollock would work well too, and have cut the fish into strips, but you could use larger pieces for a main dish. A few words of praise for carom seeds (*ajwain*)—they may not look like much, but these tiny seeds have an intense, lovage-thyme flavor, and work especially well with northern Indian fish dishes. Be judicious with it; a little goes a long way—I'd buy a small packet and keep any extra in the freezer.

1½ oz (50 g) ginger root, peeled and finely grated

4 garlic cloves, crushed

¾ tsp coarsely ground black peppercorns

juice of 1 lemon

1 lb 5 oz (600 g) skinless, line-caught haddock fillets, cut into ½ in (1 cm) wide, finger-length strips

sea salt

FOR THE BATTER

scant 1 cup (75 g) chickpea (gram) flour

3 tbsp rice flour

½ tsp carom seeds (*ajwain*) or dried thyme

1 tsp ground turmeric

2 tsp Kashmiri chile powder

2 tbsp chopped cilantro

2 cups (500 ml) sunflower oil, for deep-frying

TO SERVE

fresh cilantro & mint relish (see page 284)

lemon wedges

In a shallow dish, mix the ginger, garlic, pepper and lemon juice and season with salt. Add the fish and coat the strips in the marinade, then leave them to one side while you make the batter.

Sift the flours into a mixing bowl and whisk in the carom seeds or dried thyme, turmeric, chile powder and chopped cilantro and season with salt. Pour in enough cold water to make a smooth batter—aim for the consistency of heavy cream.

To deep-fry, fill a large wide, sturdy pan no more than two-thirds full with oil. The oil is ready for frying when it reaches 350°F (180°C) on a food thermometer, or when a cube of bread dropped into the oil browns in 30 seconds.

Dip the fish strips in the batter and fry them in batches for about 3-4 minutes, until golden and crisp. Drain each batch on paper towels while you fry the remainder. Serve with cilantro and mint relish on the side and lemon wedges for squeezing over, if you like.

SALMON & MUSTARD SEED FISHCAKES

Serves 6–7

As a child, I thought all fishcakes were seasoned with ginger and chiles, and it was something of a disappointment to realize that English fishcakes were often, well, a bit boring. My children had the same reaction when they tasted tartare sauce in Britain for the first time and realized that it wasn't always spiked with green chiles and garlic.

---

1 lb 5 oz (600 g) starchy potatoes (such as Russets)

14 oz (400 g) skin-on salmon fillets

grated zest and juice of 1 lemon, plus extra wedges to serve

4 tbsp sunflower oil, plus extra for shallow frying

1 tsp brown mustard seeds

2 onions, diced

1½ oz (40 g) ginger root, peeled and finely grated

2 red chiles, deseeded and finely chopped

1½ tsp roasted and ground cumin seeds

1 egg, lightly beaten

3 tbsp chopped cilantro leaves

¾ tsp coarsely ground black pepper, plus extra to season

sea-salt flakes

4 tbsp good-quality store-bought tartare sauce mixed with 2 tsp finely chopped pickled jalapeño chiles, to serve

FOR THE COATING

4 tbsp all-purpose flour, seasoned with salt and black pepper

2 eggs, beaten with a pinch of salt

2 cups (175 g) fresh white breadcrumbs

Peel and halve the potatoes, or quarter them if large. Bring a pot of salted water to a boil, add the potatoes and cook on medium-low heat until tender. Drain and mash them while they are still hot and then leave to one side to cool. Preheat the oven to 425°F (220°C).

Line a roasting pan with parchment paper and put the salmon fillets on top, skin-side facing down. Sprinkle half the lemon juice over the fish and season it with sea-salt flakes and black pepper. The zest from the whole lemon and remaining juice will be used later.

Cover the fillets with foil and transfer the pan to the oven for 8–10 minutes, until the salmon flakes easily and is still moist. Once it is cool enough to handle, break the fish into large flakes and discard the skin.

Heat the 4 tablespoons of oil in a karahi or wok on medium-high heat. Add the mustard seeds and swirl them around for about 30 seconds—they should start popping straight away. Turn down the heat to medium and stir in the onions, ginger and red chiles and fry for 5–7 minutes, until the onions have softened.

Add the mashed potato, lemon zest and the remaining lemon juice, along with the cumin, beaten egg, cilantro and pepper. Season with salt and fold in the salmon.

Using damp hands, shape the mixture into 14 round patties, each 2 in (5 cm) in diameter and ½ in (1.5 cm) thick. Set to one side.

For coating the fishcakes, spoon the seasoned flour onto a plate, have the beaten egg in a shallow dish, and the breadcrumbs on a tray.

One by one, dust the fishcakes in the flour, then coat them in beaten egg, and after shaking off any excess egg, coat them all over in breadcrumbs. Transfer them to a baking sheet lined with parchment paper and chill for 15–20 minutes to firm up.

Heat a ½ in (1 cm) depth of oil in a deep-sided frying pan on medium heat. Fry the fishcakes in batches for 3–4 minutes on each side, until golden and crisp. Drain each batch on paper towels while you fry the remainder. Sprinkle the fishcakes with sea-salt flakes and serve them with green chile tartare sauce and lemon wedges.

GROUND LAMB KEBABS WITH GREEN CHILES, GINGER & GARLIC   Serves 4–6

You'll find many recipes for making these pan-grilled patties, but this one is distinctive for its tart pomegranate-powder seasoning and caramelized tomato topping. Although the ingredient list is lengthy, it's an easy dish to put together and you can make and shape the mixture the day before. These are also good made with beef, if you prefer.

1 tbsp chickpea (gram) flour, sifted

1 tsp roasted and ground cumin seeds

1 tsp garam masala (see page 19)

¾ tsp red chile flakes

1 tsp cracked black peppercorns

1 tsp ground coriander

1 tbsp pomegranate powder (*anardana*) or the juice of 1 lime

2 eggs

6 large garlic cloves, crushed

1½ oz (50 g) ginger root, peeled and finely grated

3 limes, juice of 1, and the remaining 2 cut into wedges

1 lb 10 oz (750 g) ground lamb (or beef)

1 large onion, finely diced

2 green chiles, finely chopped with seeds

1 handful of cilantro, leaves and stems chopped

2 large tomatoes, thinly sliced

3–4 tbsp sunflower oil

sea salt

Roast the chickpea flour in a small, dry and sturdy pan on medium heat for about 1 minute, stirring all the time, until it releases a nutty aroma. Tip it into a small bowl and add the cumin, garam masala, chile flakes, black pepper, ground coriander and pomegranate powder and leave the mixture to one side to cool.

In a large bowl, lightly beat the eggs with the garlic, ginger and lime juice and add the ground meat and the spiced chickpea flour.

Stir in the onion, green chiles and cilantro and season generously with salt. Beat the ground meat for 10 minutes to lighten the texture—I like to use a food mixer fitted with a beater attachment.

Using damp hands, divide the meat into 2½ oz (75 g) portions—you should have 15–16 kebabs. Flatten each one into an oval shape, slightly larger than the size of your palm—about 4¾ in (2 cm) in length and 3 in (7 cm) wide, with a thickness of ¼ in (5 mm). Put the kebabs on baking sheets lined with parchment paper and leave them in the fridge for at least 30 minutes, or cover and leave overnight if you have the time.

Press a slice of tomato onto one side of each kebab. Heat a large frying pan or ridged grill pan on medium heat with 1–2 tablespoons of the oil. Fry the kebabs in batches, tomato-side facing down, for 3–4 minutes and then flip them over with a spatula and cook for another 3–4 minutes, until tender. If the sediment starts to stick to the pan between batches, pour off any excess oil, wipe the pan out with paper towels, and use fresh oil to fry the next batch. Serve with lime wedges for squeezing over.

PEPPERY LAMB KEBABS WITH PICKLED ONION & BEET

Serves 6–8

For best results, give the lamb a full two days to marinate in the peppery-lime yogurt, so that the meat can really tenderize and absorb all the toasted spice flavors too. The skewers will then cook under the broiler in just a few minutes.

1½ oz (50 g) ginger root, peeled and coarsely chopped

1 large head garlic, cloves separated and coarsely chopped

3 juicy limes

1 tsp cracked black peppercorns

2 green chiles, deseeded and finely chopped

2 lb 3 oz (1 kg) boneless lamb leg, cut into 1 in (3 cm) cubes

⅔ cup (150 g) strained full-fat Greek yogurt

2 tsp Kashmiri chile powder

2 tsp roasted and ground cumin seeds

1 tbsp roasted and ground fennel seeds

2 tsp garam masala (see page 19)

3 tbsp unsalted butter, melted

sea salt

FOR THE PICKLED ONION AND BEET

1 small red onion, finely sliced

1 small raw beet, peeled and sliced

3½ tbsp white wine vinegar

1 tsp sugar

Put the ginger, garlic and lime juice in a small food processor and blend until smooth. (Alternatively, you can use a handheld immersion blender and a bowl.) Transfer the mixture to a large mixing bowl and stir in the cracked peppercorns and the green chiles.

Add the lamb, season it with plenty of salt, and massage everything into the meat with your hands for a minute or two—I like to use disposable gloves for this. Leave to one side for 30 minutes.

Mix the strained yogurt with the chile powder, cumin, fennel and garam masala, and mix this with the lamb, making sure that the meat is evenly coated. Cover the bowl and leave the meat for 1–2 days in the fridge. The lengthy marinating helps ensure that the kebabs cook quickly to a lovely tenderness.

To make the pickled onion and beet, put the sliced onion and beet in a small bowl. Pour over the vinegar, stir in the sugar and season with salt. Leave to one side for at least an hour, or overnight if you have the time.

Take the lamb out of the fridge an hour before cooking and thread the pieces onto skewers, leaving a ½ in (1 cm) gap between each piece. I use metal skewers, but if you are using bamboo ones, soak them in water 20 minutes before cooking, to stop them scorching under the broiler.

Heat the broiler to its hottest setting and arrange the skewers on a rack over a foil-lined broiler pan. Cook for 3–4 minutes on each side, turning once, until they have browned all over, then brush them with the melted butter. The marination will have tenderized the meat, so they won't take long to cook. These kebabs are best served pink in the center. Serve with the pickled onion and beet.

LAMB RIB CHOPS WITH MANGO POWDER, JAGGERY & TAMARIND Serves 4–6

Because lamb rib chops are quick to cook, their spice-paste coating will retain its fruity flavor without scorching in the pan. If you're short on time, you could skip making the tamarind masala and serve the lamb straight after frying—it's what my mom would do, and the lamb will still taste fantastic. However, I think the sweet-sour notes of the masala topping give it an extra lift.

---

2 tsp Kashmiri chile powder

1 tbsp mango powder (*amchoor*)

½ tsp ground turmeric

1 tsp garam masala (see page 19)

3 tbsp white wine vinegar

2 tbsp sunflower oil

12 lamb rib chops

sea salt

sesame & green chile chutney (see page 285), to serve

FOR THE MASALA

1 onion, finely chopped

4 garlic cloves, coarsely chopped

1 oz (25 g) ginger root, peeled and coarsely chopped

½ tsp ground cinnamon

scant 1 cup (200 ml) hot water, plus extra if needed

2 tsp jaggery or light brown sugar

1 tbsp tamarind pulp (see page 21), or to taste

Mix the chile powder with the mango powder, turmeric, garam masala, vinegar and oil and season with salt. Rub the paste over the lamb—it's best to wear disposable gloves for this so that the turmeric doesn't stain your hands.

Put the lamb ribs on a tray, cover and marinate in the fridge for at least 1 hour, or overnight if you have the time.

Heat a dry, sturdy frying pan on medium heat and cook the lamb chops in batches for 2–3 minutes on each side, until they are just tender and pink in the middle. Turn them on their side so that the fatty edge faces downwards and fry for 1 minute more. Transfer to a tray and keep warm.

To make the masala, pour off any excess fat from the lamb pan, leaving behind 3 tablespoons. Add the onion and fry for about 10–12 minutes on medium-low heat, until golden.

Put the garlic, ginger and cinnamon in a small food processor with 3½ tbsp of the hot water and blend to a smooth paste. You might need to add a little more water to help it on its way. (Alternatively, you can use a handheld immersion blender and a bowl.)

Add the paste to the onions and fry for 2 minutes. Stir in the jaggery and remaining ⅔ cup (150 ml) of hot water and simmer for 2–3 minutes, until the water has evaporated and the masala thickened. Add enough tamarind pulp to sharpen and then take the pan off the heat.

Arrange the lamb on a serving plate and spoon over the onion and tamarind masala. Top with dollops of sesame & green chile chutney before serving.

NORTHWEST INDIA

GROUND LAMB & GREEN CHILE WRAPS
Serves 4–6

The garlicky ground meat in this recipe is tart with yogurt, sharp with hits of chile and softened with warming cumin. I serve it inside chapatis or tortillas, but it's also lovely when piled onto hot buttered toast. Don't be put off by the abundance of chiles—the heat comes from the seeds, but we're using deseeded ones here. Choose fat green chiles because they are milder than the thinner variety—pale green Turkish ones or even fresh jalapeños will both work well.

FOR THE TOPPING

1 banana shallot, thinly sliced lengthways

¾ oz (20 g) ginger root, peeled and finely sliced into thin matchsticks

juice of 1 lime

¼ tsp Kashmiri chile powder

¼ tsp roasted and ground cumin seeds

½ tsp sugar

2 tbsp chopped cilantro leaves

sea salt

FOR THE GROUND MEAT

1 lb 5 oz (600 g) ground lamb

⅔ cup (150 ml) full-fat Greek yogurt

1 tsp ground turmeric

1 tsp cumin seeds

⅔ cup (150 ml) sunflower oil

4 onions, 3 sliced and 1 diced

1 large head garlic, cloves separated and peeled

8 fat green chiles (7 oz/200 g), deseeded and cut into ½ in (1 cm) pieces

8–10 chapatis (see page 279) or 6 in (15 cm) diameter tortillas

First, make the topping. Put the shallot and ginger in a small bowl and mix with the lime juice. Stir in the chile powder, cumin and sugar and season with salt. Leave to one side for at least an hour. (You could make this the day before and leave it covered in the fridge.)

When you're ready to cook, prepare the ground meat. Put the meat in a large bowl and add the yogurt, turmeric and cumin seeds and mix well. Leave to one side for at least 30 minutes.

Heat the oil in a sturdy pan on medium heat and fry the sliced onions for 10–15 minutes, stirring regularly, until golden.

Turn the heat to high, add the seasoned ground meat and fry for 10 minutes, or until the meat loses its raw appearance. Pour over enough hot water to cover the ground meat by three-quarters and add the chopped onion, garlic cloves and chiles. Turn the heat to low, cover the pan, and simmer for 15 minutes.

Remove the lid, increase the heat to medium and continue cooking for about 15 minutes, until the liquid evaporates and the ground meat starts to brown—you'll need to keep an eye on it and stir it every few minutes. Add a small ladleful of water if the ground meat starts to catch on the bottom of the pan.

Warm the chapatis or wraps on a griddle or in the microwave oven for 30 seconds and lay them on a counter. Put a heaped tablespoon of warm green chile ground meat down the center of each one and then scatter with chopped cilantro and finish with a few lime-steeped shallot slices and ginger strips. Roll the bread around the filling, cut the wraps in half if you like, and serve straight away.

LAMB RIBS SIMMERED IN FENNEL SEED & GINGER MILK Serves 3

This recipe is loosely based on how many Kashmiri Pandit home cooks like to make this dish. I love how the glistening fat on these fried ribs yields to tender lamb imbued with the flavor of sweet fennel, smoky brown cardamom and punchy ground ginger. Lamb ribs often don't get the attention they deserve, which is a shame, because they're affordable, available from most supermarkets and make a great snack with drinks.

---

2 lb 3 oz (1 kg) lamb ribs (about 9 single ribs)

1 tbsp garam masala (see page 19)

1 tbsp roasted and ground fennel seeds

1 tsp ground ginger

3 brown cardamom pods, pierced

8 green cardamom pods, pierced

4 Indian bay leaves (*tej patta*) or a 1 in (3 cm) cinnamon stick

generous pinch of ground asafoetida (*heeng*; optional)

3 cups (750 ml) whole milk

½ cup (100 g) ghee (see page 18), or ½ cup (120 ml) sunflower oil and 2 tbsp unsalted butter, for frying

sea salt

Preheat the oven to 320°F (160°C). Put the ribs in a large Dutch oven or heavy pot and add the garam masala, ground fennel, ground ginger, brown and green cardamom pods, Indian bay leaves or cinnamon stick, and asafoetida (if using). Pour over the milk, add enough water to cover the ribs and season with salt. Place the pot on medium heat and bring to a simmer, stirring often.

Cover the pot and transfer it to the oven for 2½–3 hours, until the meat is tender and almost falling off the bone. Alternatively, continue cooking the ribs over a low heat on the stove. Using tongs, carefully lift the ribs from the spiced milk to a wire rack and leave to cool. Transfer them to a tray, cover and refrigerate for 2–3 hours.

Heat the ghee or oil (but not the butter just yet) in a large frying pan on medium-high heat and fry the ribs for 2–3 minutes on both sides, until golden. If you are using oil, add the butter when you flip the ribs over after one side has colored. Drain and serve straight away.

SPICED BROTH

Any leftover milky spiced stock makes a comforting, light and fragrant broth. Chill the cooled stock for 2–3 hours and then lift off and discard the fat, which will have solidified by now. Strain the stock and bring it to a boil in a saucepan on medium heat. Stir in 3 tablespoons of basmati or short grain rice, turn the heat to low and simmer half-covered for 7–10 minutes, until the rice is cooked. Season with salt, stir in 2 tablespoons of shredded mint or chopped cilantro and serve in deep bowls.

GRILLED CHICKEN KEBABS IN SPINACH & CILANTRO CREAM

Serves 4–6

Two different marinations provide richness and depth of flavor to these tender, grilled chicken pieces. While the first marination imparts robust garlicky character, the second one—herby spinach cream, sharpened with chiles—brings garden-fresh greenness and delicacy.

---

6 skinless, boneless chicken thighs (about 1 lb 12 oz/800 g)

2 rounded tbsp full-fat Greek yogurt

juice of 2 limes

1 oz (30 g) ginger root, peeled and finely grated

6 garlic cloves, crushed

½ tsp ground black peppercorns

½ tsp garam masala (see page 19)

FOR THE SECOND MARINATION

5 cups (160 g) baby spinach leaves

1 large handful of cilantro, leaves and stems coarsely chopped

2 tbsp mint leaves

2 green chiles, coarsely chopped with seeds

2 tsp sugar

½ cup (125 ml) heavy cream

2 tbsp sunflower oil

1 tsp store-bought or homemade *chaat masala* (see page 19; optional)

sea salt

1 lime, cut into wedges, to serve

Cut the chicken into 1½ in (4 cm) pieces and mix them with the yogurt, lime juice, ginger, garlic, pepper and garam masala. Cover the bowl and marinate the chicken in the fridge for at least 1 hour, or overnight if you have the time.

Heat a sturdy, dry pan on high heat. Add the spinach and cook for about 40 seconds, until the leaves have wilted, then scoop them into a colander set over a bowl. Squeeze any excess water from the leaves with your hands once they are cool enough to handle.

Put the spinach in a food processor and add the cilantro, mint, green chiles and sugar, then season with salt. Blend everything until it's finely chopped and then pour in the cream and give it a quick pulse until it becomes a smooth paste.

Lift the chicken pieces from the yogurty marinade and mix them with the spinach and herb paste. Leave to marinate for 30 minutes at room temperature.

Heat the broiler to its hottest setting. Thread the chicken onto skewers, leaving a ½ in (1 cm) gap between each piece. I use metal skewers, but if you are using bamboo ones, soak them in water 20 minutes before cooking, to stop them scorching under the broiler. Line a broiler pan with foil, arrange the skewers on the rack and drizzle them with the oil.

Grill the chicken for 5 minutes on each side, until the edges have browned and the juices run clear when pierced with a knife. Sprinkle with *chaat masala*, if using, and serve with lime wedges for squeezing over.

COMMUNITY ROOTS
SOUTH

ANITA DE CANAGA, PONDICHERRY

The road from Chennai, Tamil Nadu, to Pondicherry runs parallel to the Bay of Bengal. Although my route is mainly inland, it offers a view of rural landscapes and an abundance of tall palms, banana trees and papayas. Bunches of fresh green coconuts are a regular sight, hanging from sturdy branches.

We park on the verge, under leafy umbrella-like shade, and the driver calls out in Tamil for "someone with a knife." The heat outside is intense and the coastal air salty. A woman squats on the ground, balances a coconut on a gnarled tree trunk, and wields a small hand-held scythe with death defying-precision. She swipes this way and that, stripping off angular wedges until the fibrous inner yields, so that she can push a straw through. The coconut water is sweet, grassy and very cooling. Her son deftly repurposes a slice of the outer shell into a spatula and scrapes and scoops out layers of soft, creamy flesh. Its jelly-like texture and rich creamy flavor is delicious and as smooth as panna cotta.

We pass the vast salt pans of Marakkanam on the East Coast Road. It's the rainy season, so many of the salt pyramids are covered with tarpaulin, yet even then, sharp splinters catch and reflect the harsh sunlight. The driver parks outside a nondescript café with darkened windows. It's lunchtime but I'm the only diner. The menu reads like an encyclopaedia, with the untold delights of Punjabi, Chinese and "English" dishes—offering everything from butter chicken to noodles and baked vegetables in white sauce. There's also a small section dedicated to local specialties, and on this page are listed chicken curry, fish curry, vegetable curry and, well, you get the idea. Despite some apprehension, the food is stunning—tender king fish steaks, simmered in a coconut, chile and tamarind masala and a bowl of boiled rice.

The rural outposts give way to signs for "Promenade Beach," evening crowds, cotton candy sellers and beachside kiosks. We've arrived at the coastal city of Pondicherry. The French governed Pondicherry (renamed Puducherry) for more than 100 years until 1954 and left a legacy of architecture, language, culture and recipes. I'm interested in the combination of French and Indian culinary customs here, described in India as "Creole."

I've booked a four-day stay at the Gratitude Heritage Home, sited in the old French Quarter. The building was built around 200 years ago and has been restored and refurbished with European-style slatted windows, teakwood beams and reclaimed Tamil and French vintage furniture. Like many historical landmarks in the area, its exterior is painted bright and cheerful. This one is an eye-catching mustard-gold, edged with white. Inside, though, it's a tranquil retreat set in the heart of what feels like a very Gallic enclave.

Pit stop on the highway between Chennai and Pondicherry.

▶ Out on the street, the road signs are still written in French. Some of the old houses need a bit of love and restoration—some of the others have been converted to hotels and restaurants, but still preserve their heritage. For breakfast, I'm served croissants and Tamil *uttapam*—thick pancakes, topped with fried onions and green chiles.

Anita de Canaga lives on the outskirts of the city in a large, light-filled home. She pours me a glass of *nannari*, a refreshing, chilled drink made from boiled and strained *sarsaparilla*, an earthy-tasting root, sweetened with jaggery and sharpened with lemon juice. It's often served to replenish and reset the body's balance on scorching hot, summer days.

I ask about her background, and she replies without hesitation "I'm a Franco-Tamil-Catholic!" Six years ago, she noticed the lack of Tamil-inspired French dishes on restaurant menus. She's right; I've seen *coq au vin* and crème brûlée on local menus, alongside typical Tamil dishes, but rarely the two styles of cooking combining on one plate. Keen to celebrate the community's culinary heritage, Anita and her parents launched a supper club, run from their home kitchen.

The French connection is from her grandparents—they worked for the French Government for 35 years and lived in Vietnam and Cambodia, returning to India in the early 1950s. Anita remembers Ava, her grandma, cooking pigeons with peas, making foie gras, and fermenting wine and coconut toddy, which she kept cool in a pitcher buried deep in the earth.

Anita's Ava took pride in her French cooking methods, often adding a Tamil twist— perhaps a few curry leaves here, popped mustard seeds there. Ava was stubborn and strong willed and ran the kitchen single-handed—even Anita's mom wasn't allowed to cook. But she had a soft spot for Anita, who, at three years old, was given permission to help peel vegetables. Anita adds, "As long as I didn't get in her way." Ava was suspicious of modern gadgets—all pounding of masalas was done by hand to extract maximum flavor. It wasn't until 1980 that an electric blender was bought for the house.

Anita remembers accompanying Ava to church on Sundays. After the service, Ava would buy a baguette from the baker and, once home, the two of them would dip hunks of bread into fresh, creamy coconut milk and enjoy it with *"decoction"* coffee. This strong brew is made from roasted ground coffee beans, boiled in water, and left to steep. A small portion is decanted into a cup and topped up with frothy boiling milk.

Anita and her mother replicate Ava's Indo-French (by-way-of Vietnam) dishes for their supper club, while her father designs and writes the menus. There might be an appetizer of crisp-fried anchovies in red chile batter, or tiny shrimp cooked with red chiles, mustard seeds and turmeric, folded with wilted spinach leaves. Spring rolls, served with a robust chile dipping sauce, are also popular. A Tamil vegetarian staple of *sambar*, usually tamarind dal cooked with vegetables, is supplemented with chopped goat meat, so that it's more like a stew.

Another spice blend, *vadouvan*, is a concentrated mix developed locally to help the French cope with the chile levels. Anita

▶ smiles and says, "It's a bit like using British curry powder but with more flavor." Mustard seeds, garlic, onions, turmeric, fennel seeds and sesame and coconut oils are mixed and shaped into balls and dried in the fierce summer heat. Her mother makes a big batch every April—this is kept in an airtight box and small amounts crumbled into hot oil, before stirring it into dals, soups and even over roasts.

I'm in Anita's kitchen and she's making *porial*, a quick, easy and usually vegetarian stir fry, but she's also adding ground chicken. Coconut oil is heated in a traditional terracotta pot, which is a great for conducting and retaining heat, and also for setting curd and chilling water. In go the mustard seeds, which start spluttering straight away, and then a spoonful of lentils for crunch. More spices and ingredients are added and the toasty smell changes from astringent to earthy, nutty and sweet. Cumin seeds, garlic, a tumble of curry leaves, are followed by sliced shallots, turmeric for sharpness, and the warming scent of aromatics. The ground meat is sealed in the pot, chopped vegetables stirred in, and everything simmered in water for a few minutes. Anita takes off the lid and adds "just enough black pepper"—that's three rounded teaspoons. I love how pepper is a key feature of this *poriyal* and not a background spice.

Although Anita lived in France for a few years, home is still Pondicherry. I follow her into the garden as she plucks banana leaves to eat from as plates. Back in the kitchen, she removes the central stem, cuts the leaf into manageable sizes and gives them a quick wipe with a damp cloth. The leaves are arranged on her dining table and topped with short-grained *seeraga samba* rice, crowned with a ladle of tart tamarind lentils. Her glorious chicken and vegetable *poriyal* is spooned on one side. Next, a dab of green mango pickle steeped in gingery, chile-flecked sesame oil. There's a pinch of salt on the leaf—Anita says that it's a seasoning, but also a symbol of the bond between host and guest. And there's also a banana, another traditional feature—it isn't supposed to be eaten, but presented to friends as a portable snack if hunger pangs strike on the homeward journey.

Pondicherry, also known as Puducherry, is renowned for its brightly colored buildings and its beaches.

1. Anita, holding her terracotta cooking pot filled with *poriyal* for our lunch.

2. The simple elegance and calm of Gratitude Heritage homestay, where I stayed in Pondicherry.

3. Anita's tropical kitchen garden.

CHICKEN & VEGETABLE PORIYAL

Serves 4

ANITA DE CANAGA

Although *poriyals* are usually made with vegetables, for this colorful dish, my friend Anita gives her chopped vegetable stir-fry a makeover by adding a little ground chicken. I love the way in which everyday ingredients are given a boost with a couple of crackling curry leaves, popped mustard seeds and softened garlic cloves. *Poriyals* are open to adaptation—you could also use ground lamb or beef and vary the vegetables, too. I sometimes add sliced cabbage instead of beans. Some fluffy boiled rice or sliced French bread will go well with this dish.

---

4 tbsp melted coconut oil or sunflower oil

1 tsp brown mustard seeds

1 tsp skinned white urad lentils (*dhuli urad dal*; optional)

1 tsp split pigeon peas (*toor dal*; optional)

1 tsp cumin seeds

4 garlic cloves, peeled and lightly bruised in a mortar with a pestle

about 15 fresh curry leaves

5½ oz (150 g) shallots, sliced

½ tsp ground turmeric

7 oz (200 g) ground chicken; or 2-3 skinless, boneless chicken thighs, finely chopped

½ tsp garam masala (see page 19)

5½ oz (150 g) fine green beans, thinly sliced

2 carrots, finely chopped

1 tsp ground black peppercorns

sea salt

Heat the oil in a large frying pan over medium-high heat and add the mustard seeds. As soon as the popping stops, turn the heat to medium and add the lentils, if you are using them: Stir in the white lentils first, followed, after a few seconds, by the yellow *toor dal* and fry for about 20-30 seconds, until golden, stirring all the time.

Add the cumin and garlic and cook for about 30 seconds, until fragrant, then stir in the curry leaves. Once the crackling quietens, add the shallots, season with salt, and fry for 3-4 minutes, until the shallots start to soften.

Add the turmeric, chicken and garam masala and continue cooking for 2-3 minutes, until the meat has sealed and has lost its raw appearance.

Stir in the green beans, carrots and enough water to moisten—about 3½ tbsp. Cover and cook on low heat for 5-7 minutes, until the chicken is tender and the vegetables still have a bite to them. Stir in the black pepper and serve straight away.

SOUTH INDIA

CHICKEN & RED PEPPER SKEWERS

Serves 3–4

It's important that you use thighs or ground chicken with a bit of fat in it for these kebabs, known as *gilafi*, because breasts will quickly dry out under a hot broiler. *Gilafi* means a type of covering, and these kebabs are rolled and cloaked in finely diced pepper and red onions before being cooked, which gives them a bejeweled appearance. You could make them without the coating, and if you do, they would be known as chicken *seekh* kebabs.

---

1 lb (500 g) ground chicken, or 5–6 (1 lb/500 g) skinless, boneless chicken thighs

1 red onion, diced

1 tsp Kashmiri chile powder

¾ tsp garam masala (see page 19)

4 garlic cloves, crushed

1 oz (30 g) ginger root, peeled and finely grated

¾ tsp roasted and ground cumin seeds

1 tbsp ground almonds

juice of 1 lime

2 tbsp chopped cilantro leaves

1 tbsp chopped mint leaves

2 green chiles, deseeded and finely chopped

1 tbsp full-fat Greek yogurt

sea salt

FOR THE COATING

1 red pepper, deseeded and finely chopped

1 small red onion, finely chopped

5 tbsp (75 g) unsalted butter, melted

TO SERVE

fresh red chile chutney (see page 285)

1 lime, cut into wedges

Put the ground chicken in a bowl. If you are using chicken thighs, roughly chop them then blend in a food processor until very finely chopped.

Mix the chicken with the red onion, chile powder, garam masala, garlic, ginger, cumin, ground almonds, lime juice, cilantro, mint, green chiles and yogurt in a bowl.

Season generously with salt and then beat for 10 minutes to incorporate plenty of air. I like to do this in a stand mixer fitted with a beater attachment. Cover the bowl and leave it in the fridge for at least 1 hour, or overnight if you have the time.

Using damp hands, divide the ground meat into 9–10 portions, each about the size of a lime. Pat each portion into an oval shape on your palm to about the length of your index finger and 1½ in (4 cm) in diameter and then mold it around a skewer. I like to use metal skewers, but if you are using bamboo ones, soak them in water for 20 minutes beforehand, so that they don't burn on the broiler.

Lightly press the diced red pepper and red onion all over the surface of each kebab and chill the kebabs for 15 minutes to set them in shape.

Meanwhile, heat the broiler to its hottest setting and line a broiler pan with foil.

Arrange the skewers on the broiler rack—you may need to cook them in two batches. Grill for 5 minutes on each side, or until completely cooked through, using tongs to turn them over. Brush the kebabs with melted butter every 2 minutes while they cook. Serve with fresh red chile chutney and lime wedges for squeezing over.

RED CHILE & CURRY LEAF CHICKEN
Serves 4

I love how the caramelized onion masala clings to these chicken pieces as they fry in the karahi, while the curry leaves deliver bursts of fresh citrussy flavor. You can buy fresh curry leaves from any South Asian grocery store, but they're also available online. I freeze mine in a plastic bag and use them straight from the freezer.

---

1 red onion, coarsely chopped

1 oz (30 g) ginger root, peeled and coarsely chopped

6 garlic cloves, coarsely chopped

2 green chiles, coarsely chopped with seeds

2 tbsp white wine vinegar

8 skinless, boneless chicken thighs (about 2 lb 3 oz/1 kg), cut into 1 in (3 cm) pieces

FOR THE MASALA

6 tbsp sunflower oil

about 15 curry leaves

4 small red onions, sliced

2 tsp roasted and ground fennel seeds

½ tsp garam masala (see page 19)

½ tsp ground turmeric

½ tsp Kashmiri chile powder

juice of 1 lime

Put the red onion in a small food processor with the ginger, garlic, green chiles and vinegar. Add 2 tablespoons of water and blend until smooth. You can also use a handheld immersion blender and a bowl for this. Turn the paste into a bowl and mix well with the chicken. Cover and leave to marinate in the fridge for at least 1 hour, or overnight if you have the time.

When you are ready to cook, make the masala. Heat the oil in a karahi or wok set on medium-high heat. Add the curry leaves and swirl them around for a few seconds, until they release their aroma. Stir in the onions and fry on medium-low heat for 8–10 minutes, until softened.

Add the marinated chicken and fry for 3–4 minutes, stirring all the time, until sealed. Stir in the ground fennel, garam masala, turmeric and chile powder and cook for 10 minutes, until the masala has browned and the chicken is tender. Add a splash of water if the masala starts to catch on the bottom of the pan. Add the lime juice and serve.

PORK WITH SICHUAN PEPPER

Serves 6

The original version of this dish comes from Nagaland and was first cooked for me by my friend Achi Dhingra. Her extended family meet in early December for Nagaland's Hornbill Festival, which celebrates the ancient cultural traditions and diversity of the region's tribal communities. Achi's mother, Kaholi Chophyhj, spends days preparing for the annual feast, the highlight of which is pork, slow cooked on an open fire with fermented bamboo shoots and smoky chiles. It's seasoned with *timur*, which tastes similar to Sichuan peppercorns. Inspired by the rich umami flavors of Achi's wonderful dish, this simplified version is my adaptation of the original.

---

10 dried Kashmiri red chiles (about 1 oz/30 g)

1 tsp Sichuan peppercorns

1 lb 10 oz (750 g) tomatoes

1 large head garlic, cloves separated, peeled and coarsely chopped

2 tsp chipotle chile paste

1 lb (500 g) boneless pork shoulder, cut into 1 in (3 cm) pieces

1 lb (500 g) boneless pork belly, cut into 1 in (3 cm) pieces

Using scissors, snip the tops off the chiles and shake to remove most of the seeds. Put the chiles in a small heatproof bowl, cover with boiling water and leave to one side for 30 minutes to rehydrate. Drain, reserving the soaking liquid.

Heat a small dry pan on medium heat and roast the peppercorns for about 30 seconds, until fragrant. Using a mortar and pestle, grind them to a powder.

Bring a large pot of water to a boil then turn off the heat. Submerge the tomatoes in the water for about 40 seconds then lift them out and plunge them straight into a bowl of cold water. Peel off the skins with a sharp knife.

Put the tomatoes in a blender with the Sichuan pepper, drained, rehydrated chiles, garlic and chipotle paste. Blend everything until smooth and season with salt.

Put the pork pieces, fat-side facing downwards, at the bottom of a sturdy Dutch oven, then set the cold pot over medium heat. After a few minutes, the pork will release its fat and start to fry. Fry the pork until browned. You may need to do this in two batches.

Preheat the oven to 320°F (160°C). Add half of the tomato-chile purée from the blender to the pork and fry until it starts to thicken. Pour in the rest and continue frying until the masala darkens and beads of oil appear around the edge of the pot—this should take around 20 minutes. Add a ladleful of the reserved chile-soaking water if the masala starts to catch on the bottom of the pot.

Pour over enough chile-soaking water or plain water to half-cover the pork. Cover the pot and cook in the oven for 1 hour 15 minutes, or until the pork is tender. This dish tastes best if made a day before it is needed. Reheat until it's piping hot to serve.

GOAN CHORIZO ROLLS — Serves 6

Goan food is varied and diverse and many dishes reflect a Portuguese heritage, with adopted recipes being adapted to suit local preferences and homegrown produce. Often made at home, Goan chorizo is fiery and seasoned with Indian spices, which include turmeric, cumin and cinnamon. I've used a ready-made hot cooking chorizo here, which keeps this recipe simple. Make this for a weekend brunch—it can be scaled up for a crowd too.

- 4 tbsp sunflower oil
- 2 large onions, thinly sliced
- 1 lb (450 g) spicy cooking chorizo, skin removed, broken into ½ in (1 cm) pieces
- 4 garlic cloves, finely chopped
- 2 green chiles, deseeded and finely chopped
- 2 large tomatoes, coarsely chopped
- 3 tbsp white wine vinegar
- 2 tbsp chopped cilantro
- 6 soft white burger buns, split and buttered
- salt and ground black pepper

Heat the oil in a frying pan on medium-low heat and cook the sliced onions with salt to season for 15–20 minutes, stirring often, until browned.

Add the chorizo and fry for 5 minutes, until it releases oil and starts to color. Stir in the garlic, green chiles, tomatoes and vinegar and continue cooking for 2–3 minutes, until the tomatoes begin to soften.

Add the cilantro, check the seasoning and generously fill the buttered buns with the mixture. Serve straight away.

LARGE
PLATES

PANEER IN GINGER & FENNEL SEED MASALA Serves 4

Fennel seeds, ground ginger and saffron are key seasonings in a Kashmiri spice box and impart warmth, astringency and sweetness. Like so many Indian curries, this Mughal-inspired dish is open to interpretation—for example, you could use lightly fried mushrooms instead of the paneer. Spinach with garlic, chile & ginger (see page 241) would make a good match to enjoy alongside.

¼ tsp saffron strands

2 tbsp hot water

9 oz (250 g) store-bought or homemade paneer (see page 20), cut into ¾ x 1 in (2 x 3 cm) rectangles

about 2 cups (500 ml) sunflower oil, for deep-frying

3 green chiles, 2 deseeded and finely chopped; 1 deseeded and finely shredded

1½ tsp roasted and ground fennel seeds

1 tsp ground ginger

2 tsp sugar

1 tbsp chickpea (gram) flour

1 tbsp full-fat Greek yogurt

scant 1 cup (200 ml) whole milk

1 tbsp melted ghee (see page 18) or sunflower oil

4 green cardamom pods, pierced

4 Indian bay leaves (*tej patta*), or 1 in (3 cm) cinnamon stick

sea salt

boiled rice or Indian flatbreads, to serve

Bruise the saffron strands in the hot water with the back of a teaspoon and leave to one side for 1 hour (or longer) to extract maximum color and flavor.

If you are using store-bought paneer, soak the cubes in hot water for 10 minutes to soften them, then discard the water and pat the pieces dry with paper towels.

Fill a karahi or wok no more than two-thirds full with the oil. The oil is ready for frying when it reaches 350°F (180°C) on a food thermometer, or when a cube of bread dropped into the oil browns in 30 seconds. Deep fry the paneer in batches, for about 1 minute per batch, until golden, then drain them on paper towels.

For the sauce, mix the finely chopped green chiles with the fennel, ginger, sugar, chickpea flour, yogurt and milk. (Keep the shredded green chile for later.)

Heat the ghee or oil in a sauté pan on medium-high heat and fry the cardamom pods and Indian bay leaves or cinnamon stick for 20 seconds, until the pods slightly darken.

Take the pan off the heat, add the spiced yogurt, then return it to the stove. Bring the sauce to a simmer, stirring, on medium-low heat, and leave it to gently bubble for 1–2 minutes. You may need to add an extra ladleful of milk or water if it is too thick—aim for the consistency of light cream. Stir in enough saffron and soaking water to color and flavor the sauce, taking care not to add too much—saffron varieties can vary in intensity, so it's a good idea to add the spice gradually.

Turn off the heat and add the paneer—the heat of the sauce will warm it. Season with salt, to taste, scatter with the shredded green chile and serve with boiled rice or Indian flatbreads.

HIMALAYAN BELT · LARGE PLATES

CHARRED BROCCOLI WITH MUSHROOMS IN COCONUT SAUCE

Serves 4

Blanched broccoli, lightly coated in gingery coconut cream, cooked to a delicious char under the broiler with the stems retaining their crisp texture. I've combined them here with golden-fried onions and mushrooms in a coconut and lime sauce—you could alternatively serve them as a side dish, straight from the broiler or grill.

FOR THE BROCCOLI

7 oz (200 g) long-stem broccoli

3 tbsp coconut cream

4 large garlic cloves, crushed

¾ oz (20 g) ginger root, peeled and finely grated

1 green chile, deseeded and finely chopped

½ tsp Kashmiri chile powder

1 tsp ground coriander

1 tsp garam masala (see page 19)

4 tbsp sunflower oil

sea salt

FOR THE MASALA

4-6 tbsp sunflower oil

1 onion, finely sliced

7 oz (200 g) cremini mushrooms, quartered

1 x 14 oz (400 ml) can of full-fat coconut milk

juice of ½ lime

2 tbsp chopped cilantro leaves

Bring a large pot of salted water to a boil on high heat and blanch the broccoli for 1 minute. Drain it in a colander, then rinse with water and pat the stems dry with paper towels.

Mix the coconut cream with the garlic, ginger, green chile, chile powder, ground coriander and garam masala and season it generously with salt. Coat the broccoli all over with half the spiced cream and save the rest for the sauce. Leave to one side while you make the masala.

Heat the 4-6 tablespoons of oil in a karahi or wok on medium heat and fry the onion for 12-15 minutes, until golden. Add the reserved spiced coconut cream and cook, stirring all the time, for a further 5 minutes, until aromatic.

Add the mushrooms and continue frying for 3-4 minutes—you may need to add a splash of water if the masala starts to catch on the bottom of the pan. Pour the coconut milk into a jug and whisk until smooth. Then, gradually pour the milk into the pan and bring to a simmer, stirring often. Sharpen with the lime juice and stir in the chopped cilantro. Keep the masala warm while you finish cooking the broccoli.

Heat the broiler to its hottest setting. Line the broiler pan with foil and lay the broccoli stems in a single layer on the rack. Drizzle them with the 4 tablespoons of sunflower oil and cook for 4-5 minutes, turning halfway, until they are just tender but still have a bite, and are evenly colored.

Ladle the warm mushrooms and coconut sauce into a serving bowl and arrange the grilled broccoli stems on top.

LENTIL KOFTAS IN TOMATO, GINGER & GARLIC MASALA

Serves 6

¾ cup (250 g) yellow moong lentils, soaked in hot water for 2–3 hours

3½ cups (850 ml) hot water (used in two parts—so keep hot)

3½ tbsp ghee (see page 18) or unsalted butter

large pinch of ground asafoetida (*heeng*)

6 tbsp sunflower oil, plus 2 cups (500 ml) for deep-frying

1 large onion, coarsely grated

1½ oz (50 g) ginger root, peeled and finely grated

5 large garlic cloves, crushed

¼ tsp ground turmeric

½ tsp Kashmiri chile powder

1 tsp garam masala (see page 19)

1½ cups (350 ml) tomato passata

2 tsp sugar

sea salt

I first came across this recipe in Anoothi Vishal's excellent book, *Mrs LC's Table*, in which she documents the food of her Kayasth family. The Kayasths are a community whose culinary culture is shaped by both Hindu and Muslim influences. These fried dal koftas have become one of our family favorites—they're fantastic at absorbing the garlicky tomato masala while retaining their shape and soft texture. Here's my adaptation of Anoothi's splendid *dal ke kofte*.

TO SERVE

1 small red onion, very thinly sliced

½ tsp roasted and ground cumin seeds

¼ tsp Kashmiri chile powder

½ tsp sea salt

2 tbsp chopped cilantro leaves

Indian flatbreads or boiled rice

Drain the soaked lentils in a sieve and transfer them to a food processor or blender. Pour over ⅔ cup (150 ml) of the hot water and process to a smooth paste.

Heat the ghee or butter in a karahi or wok on medium heat. Add the asafoetida and, after 10 seconds, the lentil paste. Season generously with salt and fry for 5 minutes, stirring all the time with a large metal spoon, until the mixture thickens to the consistency of stiff mashed potatoes. Spread the paste on a baking sheet and leave to one side.

Wash the karahi or wok and return it to the stove. Heat the 6 tablespoons of oil on medium heat, add the grated onion and fry for 10 minutes, until golden. Stir in the ginger and garlic and cook for a further 1 minute to soften. Add the turmeric, chile powder and garam masala, and after a few seconds, the passata and sugar. Turn the heat to low and simmer without a lid for 20-25 minutes, stirring often, until the masala thickens to a soft dropping consistency and beads of oil appear around the edge of the pan.

Mix 2 tablespoons of this masala with the lentil paste. Using damp hands, shape it into 26-28 balls, each about the size of a small walnut, and arrange them on a baking sheet lined with parchment paper. Set aside.

To deep-fry, fill a large wide, sturdy pan no more than two-thirds full with oil. The oil is ready for frying when it reaches 350°F (180°C) on a food thermometer, or when a cube of bread dropped into the oil browns in 30 seconds. Fry the koftas in batches for 3-4 minutes each, until golden all over. Drain on paper towels while you fry the remainder.

Pour the remaining 3 cups (700 ml) of hot water into the remaining tomato masala in the pan and bring it to a boil on medium heat. Add the koftas, turn the heat to low and simmer without a lid for 5 minutes, until the koftas have softened.

To serve, first mix the onion in a bowl with the cumin, chile powder and salt. Scatter the koftas with the chopped cilantro and serve with the spiced onions on the side. Accompany with Indian flatbreads or boiled rice.

ROAST PORTOBELLO MUSHROOMS WITH CANNELLINI BEANS Serves 4

These large, open-textured mushrooms develop a meaty flavor as they braise in the oven and their buttery garlicky juices work well with the smoky earthiness of brown cardamom-infused tomato sauce. You could use canned chickpeas, black eye peas or butter beans instead of the cannellini, if you prefer.

5 tbsp (75 g) unsalted butter, softened

3 garlic cloves, crushed

¾ oz (20 g) ginger root, peeled and finely grated

2 green chiles, deseeded and finely chopped

1 tsp roasted and ground cumin seeds

4 Portobello mushrooms (about 10½ oz/300 g in total)

1 lime, for squeezing

FOR THE BEANS

4 dried Kashmiri red chiles

2 tbsp ghee (see page 18), or 3 tbsp sunflower oil

2 brown cardamom pods, pierced

1 large onion, diced

½ tsp ground turmeric

scant 1 cup (200 ml) tomato passata

1 x 14 oz (400 g) can of cannellini beans

1 tbsp chopped cilantro leaves

sea salt

boiled rice or crusty bread, to serve

First, prepare the chiles for the beans. Snip the tops off the Kashmiri chiles, shake out most of the seeds, and put them in a small bowl. Cover them with about 1½ cups (350 ml) of hot water and leave them to soak for at least 1 hour, until softened, then scoop them out and reserve the soaking water. Roughly chop the chiles and leave to one side.

When you're ready to cook, preheat the oven to 340°F (170°C). Mix the butter with the garlic, ginger, green chiles and cumin. Put the mushrooms in an ovenproof frying pan, rounded side facing downwards, and dot the gills with the spiced butter. Squeeze over the lime, cover with parchment paper, then seal the pan with foil and bake for 45 minutes, until the mushrooms are tender but still hold their shape.

Meanwhile, make the tomato masala. Heat the ghee or oil in a small pot on medium-high heat and add the brown cardamom pods. Fry pan about 30 seconds, then turn the heat to medium, add the onion, season with salt, and fry for 10-12 minutes, until golden.

Stir in the turmeric and cook for a few seconds to remove any raw flavor, then add the passata and chopped Kashmiri chiles. Pour in a scant 1 cup (200 ml) of the reserved soaking water from the chiles and simmer, uncovered, for 10 minutes, until the masala thickens to a coating consistency. Drain the beans in a colander, rinse them under running water, and add them to the pan. Cook for a further 10 minutes, until tender.

Take the mushrooms out of the oven, remove the foil and parchment paper, then flip the caps over so that any juices drip into the pan. Using a spatula, transfer the mushrooms to a plate, gills facing upwards and keep warm.

Bubble the buttery juices left behind in the frying pan on medium-high heat for 1 minute, then stir in the tomatoey beans and simmer for 3-4 minutes.

Divide the beans among 4 plates and top with the mushrooms. Scatter with chopped cilantro and serve with boiled rice or crusty bread.

PANEER WITH GREEN PEPPER & TOMATOES

Serves 4

We'd often have this simple and satisfying dish for lunch in Delhi, accompanied by hot chapatis, homemade yogurt, and a dab of pickle on the side. I've used a green pepper here because it's more assertive than the sweeter red variety.

---

3 tbsp sunflower oil

1 tsp cumin seeds

1 red onion, thickly sliced

1 green pepper, deseeded and thickly sliced

¾ oz (20 g) ginger root, peeled and finely grated

3 garlic cloves, crushed

2 green chiles, deseeded and chopped

½ tsp ground turmeric

½ tsp Kashmiri chile powder

½ tsp garam masala (see page 19)

3 tomatoes, each cut into 8 wedges

8 oz (225 g) store-bought or homemade paneer (see page 20), cut into 1 x ¾ in (3 x 2 cm) rectangles

squeeze of lime

sea salt

Heat the oil in a karahi or wok on medium-high heat. Add the cumin seeds and sizzle for 30 seconds, until fragrant. Stir in the onions, season with salt and fry for 5–7 minutes, until they start to soften.

Turn the heat to medium, add the green pepper, ginger, garlic and green chiles, and fry for another 3–4 minutes.

Stir in the turmeric, chile powder, garam masala and tomato wedges. Turn the heat to low, cover the pan and cook for 10 minutes, until the tomatoes and peppers have softened.

If you are using store-bought paneer, soak the pieces in hot water for 10 minutes so that it softens, then drain and discard the water. You don't need to soak homemade paneer.

Remove the lid of the masala pan and turn off the heat. Fold the paneer into the masala, add the squeeze of lime and cover the pan for 5 minutes before serving so that the flavors can mellow.

KONKAN EGG CURRY

Serves 4–6

Egg curry is the kind of dish that rarely appears on restaurant menus, but for me, the sight of a hard-boiled egg surrounded by a moat of masala epitomizes all that's great about home cooking. Many will personalize an individual recipe to reflect the tastes of their community. Perhaps they'll add a teaspoon of mustard seeds and a tablespoon of fresh curry leaves to hot oil before frying the onions, or they might stir in chopped tomatoes after the onions have softened. There's no single, definitive recipe—and if you have never made an egg curry before, this is a good one to start with.

⅔ cup (125 g) frozen grated coconut, defrosted, or 1 cup (75 g) desiccated coconut, soaked in hot water to cover for 30 minutes

¾ tsp coarsely ground black peppercorns

1 oz (25 g) ginger root, peeled and coarsely chopped

¾ tsp Kashmiri chile powder

2⅓ cups (550 ml) hot water (used in two parts so keep the remainder hot)

6 tbsp sunflower or coconut oil

2 large onions, thinly sliced

1 tbsp tamarind pulp (see page 21)

6 hard-boiled eggs, peeled and halved

1 tbsp chopped cilantro

sea salt

boiled rice, to serve

Put the defrosted or soaked coconut in a food processor or blender with the black pepper, ginger, chile powder and ⅔ cup (150 ml) of the hot water. Blend everything until smooth. (You can alternatively use a handheld immersion blender and a bowl for this.)

Heat the oil in a karahi or wok on medium heat. Add the onions, season with salt and fry for 7–10 minutes, until softened. Add the coconut paste and continue cooking, stirring often, for 10 minutes, until the masala darkens and thickens to a soft dropping consistency. Add a ladleful of water if it starts to catch on the bottom of the pan.

Pour in the remaining hot water and simmer for 5–10 minutes, until the masala has the consistency of heavy cream.

Stir in the tamarind pulp, simmer the masala for 1 minute, then turn off the heat and add the hard-boiled eggs—the warmth of the masala will warm the eggs. Scatter with the cilantro to serve. This curry goes well with boiled rice.

CAULIFLOWER CHEESE WITH SCALLIONS & JALAPEÑO CHILES

Serves 6–8

2 cauliflowers

1 tsp ground turmeric

juice of 2 limes

1 tsp Kashmiri chile powder

½ tsp coarsely ground black peppercorns

4 tbsp sunflower oil

sea salt

green salad and crusty French bread, to serve

FOR THE SAUCE

5 tbsp (75 g) unsalted butter

4½ oz (125 g) scallions, finely chopped

⅓ cup (45 g) all-purpose flour

4¼ cups (1 liter) whole milk, hot

1 tsp roasted and ground cumin seeds

¼ tsp grated nutmeg

½ tsp English mustard

1 rounded tbsp pickled green jalapeño chiles, drained, rinsed and finely chopped

2½ oz (75 g) semi-dried sunblush tomatoes, chopped

6 oz (175 g) mature cheddar, grated

3½ oz (100 g) gruyère, grated

Mention a "*bake*" to anyone over 50 in Delhi and they'll know exactly what you're talking about. It was a perennial feature of dinner party tables in the early 1980s. Alongside elaborate northern Indian dishes, there would usually be a shallow Pyrex dish, filled with diced vegetables coated in Western-style white sauce and topped with grated cheese. In those days, most people only had access to canned cheese—which didn't melt under the broiler. The *bake* was a token "European" offering and was usually anointed with Tabasco sauce to compensate for the lack of seasoning. I've long felt a need to improve the lot of the much-maligned *bake*, manifested now by this globally inspired cauliflower cheese. It's the girl boss of all *bakes* and crammed with bold flavors. All it needs with it is a green salad and crusty French bread.

FOR THE TOPPING

scant 1 cup (75 g) fresh white breadcrumbs

2½ oz (75 g) mature cheddar, grated

½ tsp Kashmiri chile powder

2 tbsp extra-virgin olive oil, for drizzling

Cut the cauliflowers into large florets—you should have about 1 lb 14 oz (850 g) after trimming.

Bring a large pot of salted water to a boil on high heat, then stir in the turmeric and lime juice. Preheat the oven to 450°F (230°C).

Add the florets, bring the water back to a boil and blanch them for 2 minutes. Drain them in a colander, then spread out in a single layer in a large roasting pan. Sprinkle with chile powder and black pepper, season with sea salt and drizzle with the sunflower oil. Using your hands, mix everything together until the florets are evenly coated—it's a good idea to use disposable gloves for this.

Transfer the roasting pan to the oven and cook for 15–20 minutes, until the cauliflower is tender and browned around the edges. Remove the pan and turn the oven down to 410°F (210°C).

Make the sauce while the cauliflower is in the oven. Melt the butter in a large saucepan, add the scallions and soften for 2 minutes on medium-low heat. Stir in the flour and cook for 2–3 minutes, until the flour turns a pale, sandy color. Turn off the heat and gradually whisk in the hot milk.

Return the sauce to medium-low heat and simmer, stirring all the time, until it is smooth and has thickened to a coating consistency.

Turn off the heat and add the ground cumin, nutmeg, mustard, jalapeño chiles and tomatoes, followed by the cheddar and gruyère. Gently fold in the cauliflower and turn everything into a buttered 6-cup (1.5-liter) baking dish.

For the topping, mix the breadcrumbs with the cheese and chile powder and season with salt. Scatter the crumbs evenly over the cauliflower, drizzle with the olive oil and bake for 15 minutes, until the cheese has browned, the crumbs are golden and the sauce is piping hot. Leave to stand for 10 minutes before serving.

SHRIMP IN COCONUT MASALA
Serves 4

Thanks to my friend Monika Bhattacharyya for sharing her fabulous family recipe. Her grandma made this classic Bengali dish for me in 1996, and it remains one of the finest shrimp curries I've tasted. You can make it with shelled shrimp, and it will still taste great, but the flavor is incomparable if you use whole shrimp, because their shells and head infuse a sea-fresh sweetness into the masala and lend color and a sense of occasion.

---

15 jumbo shrimp (about 1 lb/500 g), shell-on and head-on

½ tsp ground turmeric

1 tsp fine sea salt

1 small onion, coarsely chopped

1 oz (30 g) ginger root, peeled and coarsely chopped

hot water, for loosening

2 tbsp ghee (see page 18)

6 green cardamom pods, pierced

1½ in (4 cm) cinnamon stick

4 Indian bay leaves (*tej patta*; optional)

1 tsp roasted and ground cumin seeds, plus an extra pinch for finishing

1 tsp Kashmiri chile powder

2 green chiles, slit lengthways, not all the way through, with seeds

2 tbsp full-fat Greek yogurt

1 tsp sugar

1 x 14 oz (400 ml) can of full-fat coconut milk

2 tbsp coconut cream

luchis (see page 282) or boiled rice, to serve

Using scissors, split the shrimp along the back from the base of the head to the tail, and devein each one with a sharp knife. Transfer them to a bowl and mix them with the turmeric and salt, then leave to one side.

Put the chopped onion and ginger in a small food processor, cover with hot water, then blend to a smooth, slack paste. Set to one side. (You can alternatively use a handheld immersion blender and a bowl for this.)

Heat the ghee in a karahi or wok on high heat and fry the shrimp, stirring all the time, for 2 minutes, until they are half-cooked and just starting to turn pink. Transfer them to a clean bowl, leaving the ghee behind in the pan.

Turn the heat down to medium-high and add the cardamom pods, cinnamon and bay leaves, if using, and swirl them around in the ghee for 30 seconds.

Stir in the onion and ginger paste and fry for 10–12 minutes on medium heat, until the onion is golden. Add a small ladleful of water if the paste starts to catch on the bottom of the pan.

Mix the 1 teaspoon of ground cumin with the chile powder and add 2 tablespoons of water to make a thin paste, then add this to the pan with the slit chiles. Stir in the yogurt and sugar after a few seconds and cook on low heat for 3–4 minutes, stirring all the time.

Pour the coconut milk into a jug and whisk until smooth, then pour it into the masala. Bring the sauce to a simmer, stirring, and simmer uncovered for 7–10 minutes, until it has the consistency of light cream.

Stir in the coconut cream and simmer for another 2 minutes, then return the shrimp to the pan and cook for 1–2 minutes, until the shells and head have turned pink all over. Sprinkle with a generous pinch of ground cumin before serving. This curry goes well with *luchis* or rice.

SHRIMP BIRYANI Serves 4–6

FOR THE SHRIMP

1 lb (500 g) raw, shelled shrimp

juice of 1 juicy lime

¼ tsp ground turmeric

½ tsp Kashmiri chile powder

sea salt

full-fat Greek yogurt and kachumber (see page 288), to serve

FOR THE SPICE PASTE

2 star anise

½ tsp black peppercorns

2 tsp fennel seeds

3 dried Kashmiri red chiles

1 oz (30 g) ginger root, peeled and coarsely chopped

1 large head garlic, peeled and cloves coarsely chopped

½ cup (80 g) frozen grated coconut, defrosted

1 tsp ground cinnamon

1 tsp garam masala (see page 19)

Biryanis are celebratory dishes—they take a while to put together and are best made when you have time to enjoy the process. This is just one of the many hundreds of biryani varieties made across South Asia, and each will have its own distinctive spicing and characteristics. All you need to go with it is a simple salad and some yogurt. Guests always love that moment when the lid comes off and there's a whoosh of aromatic steam at the table.

FOR THE MASALA

4-6 tbsp coconut oil or sunflower oil, or ¼ cup (50 g) ghee (see page 18)

2 large onions, finely sliced

about 30 fresh curry leaves

scant 1 cup (200 ml) tomato passata

scant 1 cup (200 ml) fish stock or water

sea salt

FOR THE RICE

4 Indian bay leaves (*tej patta*), or 1 in (3 cm) cinnamon stick

6 green cardamom pods, pierced

1½ cups (300 g) basmati rice, soaked in water for 30 minutes

2 tbsp unsalted butter

juice of 1 juicy lime

2 tbsp coarsely chopped mint leaves

1 tbsp coarsely chopped cilantro leaves

Put the shrimp in a bowl and mix with the lime juice, turmeric and chile powder and season with salt. Leave to one side while you make the masala.

Heat a dry sturdy frying pan on medium heat and roast the star anise, peppercorns, fennel seeds and chiles, stirring all the time, for 1 minute, or until the chiles have darkened.

Put the spices in a food processor or blender and add the ginger, garlic, coconut, cinnamon and garam masala. Pour over 1 cup (250 ml) of water and blend until smooth. Transfer the paste to a small bowl and leave to one side.

For the masala, heat the oil or ghee in a large ovenproof pot on medium heat. Add the onions, season with salt and fry until they are golden (about 10-12 minutes). Then, stir in the curry leaves and, after a few seconds, the coconut-spice paste. Cook, stirring often, for 5-7 minutes, until the water has evaporated and the paste has darkened.

Pour in the passata and simmer uncovered for 5 minutes. Add the stock or water and cook for another 7-10 minutes, until it reduces to a coating consistency. Ladle the masala into a bowl and keep it warm.

Preheat the oven to 320°F (160°C). For the rice, bring a large pot of salted water to a boil on medium-high heat and add the bay leaves or cinnamon and the cardamom pods.

Drain the rice from the soaking water and add it to the boiling water. Cook for 3-4 minutes, until the grains are half-cooked, then drain them in a colander.

Put half the hot rice into the same pot as you made the masala—there's no need to rinse the pot beforehand. Ladle over the tomato masala, followed by the shrimp, then cover with the rest of the rice.

Dot the rice with the butter, drizzle with the lime juice and scatter over the mint leaves and cilantro.

Cover the biryani with wet parchment paper followed by a layer of foil and a tight-fitting lid. Bake for 15 minutes, until the rice is fully cooked and the shrimp are pink and opaque. Serve with yogurt and kachumber on the side.

MUSSELS IN GINGER, COCONUT & RED CHILE BROTH

Serves 6

Pondicherry (more recently known as Puducherry) used to be a French colony and classic dishes of French heritage have evolved over the years to reflect the taste preferences of residents. This is an area famed for its fish and seafood and I love the gentle, coconutty backdrop of this broth, and the way in which it accommodates aromatic lemongrass and chiles, and zesty fresh ginger.

- 2 lb 3 oz (1 kg) whole mussels (in their shells), cleaned
- 7 tbsp (100 g) unsalted butter
- 2 onions, diced
- 2 bird's eye red chiles, deseeded and finely chopped
- 1 oz (30 g) ginger root, peeled and finely grated
- 4 large garlic cloves, finely chopped
- 2 lemongrass stems, split lengthways and lightly bruised
- ⅔ cup (150 ml) dry white wine
- 1 cup (250 ml) fish stock
- 1 x 14 oz (400 ml) can of full-fat coconut milk
- 2 tbsp coconut cream
- sea salt and coarsely ground black pepper
- juice of 1 large lime, to taste
- 3 tbsp chopped cilantro leaves

Clean the mussels under cold running water—give any open ones a firm tap against the countertop and discard those that don't close.

Melt the butter in a large sauté pan on very low heat. Add the onions, chiles, ginger, garlic and lemongrass, cover the pan and soften the mixture for 15 minutes without coloring.

Add the wine, turn the heat up to medium, and reduce the liquid by half. Pour in the stock and bring the liquid to a boil, then tip in the mussels. Increase the heat to high, cover the pan, and cook the mussels for 5–7 minutes, until their shells have opened. Discard the lemongrass along with any mussels that remain closed.

Whisk the coconut milk and coconut cream until smooth, then pour it into the broth and bring it to the simmer. Season with salt and black pepper, sharpen with lime juice, and stir in the cilantro before serving.

CLAMS WITH CHORIZO & RED CHILE MASALA

Serves 6

The clatter of clams as they tumble into the pan is one of my favorite sounds. I've traveled to the Goan coast for inspiration here and combined sea-fresh clams with fiery garlicky chorizo and cooked them in a coconut-tomato-tamarind masala, sharpened with fresh red chiles. Soak this splendid masala up with crusty bread or a heap of boiled rice.

- 10½ oz (300 g) hot cooking chorizo, skinned and coarsely chopped
- ½ cup (100 g) frozen grated coconut, defrosted
- 2 fresh red chiles, deseeded and coarsely chopped
- 6 large garlic cloves, coarsely chopped
- 1 oz (30 g) ginger root, peeled and coarsely chopped
- 1 tsp roasted and ground cumin seeds
- 2 tsp ground coriander
- ¾ tsp garam masala (see page 19)
- ¼ tsp ground turmeric
- ½ tsp ground cinnamon
- 2 lb 3 oz (1 kg) fresh clams
- 4 tbsp coconut oil or sunflower oil
- 2 onions, diced
- 1½ cups (350 ml) tomato passata
- 2 tsp sugar, plus extra if needed
- 1 rounded tbsp tamarind pulp (see page 21), or 6 pieces of kokum (see box)

Fry the chorizo in a large, heavy-based sauté pan on medium heat for about 5–7 minutes, until it releases its oil and browns at the edges. Transfer it to a small bowl, leaving behind any oil in the pan.

Put the coconut in a blender. Add the red chiles, garlic, ginger, cumin, ground coriander, garam masala, turmeric and cinnamon, and pour in ⅔ cup (150 ml) of water. Blend to a smooth paste and set aside.

Put the clams in a colander and discard any that are damaged or remain open when sharply tapped on the counter. Rinse them in a colander under cold, running water.

Add the coconut or sunflower oil to the oil left behind in the pan and fry the onions for about 7–10 minutes on medium heat until softened. Add the coconut paste and cook, stirring all the time, for 3–4 minutes, until most of the water has evaporated.

Add the passata and sugar, return the chorizo to the pan, and bring the sauce to a boil. Stir in the clams and tamarind pulp or kokum soaking water. Cover the pan and cook on high heat for 8–10 minutes, shaking the pan every few minutes, until the shells have opened (discard any that remain shut). Taste the masala, adding more sugar if it is too tart. Divide the clams between 6 deep bowls and ladle over the sauce equally. Serve with crusty bread or boiled rice.

> Kokum is a tangy fruit, and the dried, dark purple rind or pulp is used as a souring agent in dishes across the coastal areas of West India. It's first soaked in boiling water, then left to one side in a covered bowl for at least 1 hour. I use the soaking water to sharpen a curry or masala and discard the soaked kokum, but you can add the fruit to the pan for added punchy flavor. It's a good idea to scoop it out of the masala once the dish is cooked, though, otherwise it will continue to infuse sourness into the sauce.

COMMUNITY ROOTS
WEST

YAEL JHIRAD, MAHRASHTRA

I'm waiting to sail from Mumbai to the coastal town of Alibag, an hour's ferry ride south of the city. I have the deck to myself as I listen to the lap of the Arabian Sea in the sultry breeze, and watch the darkness give way to early morning. Today is one of India's many public holidays, and a crowd of festive families and romancing couples soon join me. We jostle for the best sea view as they pose for selfies and chatter about the day ahead.

There's a collective cheer as the ferry edges out of the wharf into open water. We pass catamarans, fishing boats, a small oil rig and then give way to an enormous container ship. The on-board kiosk does brisk business in *vada pav*, hot potato dumplings, served with fried green chiles, peanut-coconut-red chile crumbs and soft bread rolls. An hour later, our ferry pulls into Mandwa Jetty, and the day trippers rush to the beaches and make plans for lunch. I'm on a 30-minute drive inland, along a straight road, which splices through paddy fields and farmland.

I've arranged to meet Yael and Ralphy Jhirad for lunch. Both are from Mumbai and of the Bene Israel Jewish community, which means *Children of Israel*. Yael tells me that they form the largest Jewish group in India and have been in the country for more than 2,000 years. She says that they were known as the "Lost Jews," who came to India fleeing from persecution. Most settled in and around Mumbai, including Alibag on the Konkan coast, and in Gujarat.

Alibag is dear to their hearts, not just for the peaceful, laid-back atmosphere, but because Bene Israel history is embedded in the landscape around. Ralphy tells me that in the 1950s, there were around 20,000 of them, but most have since emigrated to Israel, leaving barely 5,000 in India today. There are other Jewish groups across the country, in Calcutta (recently renamed Kolkata) and Cochin (known now as Kochi) for example, but like the Bene Israel, they are diminishing in numbers. Although each has a distinctive style of cooking, they share the same faith and follow the tenets of Jewish kitchen practice. Dietary laws are observed, including the separation of dairy and meat, and the avoidance of pork, shellfish and fish without scales.

Their light-filled apartment features family photos alongside framed images of them meeting international Jewish public figures. I'm shown books about Indian Jewish heritage, some of which Ralphy has contributed to. A sea breeze blows through the open balcony doors into the sitting room. They welcome me with warmth and share an easy-going joviality as we chat over chai and *methi khari*—crisp, flaky cookies, speckled with dried fenugreek leaves.

The Arabian Sea—a view from my ferry as it set sail from Mumbai to Alibag.

▶ I ask about their last name, Jhirad, which isn't Jewish, and Ralphy tells me that every Bene Israel settler adopted the name of the Indian village where their forebears lived. Over the centuries their community adapted to local ways of life, while retaining its Jewish identity. Although they converse in Hindi, English and Marathi (the local language), prayers are said in Hebrew.

Ralphy comments, "Because we in India are quite remote from global Jewish communities, it's important for us to keep our cultural traditions alive and remain connected to them." They both make a generous cultural contribution to Bene Jews by organizing social activities, religious rituals and welcoming international visitors to the table. Of course, it's a bonus that Yael is such a good cook.

They keep a kosher kitchen, and nothing is cooked during the Shabbat, observed from Friday nightfall until Saturday evening. For regular weekday meals, it isn't always easy to find kosher meat and so they eat vegetarian meals—perhaps dal, a dry-cooked vegetable masala, potato curry and rice. Yael's cooking is influenced by seasonal, local produce and Maharashtrian kitchen traditions. They live on the Konkan coast where there's an abundance of fish, which they enjoy with rice rather than chapatis. Fresh coconut makes a splendid substitute for dairy produce and doesn't violate the religious edict of not combining meat and dairy.

In the 1970s, every Friday, Yael's father and the other men of the community would go to the market early in the morning to buy live chickens and have them slaughtered by the kosher custom. As so few households had fridges, everything was sourced fresh and cooked straight away, and chicken curry and rice became an established weekly fixture. She also remembers, as a child, accompanying him to the Sunday fish market in Mumbai, a joyous noisy and chaotic place, where he loved to haggle and joke with local fisherwomen.

Other local traditions including breaking the Yom Kippur fast with *nan khatai*, shortbread-like cookies. Modern ovens are a recent innovation in many parts of India. In the past, dough was made at home and taken to a communal oven for baking. For Passover, yeasted breads and cakes are avoided, as well as food made from fermented grains, lentils and pulses. During this time, Yael doesn't cook with processed and preserved ingredients—these include dried spices unless they have been certified as kosher. So, although tart-tasting kokum and tamarind aren't allowed, Yael compensates by adding lime juice, green mangoes or tomatoes.

We're having Bene Israel fish curry for lunch today. In her neatly appointed kitchen, glistening, plump pomfret have been cut into steaks and fresh coconut puréed with fresh turmeric, cumin, garlic, chiles and lemon to sharpen. This silken paste, as green as a bowling lawn, is tipped in a karahi—Yael adds a little water and puts the fish on top. It's then drizzled with olive oil (sent by her grown-up sons) and curry leaves scattered over. And that's it. The curry simmers until the fish is just tender, Yael instinctively clocks its readiness with precision. The pearly-white flesh has a lovely, sweet flavor, which stands up well to the strident flavor of the herby,

▶ lemony, garlicky sauce. I'm impressed by the simple way in which it is made—there is no frying, and there are no complex spice blends, which makes me wonder why many people find cooking fish so intimidating.

The rice is ready and has been boiled with fresh turmeric root and cloves for astringency and cardamom for sweetness. Yael announces that there is just enough time for a "fish fry," and reappears a few minutes later with a plate of fried silver-skinned *surmai* pieces, burnished with chile powder, turmeric and ground cumin. They are delicious—rarely have I tasted fish quite this fresh.

After lunch, we visit their local beach. It's a picture-perfect postcard location—sandy shore, brilliant blue sky and shimmering sea—but punctured by the sound of Bollywood beats blasting out from a car. We breathe in the air, admire the view and quickly move on. By now it's mid-afternoon and the sun is fierce. We drop in at the iconic D. Samson Soda Shop. It's a small, 80-year-old Jewish landmark and a favorite roadside meeting place for those who like to catch up over bottles of soda. On the walls, there's a pink Star of David, pictures of Moses, family photographs and press cuttings. Furnished with rickety benches and wobbly tables, it's not likely to win awards for the décor, but there's a cheerful, almost pub-like camaraderie among locals here. And the ice-cream sodas are brilliant, too.

1. Yael with her fabulous fish curry.

2. Yael and her husband, Ralphy in their younger years.

3. Bene Israel fish curry, about to go on the stove.

BENE ISRAEL FISH CURRY Serves 4

YAEL JHIRAD

This fabulous curry with its emerald-green masala is underpinned by plenty of leafy cilantro, shot through with fresh, citrus-tasting turmeric, green chiles and creamy coconut. Yael and her husband made this curry for our lunch at their home in Alibag, a coastal town near Mumbai. It's an area renowned for its fish, and the tilapia used in this curry was caught just a few hours before we sat down to eat. All you need to bring the ingredients together is an electric blender and a deep-sided frying pan for poaching the fish. I'd use steaks rather than fillets, because the bones and skin infuse extra flavor into the curry.

---

1 large handful of cilantro, leaves and stems coarsely chopped

¼ cup (50 g) frozen grated coconut, defrosted

¼ oz (5 g) turmeric root, coarsely chopped, or ¼ tsp ground turmeric

¾ tsp cumin seeds

6 garlic cloves, coarsely chopped

5 green chiles, deseeded and coarsely chopped

about 15 fresh curry leaves

1 x 1 lb 14 oz (850 g) whole pomfret, scaled and cleaned, without its head, its body cut crossways into 1 in (3 cm) thick steaks

juice of ½ lime

2 tbsp melted coconut oil, sunflower oil or olive oil

sea salt

boiled rice, to serve

Put the cilantro, coconut, turmeric, cumin, garlic and green chiles in a small food processor or blender. Add salt to season and 1 cup (250 ml) of water and process until smooth. Pour the sauce into a wide, deep-sided frying pan, large enough to hold the fish in a single layer.

Scatter the curry leaves over the sauce and put the fish steaks on top in a single layer. Season with a little more salt, spoon over the lime juice and drizzle with the oil. Leave to one side for 10 minutes.

Bring the sauce to the simmer, uncovered, on medium heat. Turn the heat down to low, cover the pan and cook the fish for 5–7 minutes, removing the lid to turn each piece over with a spatula halfway through, until tender. Serve straight away with boiled rice.

SALMON WITH RED CHILE & GROUND FENNEL

Serves 4

My dad loved salmon, and during the last few years of his life, he'd have lunch with me at home. "Fish on Fridays" was a weekly ritual and this quick-to-assemble dish, with its sweet-sharp citrussy marination, was one of his favorites. I'd often serve it with potato vinaigrette and a leafy salad, but sometimes, I'd flake the cooked salmon into buttery rice with plenty of chopped cilantro—just as my mom used to do.

---

2 red chiles, deseeded and finely chopped

¾ oz (20 g) ginger root, peeled and finely grated

juice of 2 limes

2 rounded tsp jaggery or light brown sugar

1 tbsp chopped cilantro leaves

1 tsp roasted and ground fennel seeds

1 tsp sunflower oil

4 skin-on salmon fillets (about 4½ oz/125 g each)

sea salt

Mix the chiles with the ginger, lime juice, jaggery or sugar, cilantro and ground fennel, and season with salt.

Line a roasting pan with parchment paper. Put the salmon fillets into the pan and spoon over the marinade. Drizzle with the oil and leave aside for 30 minutes.

Preheat the oven to 425°F (220°C). Roast the fish for around 7–10 minutes, until just tender.

HAKE STEAKS WITH COCONUT & TAMARIND

Serves 4

It's a myth that fish needs a light touch and gentle spicing. Most of my recipes involve punchy and often pungent flavors, and this curry, with its burst of tamarind and warming chiles, is a brilliant match with hake. Here, the soothing flavor of creamy coconut milk in the masala softens earthy-tasting cumin, sharp mustard seeds and astringent coriander. The strength of the masala is very much in your hands—leave the chile seeds in if you want to dial up the heat level.

FOR THE ROASTED SPICE PASTE

6 dried Kashmiri red chiles

1 tsp cumin seeds

1 tsp brown mustard seeds

1 tsp coriander seeds

½ tsp black peppercorns

5 garlic cloves, unpeeled

1 red onion, diced

1 oz (30 g) ginger root, peeled and coarsely chopped

scant 1 cup (200 ml) canned full-fat coconut milk

⅔ cup (150 ml) hot water

FOR THE CURRY

6 tbsp coconut oil or sunflower oil

about 15 fresh curry leaves

1 large red onion, finely sliced

½ tsp ground turmeric

1½ cups (350 ml) fish stock or water

1 tbsp tamarind pulp (see page 21)

scant 1 cup (200 ml) full-fat coconut milk

4 hake steaks (about 7 oz/200 g each)

sea salt

Snip the tops off the chiles with scissors and shake out most of the seeds (or leave them in for extra heat). Heat a small sturdy pan on medium heat. Add the chiles and the cumin, mustard and coriander seeds, as well as the peppercorns and garlic cloves and dry roast for 2 minutes, stirring all the time, until the spices release their fragrance. Transfer everything to a plate and leave to cool before removing the skin from the garlic.

Put the roasted spices and garlic in a small food processor and add the onion, ginger and coconut milk. Pour over the hot water and blend to a thick paste. (You can alternatively use a handheld immersion blender or blender for this.)

Heat the oil in a karahi or wok on medium-high heat and add the curry leaves—they will splutter as they hit the oil, so stand back. After a few seconds, add the onions and salt to season and fry the leaves until they are golden.

Turn the heat down to low and add the turmeric followed by the spice paste. Cook, stirring often, until the paste darkens and beads of oil appear around the side of the pan. Add a splash of water if the masala starts to stick.

Pour in the fish stock or water and simmer, uncovered, for 10 minutes, until the masala has a broth-like consistency. Stir in enough tamarind pulp to sharpen the masala (you may not need it all).

Add the coconut milk and fish and simmer, uncovered, for 6–8 minutes, until the fish is tender—the masala should have the consistency of light cream. Serve with boiled rice.

COMMUNITY ROOTS
WEST BENGAL

SNIGDHA CHATTERJI, HARYANA

"I've braved the crowds and chaos of Bristol fish market to bring this *hilsa* home; God only knows if I've been ripped off," shrugs Snigdha. "All these chaps say that their *hilsa* is the best, because it's from the rivers of Bangladesh, but I'll believe this only when I taste it." I warm to her direct, no-nonsense introduction and love that we're talking about fish within minutes of my arrival. I doubt that much escapes her notice, not least a vendor whose fish doesn't come up to expectation.

As I'm about to find out, *hilsa*, or *ilish* in Bengali, is revered for its oily, sweet flavor—and although found in both sea and fresh water, the prized ones are caught from rivers. It's related to the herring family and loaded with tiny bones. And Snigdha's Bristol fish market is not in Bristol, England, but in Gurgaon (also known as Gurugram), near New Delhi.

Snigdha and her husband Shukdev live in a gated apartment block in Haryana, just outside Delhi. They worked in Dubai for many years, where she was a corporate secretary and Shukdev a food technologist, before retiring and returning to India. We are in their sitting-dining room, which is furnished in dark wood and fronted by a balcony filled with leafy green plants. There's a large chandelier over the dining table and a display cabinet for chinaware and cut glass. Their daughter, Shomita, arrives and animatedly joins our conversation about *hilsa*.

Although Snigdha was born and raised in Delhi, her parents were from West Bengal and the family takes their Bengali heritage seriously. We move into the kitchen, where the counter is dominated by a flat, pitted grinding stone. Her home helper is breaking down mustard seeds and green chiles on it with a small, smooth-textured stone. He occasionally splashes the surface with water droplets, which helps the paste on its way to a silken consistency. The rocking movement brings out natural flavors in a way that wouldn't be replicated in an electric blender.

This paste is mixed with turmeric and red chile yogurt, and Snigdha uses it to coat the fish with her fingers, gently massaging the masala into the flesh. Golden mustard oil is poured into a steel tin—it's the cooking medium of choice for Bengalis, who love its pungency (see page 222). The pieces of *hilsa* are arranged in the pan, strewn with whole green chiles, and tightly sealed before being steamed. On the hob next to it, rice is put to boil.

As the fish cooks, Snigdha tells me that, decades ago, local fishing communities around the Bay of Bengal would have been mindful of the ebb and flow of *hilsa* and its habits, but intensive fishing has been less kind to

A local shop, decked out for Diwali customers.

▶ the environment. And although *hilsa* is the favorite fish from the region, there's a growing recognition that its dwindling stocks need to be protected.

We talk about her daily routine. Lunch is the main meal of the day and Bengali dishes are usually sequenced as separate courses. A bitter-tasting vegetable is served at the beginning, because it's believed to have medicinal cleansing properties. Snigdha tells me that this benefits the liver and stimulates the appetite, especially during the hot and humid months. One of her favorite appetizers is small bitter gourds, split and stuffed with spiced mashed potato and fried in mustard oil.

Next, a dal, spiced with cumin seeds, ginger and aromatics. It's accompanied with a simple, lightly fried vegetable and a little rice. As Bengalis, they don't often eat chickpea and kidney beans, because these can be quite heavy—preferring instead easily digestable dals, such as pink masoor or yellow moong. Snigdha often cooks thinly sliced cauliflower florets in mustard oil with dried, broken red chiles and *panch phoran*— a blend of five contrasting spices (see page 20). She tells me that it's important to have a light touch when spicing vegetables, and a pinch of sugar stirred into her vegetable dishes makes a good contrast to the bitter notes of the first course.

Then comes the fish or an occasional meat course. We're going to have the *hilsa*, which is still steaming on the stove. It'll be served with rice and one of Snigdha's famed homemade chutneys. Today there's a sweet-sour tomato one, studded with plump raisins and flecked with popped mustard seeds. It's wonderful, the kind of relish I'd happily pile into a cheese sandwich. Snigdha sighs and wishes that she'd saved a spoonful of "plastic chutney" for me to try. I'm quite relieved that she hasn't, until I realize it's a nickname given to shredded, sweetened pineapple, cooked with ginger, raisins and lime juice. The name comes from its translucent strands, which look like thin strips of plastic.

Yogurt isn't served with the main meal. It's eaten with sugar as a quick-fix dessert on the rare occasion when there aren't any syrupy sweetmeats (*mithai*) or milky puddings in the house. Bengalis love sweets, which are enjoyed in pretty much the same way as I dip into my cookie jar throughout the day.

When Snigdha entertains, there will be at least eight or nine dishes on the table, but even for everyday meals, a homemade fish or meat curry, dal, rice and two vegetables is the norm.

The *hilsa* is now ready, its steel box carefully lifted out of boiling water and the lid prised open. Drifts of mustardy steam fill the air, and there's a slick of oil around the fish, which will now be infused with its spiced juices. The *hilsa* is carefully transferred to a shallow serving bowl and Snigdha makes a point of telling me that she's not going to bother with a chopped cilantro garnish—it would only detract from the mustardy masala.

As a mound of steamy rice is piled onto my plate, I own up to being a bit nervous about navigating my way around the bones in my fish. The family smiles and tells me that choking is commonplace and learning how to eat bony fish is a skill ingrained from

▶ childhood. I recall my own fish-finger lunches and am not reassured.

Snigdha tells me that because Bengalis love fish so much, they train their tongue to separate bones from the flesh while the fish is being chewed. Less practiced, I separate mine on the plate with my fingers—and it's quite a process. Almost everyone has a tale to share about *hilsa* bones getting stuck in the throat—and it's delivered with humor. Snigdha's daughter Shomita advises that if it happens to me, I'm to take a ball of boiled rice, pop it in my mouth and swallow it straight away. Or I'm to reach for the fruit bowl quickly and eat a banana. As if on cue, she starts to clear her throat—and the bowl of rice is pushed in her direction while the conversation carries on without missing a beat. These *hilsa* steaks are perfectly cooked, and their buttery roe, like the flesh, is rich and sweet-tasting, making a lovely contrast to the horseradish-like kick of the masala. It's an outstanding curry with big bold flavors and one that is recognized as one of the most-loved dishes in the Bengali recipe repertoire.

Snigdha was an eighteen-year-old bride when she married Shukdev 56 years ago. I ask if Shukdev shares the family's love of fish. He quips, "My mother used to take the bones out of *hilsa* before I was married, but my wife here wasn't having any of it." Snigdha laughs and adds wryly, "Of course I refused—how can you be a bonafide Bengali if a few bones get in the way of enjoying what is India's, no the world's, finest culinary tradition?!"

1. Nothing escapes Snigdha's exacting eye when she cooks. Here, she has just made the fish dish and is waiting for her daughter to join us for lunch.

2. Grinding mustard seeds and green chiles in the traditional way, on a pitted grinding stone. A smoother stone is used to crush the seeds with a rocking motion. This method produces a silken texture, which is often quite hard to replicate in many modern food processors.

3. Snigdha's finished dish.

STEAMED HAKE WITH MUSTARD MASALA

Serves 4

SNIGDHA CHATTERJI

This mustardy, turmeric-hued, steamed fish dish is traditionally made with *hilsa*, an exceptionally bony oily fish, which is part of the Indian herring family. It's a much-loved delicacy among Bengalis and Bangladeshis and is usually cooked in pungent mustard oil, which mellows to sweetness when heated.

Although pure mustard oil has been a key pantry staple in Bengali kitchens for centuries, it isn't common in the West. Some shops in the West now sell blended mustard and canola oils, which have been given the green light for cooking. I've adapted this recipe for boneless hake fillets, and I've pre-soaked the mustard seeds so that they're easier to pound, and sharpened the creamy yogurt with lime, but the flavor remains close to Snigdha's original, and is truly delicious.

---

2 tsp brown mustard seeds, soaked in hot water to cover for 2–3 hours

3 green chiles, deseeded and finely chopped, plus 4 whole green chiles for steaming

½ tsp ground turmeric

½ tsp Kashmiri chile powder

3 tbsp full-fat Greek yogurt

juice of ½ lime

4 skinless hake fillets (about 7 oz/200 g each)

½ cup (120 ml) mustard oil

sea salt

boiled rice, to serve

Drain the mustard seeds into a sieve, and, using a mortar and pestle, pound the seeds and chopped green chiles with 3–4 tablespoons of water until they break down into a paste. Transfer to a bowl and stir in the turmeric, chile powder, yogurt and lime juice. Season generously with salt and add about 3½ tablespoons of water, or enough for a coating consistency.

Put the fish fillets on a tray, spread the mustardy yogurt over both sides, and leave to one side for 15 minutes. Spoon the oil into an 8 in (20 cm) diameter, 4¼ cup (1 liter) heatproof dish. Arrange the fish in a single layer on the oil and put a whole chile on top of each fillet. Cover the dish with foil and secure it around the rim with string.

Transfer the dish to a large, deep-sided frying pan and pour in enough hot water to reach three-quarters of the way up the side of the dish. Put a lid on the pan, bring the water to a boil on medium heat and steam the fish for about 15 minutes, until the fillets are opaque and the flesh flakes easily. Serve straight away with boiled rice.

CHICKEN IN CUMIN & GROUND CORIANDER YOGURT

Serves 4–6

This is a simple and comforting curry made with everyday spices and simple ingredients. Because winters can be long and harsh for Himalayan hill and mountain communities, dried ginger rather than fresh is often the preference because of its long shelf life. It's a spice that blends well with the earthy notes of toasted cumin and astringency of ground coriander.

8 skinless, boneless chicken thighs (about 2 lb 3 oz/1 kg)

½ cup (125 ml) full-fat Greek yogurt

½ tsp ground turmeric

1 large onion, coarsely chopped

6–8 tbsp sunflower oil

4 cloves

4 green cardamom pods, pierced

3 brown cardamom pods, pierced

6 garlic cloves, crushed

1 tsp ground ginger

2 tsp ground coriander

1 tsp roasted and ground cumin seeds

1 tsp Kashmiri chile powder

about 1 cup (250 ml) hot water

2 tbsp chopped cilantro leaves

sea salt

boiled rice, to serve

Put the chicken in a shallow dish and season with salt. Mix the yogurt and turmeric and coat the thighs with it. Leave to one side while you make the masala.

Put the onion in a small food processor, add enough water to cover and blend it until smooth. (You can alternatively use a handheld immersion blender and a bowl for this.)

Preheat the oven to 350°F (180°C).

Heat the oil in a large, sturdy Dutch oven on medium-high heat and add the cloves and green and brown cardamom pods—sizzle for about 30 seconds, until aromatic.

Stir in the onion paste and fry, stirring often, until golden. Add the yogurt-coated thighs and garlic and continue frying for 5–7 minutes, until sealed and the thighs have lost their raw appearance.

Add the ginger, ground coriander, cumin and chile powder and fry them for 1 minute. Pour in enough of the hot water to come halfway up the chicken, then cover the pot with a lid, transfer it to the oven and cook for 15–20 minutes, until the chicken is tender. Scatter with the chopped cilantro and serve with boiled rice.

HIMALAYAN BELT

HOMESTYLE PUNJABI CHICKEN CURRY

Serves 4–6

This curry recipe started off in my Mom's childhood kitchen in Old Delhi before being transported to a village in Cumbria. My school friends used to say that our house smelled like Christmas Day when mom was making it. It's one of those staples that's open to interpretation—I like adding an extra stick of cinnamon or simply not using the brown cardamom pods if I've exhausted supplies. I might leave in the seeds of green chiles for extra stridency, simmer halved floury potatoes with the chicken, or use chicken stock instead of water for a more robust flavor. This is one of my favorite family-friendly dishes.

---

1 large onion, coarsely chopped

6 large garlic cloves, coarsely chopped

1½ oz (50 g) ginger root, peeled and coarsely chopped

½ cup (125 ml) sunflower oil

2 tsp cumin seeds

2 in (5 cm) cinnamon stick

3 brown cardamom pods, pierced

6 green cardamom pods, pierced

4 Indian bay leaves (*tej patta*), or 1 in (3 cm) cinnamon stick

1 x 14 oz (400 g) can of chopped tomatoes

1 tsp Kashmiri chile powder

1 tsp ground turmeric

1 tsp garam masala (see page 19)

1 tsp sugar

8 large skinless, boneless chicken thighs (about 2 lb 10 oz/1.2 kg)

2 green chiles, halved lengthways, seeds removed

sea salt

2 tbsp chopped cilantro leaves, to serve

Indian flatbreads or boiled rice, to serve

Using a food processor or handheld immersion blender, process the chopped onion to a smooth paste with enough water to cover, then transfer to a small bowl and leave to one side. Blend the garlic and ginger to a paste with water to cover in same way.

Heat the oil in a sturdy Dutch oven on medium-high heat. Add the cumin seeds, cinnamon, brown and green cardamom pods and bay leaves (or cinnamon stick). Swirl the spices around for 30 seconds, until they release their aroma.

Add the onion paste and fry, stirring often, for about 10 minutes, until golden. Stir in the garlic and ginger paste and continue cooking for 2 minutes, until any water has evaporated.

Stir in the tomatoes, chile powder, turmeric, garam masala and sugar, and cook for about 5 minutes, stirring often, until the tomatoes have thickened.

Add the chicken and green chiles and cook in the tomato masala for 5 minutes, stirring all the time until the thighs are sealed and have lost their raw appearance. Pour over enough hot water to cover the chicken by three-quarters, season with salt and simmer for 15 minutes without a lid until the masala has reduced to a coating consistency and the chicken is tender. You might need to add a little more water if it is too thick. Sprinkle with the cilantro and serve with Indian flatbreads or boiled rice.

CHICKEN CURRY WITH TOMATOES & TAMARIND

Serves 4–6

Chicken *chitanee* probably started off as a simple soup. Over the years it evolved into a curry seasoned with fragrant spices, sweetened with a little sugar and sharpened with tamarind and tomatoes. This version was originally made by Calcutta's (more recently known as Kolkata) Jewish community, who came as traders from Iraq, Iran and Syria in the eighteenth and nineteenth centuries. Most have long since emigrated, but they have left behind a fine culinary legacy.

- 4 tbsp sunflower oil
- 1 large onion, thinly sliced
- 5 garlic cloves, crushed
- 1 oz (30 g) ginger root, peeled and finely grated
- 1 tsp ground turmeric
- 2 tsp ground coriander
- 1 tsp roasted and ground cumin seeds
- 1 tsp Kashmiri chile powder
- ½ tsp coarsely ground black peppercorns
- 2 green chiles, halved lengthways and deseeded
- 4 skinless, bone-in chicken thighs (about 1 lb/500 g)
- 4 skinless, bone-in chicken drumsticks (about 1 lb/500 g)
- 1 x 14 oz (400 g) can of chopped tomatoes
- 2 tbsp tamarind pulp (see page 21)
- 2 tsp sugar, plus extra if needed
- 1 cup (250 ml) chicken stock or water
- juice of 1 lime
- sea salt
- boiled rice, to serve

Heat the oil in a large Dutch oven on medium heat. Add the onions and fry for 10–12 minutes, until golden, then add the garlic and ginger and fry for 1 minute. Preheat the oven to 350°F (180°C).

Stir in the turmeric, coriander, cumin, chile powder, black pepper and green chiles, and fry the spices on medium heat, stirring all the time, for a few seconds, until aromatic.

Add the chicken pieces and cook for 5 minutes, until the meat has lost its raw appearance and is sealed. Stir in the tomatoes, tamarind, sugar and chicken stock and season with salt. Bring the curry to a simmer, cover, transfer the pot to the oven and cook for 20 minutes, until the chicken is tender and the masala has a coating consistency.

Add enough lime juice to sharpen, and adjust the seasoning, adding more sugar if the masala needs it—aim for a sweet-tart flavor. Serve with boiled rice.

CHICKEN IN ROASTED COCONUT MASALA

Serves 4–6

Roasted coconut, sweet cinnamon and fennel seeds provide the foundation for this glorious curry from the Konkan coast in West India. These mellow flavors are then given a punchy flourish with sharp-tasting chiles, tamarind and tomatoes. I've used Sichuan peppercorns and tamarind instead of traditional *tefla* berries and kokum as they're easier to find in stores. When tomatoes are out of season, I prefer to use canned tomatoes because they have more flavor. This curry tastes best if you make it the day before you intend to serve.

---

8 skinless, bone-in chicken thighs (about 2 lb 3 oz/1 kg)

½ tsp ground turmeric

1 tsp sea salt

FOR THE MASALA

8 dried Kashmiri red chiles

¼ tsp black peppercorns

½ tsp Sichuan peppercorns

2 tsp fennel seeds

¼ tsp cloves

8 green cardamom pods, seeds only

1 tsp ground cinnamon

½ cup (100 g) frozen grated coconut, defrosted; or ½ cup (50 g) desiccated coconut

scant ½ cup (100 ml) melted coconut oil or sunflower oil

2 onions, diced

1 x 14 oz (400 g) can of chopped tomatoes

1 tbsp tamarind pulp (see page 21), or to taste

sea salt

boiled rice, to serve

Put the chicken thighs in a bowl and rub them with the turmeric and salt. It's best to use disposable gloves for this to avoid staining your fingers orange. Set to one side while you make the masala.

Using scissors, snip the tops off the chiles and shake out and discard most of the seeds.

Heat a sturdy, small frying pan on medium-low heat and add the red chiles, black and Sichuan peppercorns, fennel seeds, cloves and cardamom seeds. Roast the spices, stirring all the time, for about 2 minutes, until fragrant. Turn off the heat, add the cinnamon and tip everything onto a plate. Leave to one side.

Roast the defrosted or desiccated coconut in the same pan on medium-low heat, until nicely golden, stirring it all the time (about 3-4 minutes).

Put the coconut and roasted spices in a blender and add 1 cup (250 ml) of water. Process everything until it becomes a smooth paste.

Heat the oil in a large Dutch oven on medium heat. Add the onions, season with salt and fry until browned—this should take around 10-15 minutes. Stir in the coconut paste and continue cooking for 5 minutes, or until the paste darkens and small droplets of oil appear around the side of the pan. Add the tomatoes and cook for another 5 minutes, until the masala thickens to a coating consistency. Preheat the oven to 350°F (180°C).

Add the chicken and cook for 5 minutes, stirring all the time, until the thighs have lost their raw appearance and are sealed. Pour over enough hot water to barely cover the chicken and bring it to a simmer.

Cover the pot and transfer it to the oven to cook for 20 minutes, until the chicken is tender. Stir in enough tamarind to sharpen the masala and season with salt. Serve with boiled rice.

WEST INDIA

CHICKEN WITH APRICOTS & CINNAMON

Serves 4–6

2 oz (60 g) ginger root, peeled and coarsely chopped

1 small head garlic, cloves separated, peeled and coarsely chopped

2 dried Kashmiri red chiles

scant ½ cup (100 ml) sunflower oil

2 in (5 cm) cinnamon stick

5 cloves

2 brown cardamom pods, pierced

½ tsp black peppercorns

1 large onion, diced

1 x 14 oz (400 g) can of chopped tomatoes

¾ tsp Kashmiri chile powder

½ tsp ground turmeric

1 tsp roasted and ground cumin seeds

1 tsp ground coriander

1 tsp garam masala (see page 19)

8 skinless, bone-in chicken thighs (about 2 lb 3 oz/1 kg)

1 cup (125 g) semi-dried apricots, soaked in hot water for 1 hour

3½ tbsp white wine vinegar

1½ tbsp jaggery or light brown sugar

scant 1 cup (200 ml) chicken stock or water

2 tbsp chopped cilantro leaves

sea salt

These chicken thighs, simmered in tomato-cinnamon masala, are sweetened with jaggery and apricots and sharpened with a little vinegar. It's a classic curry that embodies the Parsi community's Persian heritage. Wild, dried *hunza* apricots (also known as *jardaloo*) are traditionally used in this dish. They are shrunken in shape, hard in texture and about the size of a large brown marble. Any shortfall in their appearance, though, is compensated by a wonderful, intense and almost caramel-like flavor. You'll find these apricots in Middle Eastern and South Asian shops. That said, I've used semi-dried ones from the supermarket here and they work well, too.

TO SERVE

store-bought fried potato matchsticks

boiled rice

Put the chopped ginger and garlic in a small food processor, add enough water to cover, and blend until smooth. (You can alternatively use a handheld immersion blender and a bowl for this.) Leave to one side.

Using scissors, snip the tops off the chiles and shake out and discard most of the seeds.

Heat the oil in a large Dutch oven on medium-high heat and fry the cinnamon, cloves, cardamom, whole peppercorns and red chiles for 30 seconds, until the chiles have darkened. Add the onion and salt to season and continue frying for 10 minutes, until golden.

Turn the heat down to medium and stir in the ginger-garlic paste, followed, after 1 minute, by the tomatoes, chile powder, turmeric, cumin, ground coriander and garam masala. Preheat the oven to 350°F (180°C).

Cook the tomatoes for 5 minutes, until thickened and beads of oil appear around the side of the pan. Add the chicken pieces and cook for about 5 minutes, until the thighs are sealed and have lost their raw appearance.

Drain the apricots and add them to the pot with the vinegar, jaggery or brown sugar, and stock or water. Bring to a simmer, cover and transfer the pot to the oven and cook for 15-20 minutes, until the chicken is tender.

Stir in the chopped cilantro and then scatter with potato matchsticks to serve. Accompany with boiled rice.

WEST INDIA

ROAST SPATCHCOCK CHICKEN WITH TURMERIC

Serves 4

I've left the skin on the chicken for this dish, because I like the way it colors and crisps in the oven as it roasts. My mother, like most home cooks in India, always pulled it off and you could do this too if you prefer. Keep a close eye on it in the oven, though, to make sure it doesn't become dry. Any leftovers taste great in a salad—shred the meat, mix it with cubed melon (any kind) and torn mint leaves, and finish the whole kaboodle with a big squeeze of lime.

---

1 whole chicken (about 3 lb 5 oz/1.5 kg)

1 tbsp cracked black peppercorns

1 tbsp Kashmiri chile powder

2 tsp ground turmeric

4 tbsp white wine vinegar

1 tbsp sunflower oil

2 tbsp runny honey

sea-salt flakes

TO SERVE

green mango salad (see page 289) or kachumber (see page 288)

full-fat Greek yogurt

Put the chicken on a chopping board, breast-side facing downwards, with the legs towards you. Using sharp scissors, cut along both sides of the backbone and remove it.

Turn the chicken over so that the skin-side is facing you and press hard on the breastbone so that the chicken flattens. Using a sharp knife, make diagonal slashes over the chicken, through the skin and flesh. Put the chicken in a snug-fitting roasting pan.

Mix the peppercorns with the chile powder, turmeric, vinegar and oil and season generously with sea-salt flakes.

I like to wear gloves for the next step to prevent the turmeric staining my fingers orange. Rub the spice mixture over both sides of the chicken, cover and leave it to marinate in the fridge for at least 1 hour, or overnight if you have the time.

Preheat the oven to 400°F (200°C), then roast the chicken for 20 minutes. Spoon over the honey—if it's thick, you might need to warm it first. Turn the oven up to 425°F (220°C) and continue roasting the chicken for another 15 minutes, until the skin browns and the juices run clear when pierced with a knife. Serve the chicken with green mango salad or kachumber and yogurt.

COMMUNITY ROOTS
WEST

ANU SHETTY, MUMBAI

Mumbai is noisy, crowded and chaotic, but never dull. It's India's financial hub and the heart of Bollywood's glittering film industry. But there's also the sharp edge of inequality—this is a city of deep pockets and empty purses. All of life is here in all its guises.

I've taken a moment to enjoy a delicious slab of guava and red-chile ice cream, bought from Parsi-owned, K. Rustom & Co ice cream shop. I love its musky floral flavor and the slow burn of chile heat, and order a second helping. Next, I visit Crawford Market, and feign disengagement as hustlers try and offload dragon fruit, bangles and wind-up toys. I escape across the road, dodging the traffic, and head for Badshah Cold Drinks. This café has been around for more than a century and is famed for its *falooda*—rose-scented milk, swirled with vermicelli and speckled with the crunch of soaked basil seeds. An hour later, I elbow my way through the dense evening crowd to Chowpatty Beach's hawkers and food stalls. I order roasted corn, singed over charcoal and coated with black salt and rubbed with lime. For mains, I settle for *pav bhaji*—crushed buttery potato masala served with soft rolls. Mumbai is a snackers' paradise.

The next morning, I'm all set to meet my friend Anu, but arrive almost an hour earlier than planned. This is an affluent residential area, and I can't locate a local *chai wallah*, but there is a glass-fronted, air-conditioned Starbucks. After almost six weeks on the road, it's hard to resist it, and I'm soon hooked up to decent wifi and surrounded by well-dressed young professionals. I love how dishes are adopted and adapted to suit local tastes across India. This menu includes a cross-continental mix of chile cheese toast, tandoori paneer rolls and pistachio glazed cardamom croissants. As lunch is around the corner I settle for an Americano.

Anu's welcoming ground floor is fronted by a spacious stone patio and furnished with a mix of old and new. I'm introduced to Maalu, Anu's fishmonger of 25 years, who sits cross-legged on the ground under the shade of a leafy canopy. This morning's catch has been generous, and I admire heaps of enormous shrimp, fresh bombay duck (known as *bombil*) and *mandeli*, which are golden anchovies. Maalu wields a curved blade with dexterity as she beheads, fillets, shells and piles prepared shrimp and fish fillets into steel thalis. Anu comments, "In Westernized kitchens we would pay a packet for fancy, bendy, filleting knives, while Maalu outdoes us all with her ancient blade."

Anu is a production designer for film sets. She's from the Bunt community, a group of people with roots in coastal Mangalore, southwest India. Their cooking style is well known, although it's yet to receive the recognition it deserves outside of the country. Typical dishes are likely to include fish, seafood and ▶

The Mumbai coastline at dawn.

▶ meat preparations made with coconut-rich masalas, sharpened with tamarind or tartly flavored fruit. Rice is the main staple here.

I tell Anu about a fish curry lunch I had at a well-known Mangalorean restaurant, where I tasted *neer dosa* for the first time. *Neer* means water in Tulu—a language spoken in the coastal region of Karnataka. These soft crèpes are made from soaked and ground rice, cooked in a covered pan, so that the texture remains soft and pliant. Anu asks about the curry itself, which in truth, wasn't much to boast about. She smiles and says that the best Mangalorean food is made with a big heart in home kitchens and rarely in restaurants.

Over a cold drink, roasted eggplant chutney and crisp millet chips, Anu shares memories of her mother, who, in the 1960s, would bake bread, make bagels, simmer French sauces and cook splendid Mangalorean dishes at the family home in Bangalore. A prudent and curious cook, she also made her own ketchup, churned butter and even kept a bottle of caramel for darkening her fruit cakes. Anu's parents died young, and after living with relatives for several years, she made the move to Mumbai in her mid-twenties. She worked in corporate business and loved the independence, the social life and the opportunities to travel. She also realized how much of a culinary inspiration her mother had been to her.

Today, Anu is making a Bunt specialty of *kori gassi*, a coconutty chicken curry, spiced with mildly flavored, colorful *byadagi* chiles, grown in north Karnataka. *Kori* in Tulu means chicken, and *gassi* means curry. We're in the kitchen with Anu's home helpers, Lulla and *Ajji*—*Ajji* means granny in Marathi, the local language of Maharashtra. A whole chicken has been chopped on the bone and rubbed with turmeric, chile powder and ginger-garlic paste. Roasted coconut and aromatic spices, including black peppercorns, fenugreek and cumin seeds, have been ground with tamarind and a handful of red chiles. Anu tells me that Kashmiri chiles or hot paprika could be substituted, and although not an exact match, this would still make for a tasty dish.

Chopped onion goes into hot oil and is fried with extra garlic, and a few minutes later, she adds the red coconut-chile paste. So much about gauging the readiness of fried masalas is about sight and smell, the rich aroma of garlic as it cooks, the way the sharpness of chiles mellows in the masala, and the little bubbles of oil around the side of the pan.

Anu adds the chicken, and after a few minutes, pours over a jug of coconut milk—not from a can or a carton, hers is made at home. Grated coconut has been blended with warm water and strained through cheesecloth. The first extraction is thick and creamy. The process is then repeated with more water, and this thin, second extraction added to the curry, along with chopped cilantro. The chicken simmers in its sauce until tender, and the masala is then enriched with the reserved coconut cream.

She opens a packet of *rotti*—these wafer-like rice crisps are as large and as thin as a sheet of printer paper. I break off a piece—it tastes like unsweetened breakfast cereal. Made from ground rice batter, they're cooked, crèpe-style, on a cast-iron griddle. Back in

▶ the day they would have been made on an open wood fire. It's hard work—Anu sources her supply from specialist Mangalorean shops.

The chicken is ready and we head to the dining table, where she snaps a few *rottis* into shards and layers them in wide pasta bowls. The curry is ladled over and the rice crisps soften within seconds as they soak in the sauce. There's no other way to eat this glorious sunshine dish than with our fingers. The red chile masala, rich with sweet coconut, is warmed with toasted ground pepper and sharpened with astringent ginger and a little sour tamarind. We almost forget to taste Lulla and Ajji's fried fish, crusted with chile-spiced semolina—it's delicious, too.

Over a light and wobbly panna cotta, made with fresh green coconut flesh, Anu tells me that she once joined a French cooking school in London and found following recipes quite restrictive. "All that regimentation and rule following, it went against the grain—I like to cook by impulse." I ask about the importance of upholding Bunt culinary tradition, and she says that convention has its place, but personal expression has a role, too. When making *kori gassi*, she improvises by cooking fresh cilantro with the sauce, and likes to squeeze in lime at the table—something her mother and aunts wouldn't have done.

And the *rotti*? I've already done an online search for UK-based stockists and drawn a blank. Could she recommend an option? Her eyes light up as she remembers backpacking and couch-surfing across South America for six months and home-schooling her son as they traveled. Along the way they made new friends, connected with old ones, and she introduced everyone to Mangalorean cooking by making *kori gassi*, seasoned with spices brought over from Mumbai. In Peru, she swapped *rotti* with quinoa, while in Chile, baked potatoes worked a treat. And further afield in Japan, sticky rice made for a marvelous partner. "Roopa, feel free to serve my curry with couscous, bulgur, pearl barley or whatever you like. All I ask is, let's remember that its soul belongs to the Bunt community."

1. Mumbai's well known ice cream parlor, K. Rustom, is a Churchgate landmark much-loved for its ice cream wafers. This one has a fantastic frozen guava and red chile filling—it was so good that I returned for second helpings.

2. Local passenger boats at Mumbai's bustling Bhaucha Dhakka ferry terminal.

3. Crawford Market in south Mumbai has long been a historic wholesale market and visitor attraction. You'll find everyday staples here alongside imported delicacies and exotic fruit and vegetables.

4. K. Rustom & Co ice cream parlor in Mumbai originally sold medicines, but soon learned that making ice cream was a far more lucrative business.

5. Returning to Mumbai on the ferry from Alibag. A sultry afternoon, cooled by a steady breeze from the Arabian Sea.

6. Maalu, Anu's personal fishmonger, preparing freshly caught fish at home.

1. Anu with her brightly colored *byadagi* chile masala.

2. Spices and coconut used in Anu's masala.

3. Anu's beautiful home is filled with artwork and artefacts from her travels.

MANGALOREAN CHICKEN CURRY

Serves 4

ANU SHETTY

This traditional curry with its chile-coconut-toasted spice paste base is a specialty made by the Bunt community in Mangalore and introduced to me by Anu Shetty in Mumbai. It's known as *kori gassi*—*kori* means chicken and *gassi* refers to a curry.

Although this looks like a complex recipe, you make the paste ahead of time, and the result is a triumph of sunshine flavors. It's important to use a whole chicken, because the bones will make their own stock in the masala, which lends depth of flavor. I've used Kashmiri chiles here, but *byadagi* chiles from Karnataka are the preferred choice—they have an especially deep red hue and mild flavor. I've suggested an alternative of serving the curry with boiled rice, because life may be too short for trying to make the traditional accompaniment of rice wafers at home.

FOR THE CHICKEN

1 whole chicken (about 3 lb 5 oz/ 1.5 kg), skin removed

1 tsp Kashmiri chile powder

½ tsp ground turmeric

1 oz (25 g) ginger root, peeled and finely chopped

4 large garlic cloves, finely chopped

sea salt

boiled rice, to serve

FOR THE RED CHILE PASTE

½ cup (100 g) frozen grated coconut, defrosted; or ½ cup (50 g) desiccated coconut covered with hot water and soaked for 1 hour

½ tsp black peppercorns

1 tsp brown mustard seeds

1 tsp cumin seeds

½ tsp fenugreek seeds

2 tsp coriander seeds

16 dried Kashmiri red chiles ▸

Put the chicken on a chopping board and chop it into 8–12 pieces. You can ask the butcher to do this for you, if you like. Keep the rib cage, wing tips and neck for added flavor.

Transfer the pieces to a large bowl and add the chile powder, turmeric, ginger and garlic and season with salt. Using your hands, coat the chicken evenly in the spices—it's a good idea to wear disposable gloves for this. Leave to one side while you make the chile paste.

Heat a large, sturdy karahi or wok on low heat and dry roast the defrosted grated coconut (if you are using soaked, desiccated coconut, you don't need to cook it), stirring all the time, for about 3–4 minutes, until it loses its moist appearance but doesn't color. Tip it into a heatproof bowl, then rinse out the pan.

Return the pan to medium heat and dry roast the peppercorns, mustard seeds, cumin, fenugreek and coriander seeds, stirring all the time, until the cumin releases a nutty aroma—this should take about 30 seconds. Add the spices to the coconut and leave to one side.

Using scissors, snip the tops off the chiles and shake out and discard most of the seeds.

Heat the same karahi or wok with the oil on medium heat and fry the chiles for about 1 minute until they swell and darken. Add them to the coconut and spices, leaving any oil behind in the pan.

Put the spices, chiles and coconut (or soaked desiccated coconut) in a blender. Add scant 1 cup (200 ml) of water and process until ▸

2 tbsp sunflower oil or melted coconut oil

1 tbsp tamarind pulp (see page 21)

FOR THE MASALA

4 tbsp sunflower oil or melted coconut oil

1 onion, finely chopped

6 garlic cloves, finely chopped

1 x 14 oz (400 ml) can of full-fat coconut milk

2 tbsp chopped cilantro leaves

3 tbsp coconut cream

smooth—you may need an extra ladleful of water to help it on its way. Stir in the tamarind and leave the paste to one side.

For the masala, add the 4 tablespoons of oil to the chile oil already in the pan. Add the onion and salt to season, and fry on medium heat for 7–10 minutes, stirring often, until the onion is golden around the edges. Stir in the garlic and continue frying for 1 minute.

Add the spiced coconut paste and cook, stirring, for about 5 minutes, until it starts to thicken. Add the marinated chicken pieces, mix well, and continue cooking for 5–7 minutes, until the chicken loses its raw appearance and is sealed.

Whisk the coconut milk until smooth and pour it over the chicken. Add enough hot water to generously cover the pieces and bring the liquid to a boil, then add the chopped cilantro. Turn the heat down to low and simmer uncovered for about 15 minutes, stirring occasionally, until the chicken is tender when pierced with a knife. You may need to top up the masala with water as it cooks—the masala should be broth-like in consistency.

You can now scoop out and discard the bony wing tips and rib cage as they have done their job and infused flavor into the curry. I like to leave the neck in the curry though—and treat it as a cook's perk. Stir in the coconut cream and simmer for 2–3 minutes to warm through before serving with boiled rice.

1. A first glimpse of the Mumbai skyline from the Arabian Sea.

2. Sweet pineapple grown in Maharashtra.

3. A relatively quiet post-Diwali afternoon at Crawford Market, Mumbai.

KERALAN ROAST CHICKEN WITH CINNAMON & CURRY LEAVES Serves 4

The onion-yogurt marinade for this chicken darkens in the oven to a lovely, caramelized brown. Its sweetness is contrasted by the citrussy flavor of crisp-fried curry leaves and star anise. Even though star anise doesn't grow in the region, it's commonly used in Keralan cooking and was introduced to the Malabar coast hundreds of years ago by Chinese traders.

---

1 whole, large chicken (about 4½ lb/2 kg), skin removed

2 star anise

juice of 2 limes

6 tbsp sunflower oil or melted coconut oil

1 tsp brown mustard seeds

about 15 fresh curry leaves

2 large onions, sliced

2½ oz (75 g) ginger root, peeled and finely chopped

1 tsp Kashmiri chile powder

2 tsp ground cinnamon

1 tsp cracked black peppercorns

⅔ cup (150 ml) full-fat Greek yogurt

sea salt

boiled rice or Indian flatbreads, to serve

Put the chicken in a roasting pan and make 2-3 diagonal slashes across the breast, wings and legs with a sharp knife. Put the star anise in the cavity and rub the bird with the lime juice and plenty of sea salt. Tie the legs together with string.

Heat the oil in a sturdy Dutch oven set on medium-high heat and add the mustard seeds—they should start popping straight away. After about 30 seconds, add the curry leaves—these will crackle as they hit the hot oil, so step back.

Turn the heat down to medium-low, add the onions and fry, uncovered, stirring often, for 15-20 minutes, until browned. Stir in the ginger and continue cooking for 2 minutes, then add the chile powder, cinnamon and black pepper and turn off the heat. Stir in the yogurt and leave the mixture to cool.

Blend the onion-yogurt mixture in a food processor or blender until smooth. You can alternatively use a handheld immersion blender and a bowl for this. Rub the paste all over the chicken, cover with parchment paper followed by foil to seal, and leave it in the fridge for at least 1 hour, or overnight if you have the time.

Preheat the oven to 425°F (220°C). Roast the chicken for 30 minutes, then remove the foil and parchment paper and continue cooking for about 50 minutes, or until the juices run clear when a thigh is pierced with a knife. Add a ladleful of hot water to the roasting pan if the masala starts to stick during the last 10 minutes of cooking. Leave the chicken to rest for 15 minutes, then serve with boiled rice or Indian flatbreads.

PARSI CHICKEN CURRY WITH POTATOES

Serves 4–6

I love the way the potatoes almost break down into this aromatic masala, absorbing the flavors of cardamom, star anise and green chiles. This comforting and delicately flavored Parsi dish uses whole spices rather than ground ones. Like most Indian home cooks, I don't bother scooping spices out of the masala once it's is cooked—most folk push them to one side of their plates.

---

4 skinless, bone-in chicken thighs (about 1 lb/500 g)

4 skinless, bone-in drumsticks (about 1 lb/500 g)

5 garlic cloves, crushed

1 oz (30 g) ginger root, peeled and finely grated

½ tsp ground turmeric

1 tsp sea salt

FOR THE MASALA

2 dried Kashmiri red chiles

1 tsp cumin seeds

4 cloves

4 Indian bay leaves (*tej patta*), or 1 in (3 cm) cinnamon stick

1 star anise

2 in (5 cm) cinnamon stick

6 green cardamom pods, pierced

½ tsp black peppercorns

¼ cup (50 g) ghee (see page 18), or 5 tbsp sunflower oil

2 onions, thinly sliced

4 small starchy potatoes (such as Russets), peeled and cut into 1½ in (4 cm) pieces

2 green chiles, deseeded and finely shredded

about 1¼ cups (300 ml) chicken stock or water

Put the chicken in a bowl and add the garlic, ginger, turmeric and salt. Mix everything so that the chicken is evenly coated. I use disposable gloves for this to prevent my fingers being stained orange. Leave to one side while you make the masala.

Using scissors, snip the tops off the chiles and shake out and discard most of the seeds.

In a small bowl, mix the red chiles with the cumin, cloves, bay leaves (or cinnamon stick), star anise, cinnamon, cardamom pods and peppercorns.

Heat the ghee or oil in a sturdy pot on medium-high heat, add the spices and fry for about 30 seconds, until they release their aroma.

Turn the heat down to low, add the onions, cover and cook for 15–20 minutes, until softened but not colored. Increase the heat to medium, stir in the potatoes and cook for 2–3 minutes. Add the chicken and fry for about 5 minutes, until the pieces have lost their raw appearance and are sealed.

Stir in the green chiles and pour over enough of the chicken stock or water to cover and bring the curry to a simmer. Half-cover the pan and cook on low heat for about 20 minutes, until the chicken is tender and the potatoes are soft and just starting to crumble around the edges. Serve with crusty bread or rice.

ROAST CHICKEN THIGHS WITH POMEGRANATE & WALNUT YOGURT

Serves 4–6

This pretty dish is simple to make and great as a party centerpiece. The chicken's yogurt marinade is enriched with walnuts and sharpened with turmeric and tart pomegranate powder (*anardana*). A fruity-tasting spice, *anardana* has a molasses-like flavor and is made from the dried and pounded seeds of wild pomegranates that grow on the slopes of Himalayan hills. You can prepare most of the ingredients ahead and the sticky glaze, made with juices from the roasting pan, gives the chicken a lovely golden sheen.

---

8 skinless, bone-in chicken thighs (about 2 lb 3 oz/1 kg)

juice of 2 lemons

1½ oz (50 g) ginger root, peeled and coarsely chopped

6 garlic cloves, coarsely chopped

1½ oz (50 g) walnuts, coarsely chopped

⅔ cup (150 ml) full-fat Greek yogurt

2 tsp jaggery or light brown sugar

½ tsp ground turmeric

2 tsp Kashmiri chile powder

1 tsp garam masala (see page 19)

2 tsp pomegranate powder (*anardana*)

2 tsp ground coriander

¼ cup (50 g) ghee (see page 18), melted, or 5 tbsp sunflower oil

sea salt

FOR FINISHING

1 handful fresh pomegranate arils

¼ cup (25 g) finely chopped walnuts

2 tbsp shredded mint leaves

Make 2 incisions across each chicken thigh with a sharp knife and arrange them in a single layer in a deep-sided dish.

Pour the lemon juice into a small food processor and add the ginger, garlic and walnuts. Season with salt and process until smooth. You can alternatively use a handheld immersion blender and a bowl for this. Transfer everything to a mixing bowl.

Stir in the yogurt, jaggery or sugar, turmeric, chile powder, garam masala, pomegranate powder and ground coriander. Spoon this marinade over the chicken thighs, making sure they are coated all over. Cover, and leave for at least 2–3 hours, or overnight in the fridge.

Preheat the oven to 425°F (220°C), then put a large, sturdy, dry roasting pan inside to heat up for 5 minutes. Put the thighs in a single layer in the hot pan, drizzle with melted ghee or oil and roast for 15–20 minutes, until tender and the juices run clear when pierced with a knife.

Scrape any juices from the roasting pan into a small saucepan and simmer for about 5–7 minutes, until reduced to a sticky glaze. Transfer the thighs to a serving plate and spoon over the glaze.

To finish, mix together the pomegranate arils, walnuts and mint and scatter the mixture over the chicken before serving.

MOM'S CHICKEN BIRYANI Serves 6

This recipe was handwritten by my mom 40 years ago—the ink has now faded and is smudged with ghee stains, but her instructions have weathered well. Purists wouldn't recognize this as a true biryani. The partially cooked rice isn't layered with chicken and its masala before going into the oven and mom didn't have time to mess with complex spice blends when cooking for the family. None of this detracts from the taste, though—the rice swells as it cooks in steam from the herby yogurt and absorbs the heady aromas.

1½ cups (300 g) basmati rice

8 skinless, bone-in chicken thighs (about 2 lb 3 oz/1 kg)

juice of 1 lemon

1 tsp sea salt

5 large garlic cloves, coarsely chopped

1 oz (30 g) ginger root, peeled and coarsely chopped

3 green chiles, chopped with seeds

1 tsp garam masala (see page 19)

1 tsp ground cinnamon

1 handful of cilantro, leaves and stems, coarsely chopped

scant 1 cup (200 ml) Greek yogurt

¼ cup (50 g) ghee (see page 18), or 5 tbsp sunflower oil

10 green cardamom pods, pierced

4 brown cardamom pods, pierced

4 Indian bay leaves (*tej patta*), or 1 in (3 cm) cinnamon stick

2 large onions, thinly sliced

scant ½ cup (100 ml) hot water

2 tbsp mint leaves, shredded

2 tbsp unsalted butter

TO SERVE

kachumber (see page 288)

full-fat Greek yogurt

Put the rice in a sieve and rinse it under cold running water until the water runs clear, then transfer the rice to a bowl. Cover with fresh water and leave it to soak for 1 hour.

About 30 minutes into the soaking time, put the chicken thighs in a shallow dish and coat them with the lemon juice and salt. Leave to one side.

Put the chopped garlic and ginger in a small food processor with the green chiles, garam masala, cinnamon, cilantro and yogurt. Blend to a paste and leave to one side.

Heat the ghee or oil in a sturdy Dutch oven on medium-high heat and add the green and brown cardamom pods, and bay leaves or cinnamon stick. Swirl everything around for about 30 seconds, then add the onions and fry for about 10–15 minutes, until browned. Preheat the oven to 300°F (150°C).

Spoon the herby yogurt into the pot, add the hot water and bring the sauce to a simmer, stirring all the time. Add the chicken thighs, then cover and cook for about 15–20 minutes on low heat, until tender.

While the chicken is simmering, bring a large pot of salted water to a boil. Drain the soaking water from the rice, tip the grains into the boiling water, and bring the water back to a boil. Cook the rice for 2 minutes on high heat, then drain it in a colander. Heap it on top of the chicken in the pot. It's important to do this while the chicken and rice are hot, so that the grains cook in the steam from the sauce. Scatter with mint leaves and dot with the butter.

Cover the pot with foil and a tight-fitting lid and transfer it to the oven for 40 minutes, until the rice is cooked. Serve with kachumber and yogurt on the side.

CHICKEN WITH COCONUT CREAM & LEMONGRASS

Serves 4–6

This fragrant dish is inspired by the cooking style of home cooks in Pondicherry (renamed Puducherry), which was once governed by France. It's infused with Indian spices but cooked in a French-inspired manner. Lemongrass is widely cultivated in this region and is often called Cochin or Malabar grass—it lends a lovely citrussy-gingery flavor and marries well with coconut. I buy my coconut cream in cartons, although many cooks in South Indian kitchens would make their own.

---

1 oz (30 g) ginger root, peeled and finely grated

5 garlic cloves, crushed

2 green chiles, deseeded and finely chopped

1 tsp roasted and ground fennel seeds

1 tsp garam masala (see page 19)

juice of 1 large lime

8 large skinless, bone-in chicken thighs (about 2 lb 10 oz/1.2 kg)

sea salt

FOR THE SAUCE

5 tbsp (75 g) unsalted butter

4 Indian bay leaves (*tej patta*), or 1 in (3 cm) cinnamon stick

1 large onion, diced

3 lemongrass stems, outer leaves removed, split in half lengthways and bruised

scant 1 cup (200 ml) chicken stock

scant 1 cup (200 ml) coconut cream

juice of 1 lime, to taste

2 tbsp chopped cilantro leaves

boiled rice or crusty bread, to serve

Mix the ginger with the garlic, green chiles, ground fennel, garam masala and lime juice, and season generously with sea salt. Put the chicken thighs in a bowl and coat them with this mixture. Cover and leave for at least 1 hour in the fridge.

Make the sauce. Preheat the oven to 340°F (170°C). Melt the butter in a Dutch oven or heavy pot on low heat and add the bay leaves or cinnamon stick, followed, after a few seconds, by the onion and lemongrass stems. Cover the pot and soften the onion without coloring for 15 minutes, stirring often.

Turn the heat to medium, add the chicken and cook, uncovered, for 5 minutes, stirring all the time, until the thighs have lost their raw appearance and are sealed. Pour in the stock and bring to a simmer. Cover the pot, transfer it to the oven and cook for about 20 minutes, until the chicken is tender.

Remove the chicken pieces from the pot and keep them warm. Squeeze any juice from the lemongrass with the back of a wooden spoon and discard the stems.

Put the pot back on medium heat and skim any extra oil from the surface. The sauce should be broth-like in consistency. Once it comes to a boil, gradually add the coconut cream and enough lime juice to sharpen. Return the chicken to the pot and simmer the sauce for 2 minutes. Scatter with the cilantro, then serve with rice or crusty bread.

COMMUNITY ROOTS
SOUTH

SUNIL & SUJA ELIAS, KERALA

The early morning rainfall had left puddles on the road—it was hot and humid, and plumes of steam rose from the tarmac. Sunil Elias, a retired spice trader, met me at Kochi airport. I'd booked to stay for four nights at his family's homestay in the village of Varapuzha, 40 minutes away.

Cochin (also known as Kochi) is a major trading port, with huge container ships in the harbor, a buoyant shipbuilding industry and a naval base. Glass-fronted office buildings and shiny shopping complexes lined our route out of the city, but there were also historical landmarks. The occasional heritage home with its sloping pagoda-style roof and pillared porch had seen better days, and Sunil wondered how long the owners would resist the promise of big money from developers keen to rebuild apartments in its place.

Maritime merchants from across the world have left footprints on Cochin and the profusion of mosques, churches, synagogues and temples are testament to past and present communities living comfortably together. As we drove, the neon lights and glass-fronted buildings fell away, and with a view unhindered by concrete, I caught my first glimpse of rural Kerala—the backwaters, marshy landscapes, small fishing boats and paddy fields.

We had arranged to meet his friends on the way to his village. The road narrowed as we approached their house and leafy trees on either side of the lane diffused the sunshine into dappled shade. Smitha and Anil live inland on a family-owned rubber plantation, and their home is surrounded by luxuriant banana trees, palms, reeds and flowers suffused in bright colors. Sunil brought a couple of vinyl records into the house, and we all paid homage to Anil's splendid music system. Smitha had generously cooked lunch, which included a fabulous fish curry, rippled through with curry leaves and enriched with creamy coconut milk. We ate appreciatively while listening to Dire Straits and David Bowie—the soundtrack to my youth. As we left, Sunil enthusiastically invited them for a "duck roast" lunch at *Teak House*, his family home.

We reach Varapuzha where Sunil lives with his wife, Suja, and their daughter, her husband and two young granddaughters. In my room, grateful for the chill of the air conditioning, I unpack and look forward to four whole days of not living out of a suitcase. Their large bungalow, although recently built, is respectful of traditional architectural design. Its terracotta tiled roof is pitched to help with water drainage during the two annual monsoon seasons and keeps the interior cool. A long veranda runs along the back of the house and a porch at the front provides extra shade and cross ventilation.

The Synagogue in Cochin, built in 1568.

▶ My guest room opens on to this veranda and faces their tiered garden. A clump of teak trees stands tall, and is surrounded by various spice trees, which include cinnamon, allspice and clove. I notice that some of the gnarled trunks provide life to a variety of orchids and twisted peppercorn vines. It's all a glorious tangle of creeping plants, leafy greens, herbs and rhizomes, with hanging chiles and flowers providing sporadic bursts of color.

Sunil joins me on the veranda as I admire the view. He tells me that whenever manure is bought for the garden, the family has no idea what they will be harvesting in a few months' time. This year's unexpected gifts included tomato plants, eggplants and okra. As we stroll across the lawn, he points out different spice varieties. Eight nutmeg trees provide around 90 lb (40 kg) of nutmeg every year, and any excess is sold to neighbors. We chew on sweet and fragrant young cinnamon leaves, surprisingly delicate clove leaves, and he plucks a couple of makrut lime leaves to go into tonight's beef patties. Sunil and Suja are Catholics and regularly cook with beef.

I walk past the family's vegetable patch and swimming pool and step down to the backwaters at the end of the garden. This network of lagoons and waterways is fed both by tidal water from the Arabian Sea and fresh water from the Periyar river. A man in a knee-length lungi paddles his slow-moving boat, barely creating a ripple as it glides past. The sun is setting, birds fly across the darkening sky and a dog barks in the distance. If ever there was a moment to capture images for a tourist brochure, this is it. The mosquitos are nipping at my ankles, and I hear the low grumble of thunder, so return to the main house. It's sundowner hour; Sunil pours a whisky and I settle for a cold beer. Dusk is short-lived and nightfall descends.

The next morning, Suja and I bond over a shared interest in cooking as she crackles curry leaves from the garden into hot coconut oil for an egg-curry breakfast. She's not very fluent in English and I have no knowledge of Malayalam, but no matter. I watch as she tips a ladle of *appam* batter into the pan and spreads it into a lace-like pancake. She made this batter the night before from coconut blended with rice, yeast, a little sugar and water, and then left it in the warmth of the kitchen to ferment. Years ago, the rice grains would have been pounded in a big stone mortar, but Indian electric "mixis" are now the workhorses of many kitchens. A saucer-shaped appam is placed, spongy side up, on my plate next to a hard-boiled egg and a spoonful of softened onion and green chile masala. Silverware has no place here and any lifting is done with the tips of fingers, which makes the curry taste all the more delicious.

Suja and Sunil's day starts at 5:30 am with black tea infused with holy basil for good health. Sunil takes breakfast requests from his granddaughters the night before, and this morning, Saira and Samantha have asked for sausages and *puttu*—a ground rice paste layered with grated coconut steamed in a cylindrical stainless-steel tube. Traditionally bamboo would have been used, but metal works just as well. Many dishes feature coconut in some form—perhaps the creamy white flesh will be pounded for chutney, blended into a batter, or the milk added to curry or a pudding. Nothing gets wasted;

▶ even the fibrous outer coating is made into coir mats, and local street hawkers do a brisk trade in bamboo-handled ladles fashioned from empty coconut shell halves.

Nothing short of three cooked meals is the norm in the Elias household. I tell them that on weekdays, I normally make do with tea and toast in the mornings, and Suja looks appalled. Now that Sunil has retired, they both share the cooking. Suja prefers to focus on fish and vegetable preparations, while Sunil cooks meat and poultry and does the shopping. I get the impression that he enjoys visiting the market and meeting friends and shopkeepers as much as he likes being in the kitchen. Now in his mid-sixties, he's often out and about on his bicycle or motorcycle. From November to March, when fish are plentiful, he'll be in the backwaters with his rod and catch the likes of pearl spot, red snapper or even eels. There's a small co-operative shop located a kilometer away and local farmers will sell their crops there—the prices are reasonable and the quality better than what's available in the city.

We're on our way to a nearby duck farm in Kadamakkudy, sited on an islet and accessible by a narrow bridge. Sunil, a keen birdwatcher, keeps a camera poised for action and is rewarded with shots of purple herons wading among the reeds and a rare sighting of a stork-billed kingfisher—its massive red beak and colorful plumage making a colorful splash against the marshy landscape. We pass a local tourist attraction, where couples and young families buy cold drinks, cotton candy, ice cream and fried snacks from roadside kiosks. A little farther along the single-track road is a toddy shop, which sells a boozy brew made from the sap of coconut palms. I'm more interested in sampling the chile-laden snacks served at this drinking den, but Sunil gently steers me away, reminding me that we have ducks to buy for tomorrow's lunch. He shares an easy-going kinship with the duck farmer and his wife, and after appraising the birds in the greenish, brackish stream, he puts in a home delivery order for the morning.

The next day, husband and wife have decided that today's "duck roast" will be a collaborative effort. I'm intrigued by how often "roast" meats are talked about. Back in the day, most Indian kitchens didn't have ovens, and if an "English-style" roast was ordered in a restaurant, it was often simmered until tender in a lightly spiced water, and then browned in a pan. Over the years, this term has been adopted, adapted and embraced by so many that it's now part of the lexicon of Indian culinary descriptions.

Two birds have already been plucked, cleaned and chopped on-the-bone. A bunch of curry leaves are arranged like flowers in a vase, the vegetables have been prepared, and spices neatly arranged in bowls. One of the blends has a particularly sweet and earthy aroma, and Suja tells me that it's "meat masala." After a few seconds of anticipatory silence, she rattles off a raft of aromatics, which I hastily scrawl in my notebook.

The duck has been sealed in a cavernous cast-iron karahi and she judiciously but confidently adds the "meat masala," followed by a spoon of ground turmeric, pungent chile powder and plenty of black pepper. ▶

1. Sunil is a keen birdwatcher and photographer, and doesn't need a map to navigate the landscape around the Keralan backwaters.

2. Heading back to Sunil and Suja's homestay in Varapuza after visiting a nearby duck farm.

3. Little Queen Embroidery Shop, located close to the Synagogue in Cochin, employs local women, and is renowned for its embroidery and lacework.

4. Top quality Keralan turmeric, pink shallots, pungent chiles and fresh coconut picked from a tree in Sunil's garden. My favorite is the peppery curry leaves, which grow in unruly bushes within arm's reach of the kitchen window.

5. Cantilevered Chinese fishing nets were introduced to the Cochin shoreline centuries ago.

6. Checking out the visitors to Kerala's backwaters.

▶ Sunil carefully stirs and coats the pieces with masala, and adds sweet red shallots and spindly green chiles, followed by fresh curry leaves and water to cover. As the "roast" bubbles on the stove, he tells me that Keralan turmeric is of particularly high quality, because it has the highest concentrate of curcumin, which provides a particularly bright yellow color and a full whack of astringent flavor. It's called Alleppey Finger Turmeric (AFT) even though it isn't grown there—its name stuck because Alleppey was the main spice trading center in Kerala until Cochin took over in 1960s.

The duck is tender and the spices have mellowed. Suja has deep-fried potatoes and gently folds them into the masala, where they will absorb the richly spiced fat. Smitha and Anil have arrived, and we all gather in the kitchen, beer in hand, waiting for Suja to tip the glistening pieces of duck into a bowl and scrape out the sticky peppery sediment from the pan. A pot of short-grained rice is ready and we all sit down to eat. There's no need for small talk as we savor the meat and nibble around the bones with spice-coated fingers. It's a lovely dish, its flavor warmed with sweet cinnamon and shallots and the duck's richness cut with sharp chiles, ginger and citrussy curry leaves.

It's my last day in Kerala, a cool breeze blows through the open veranda doors and Sunil asks if he can play some music while we eat. This time it's not rock legends but Hindi film songs from the 1950s, the same ones that my late dad used to listen to in the car when I was a child. I ask who the vocalist is on this recording—it's a beautiful, melodic voice. Sunil smiles—he is the singer.

1. Sunil showing off his dark and peppery duck roast.

2. Sunil and Suja in their younger days.

3. Beautiful, marble-sized shallots, juicy ginger from the garden and fresh green chiles going into the masala for our duck roast.

KERALAN DUCK ROAST

SUNIL AND SUJA ELIAS

Serves 4–6

---

1 tsp fennel seeds

½ tsp fenugreek seeds

1 whole duck (about 4 lb 6 oz/2 kg), skin on

3 tbsp melted coconut oil or sunflower oil

¾ tsp ground turmeric

1 tsp Kashmiri chile powder

2 tsp ground coriander seeds

1½ tsp ground black peppercorns

1 tsp garam masala (see page 19)

3 large banana shallots, coarsely chopped

1 large garlic head, cloves separated and peeled

1½ oz (50 g) ginger root, peeled and finely shredded

4–5 green chiles, halved lengthways and deseeded

about 30 fresh curry leaves

sea salt

Heat a small, sturdy pan on medium-low heat and add the fennel and fenugreek seeds and cook for about 1 minute, stirring all the time, until the fennel releases a sweet, toasted aroma and the fenugreek darkens. Tip the spices onto a plate and when they are cool enough to handle, pound them to a powder in a pestle with a mortar and leave to one side.

Put the duck on a chopping board, and with a sharp knife, cut the bird into 8 portions. Keep the ribs, neck and wing tips for adding to the pot—they will add to the rich, meaty flavor as the curry simmers.

Transfer the duck pieces to a tray lined with double-thickness paper towels, skin-side facing upwards. Sprinkle the skin generously with salt, cover with parchment paper and keep in the fridge for 2–3 hours, or overnight if you have the time.

Pat the duck dry with paper towels and arrange the pieces in a single layer, skin-side facing downwards, in a large, cold, heavy-bottomed Dutch oven—you'll probably need to do this in two batches. Cook each batch on low heat for about 10 minutes, until the skin has released its fat and browned. Increase the heat to medium, turn the pieces over and fry for a further 2 minutes to seal the meat, then transfer it to a tray while you cook the next batch.

Preheat the oven to 340°F (170°C).

Add the coconut or sunflower oil to the duck fat left behind in the pot and set it on medium heat. Return the duck to the pot and add the turmeric, chile powder, ground coriander, pepper, garam masala and the ground fennel and fenugreek seeds. Season with salt.

Stir well and fry the duck and spices together for 5 minutes, until the spices lose their raw flavor and evenly coat the pieces. Pour over enough hot water to three-quarters cover the duck and then bring the liquid to a simmer.

Although this dish is known as a "roast," it doesn't go into an oven—it's cooked in a karahi on the stovetop. Sunil and his wife are wonderful cooks. Their Keralan duck curry is simmered in a masala darkened with freshly ground black pepper and garam masala. I love the finishing flourish of fried potatoes, especially as they soak up the delicious, spiced duck fat. This is a great recipe to make on a rainy day—I'd set an afternoon aside for the preparation, and before you start, pour a large glass of wine, turn the radio on, then line up the ingredients. Your kitchen will smell wonderful as the duck simmers.

This is one of those dishes that mellows and deepens in flavor if it's made a day ahead of serving. You can prepare the fried potatoes to finish while the duck is cooking, or even further in advance, if you prefer.

TO FINISH

3 potatoes (such as Russets)

about 2 cups (500 ml) sunflower oil, for deep-frying

Stir in two-thirds of the shallots, all the garlic, ginger and green chiles, and half the curry leaves. Cover, transfer the pot to the oven and cook for 1 hour 30 minutes, or until the duck is tender.

Meanwhile, make the fried potatoes to finish. Peel and slice each potato into ¼ in (5 mm) thickness "fries." Rinse them in a colander under running water and then soak in fresh water for 30 minutes.

To deep-fry, fill a large wide, sturdy pot no more than two-thirds full with oil. The oil is ready for frying when it reaches 350°F (180°C) on a food thermometer, or when a cube of bread dropped into the oil browns in 30 seconds.

Drain the fries from their soaking water and pat them dry with paper towels. Fry them in the hot oil for about 5–7 minutes, until pale golden—you may need to do this in two batches. Drain each batch on paper towels, season the fries with salt and leave them to one side.

Transfer the cooked duck to a plate and discard the wing tips and rib cage. Reduce the masala, without a lid, on high heat, until it darkens and thickens to a coating consistency (about 5–7 minutes). Stir in the remaining shallots and curry leaves, then turn the heat down to low and return the duck to the pot. Stir well, add the fried potatoes and carefully mix them through the masala just before serving.

If you're making this dish the day before serving, cool the duck to room temperature and then cover and chill it overnight. The next day, reheat it on the stovetop in an uncovered pot, stirring occasionally. Add a ladle of water as the duck warms to lift any sediment from the bottom of the pot. Fold in the fried potatoes when the duck is piping hot, then cover the pot and leave it to one side, off the heat, for 3–4 minutes before serving. The heat from the masala will warm the potatoes.

CINNAMON-SPICED DUCK BREASTS WITH ORANGE & GINGER SAUCE

Serves 4

As many of us know, duck a l'orange was the height of sophistication during the 1970s and mom regularly made it for dad's birthday—it was the only way she knew of cooking duck. Only recently have I appreciated that fragrant Indian spices, crackling curry leaves and the bite of chiles make a marvelous contrast to the richness of duck. I've played around with Keralan flavors here—the orange provides zesty freshness, while tamarind brings a burst of sharpness, softened by a little butterscotch-like jaggery. You could use pork chops instead of duck breasts if you prefer.

---

4 skin-on duck breast fillets

2 tsp Kashmiri chile powder

¼ tsp ground turmeric

1 tsp ground cinnamon

1 tsp sea-salt flakes

FOR THE SAUCE

2 tbsp sunflower oil

½ tsp brown mustard seeds

about 15 fresh curry leaves

1 star anise

1 large onion, thinly sliced

¾ oz (20 g) ginger root, peeled and finely chopped

1 green chile, deseeded and finely chopped

1 tbsp tamarind pulp (see page 21)

2 tsp jaggery or light brown sugar

½ cup (125 ml) chicken stock or water

finely grated zest and juice of 1 orange

boiled rice, to serve

Using a sharp knife, score the duck breasts diagonally across the fatty skin, in close parallel lines taking care that you don't go through to the flesh. Mix the chile powder with the turmeric, cinnamon and salt and rub the spice mixture over both sides of each duck breast (I wear disposable gloves for this). Leave to one side.

Heat the oil in a small Dutch oven or heavy pot on medium-high heat and add the mustard seeds—they should sizzle straight away. Fry for 30 seconds, until the popping stops, then add the curry leaves and star anise—stand back, because the leaves will splutter as they hit the hot oil.

Turn the heat down to medium, add the onion and fry for 10–12 minutes, until golden. Stir in the ginger and green chile and cook for 1 minute.

Add the tamarind pulp and jaggery or sugar followed by the stock and simmer for 2–3 minutes, then stir in the orange zest and juice and cook on gentle heat for 2–3 minutes. Cover and leave to one side.

Pat the duck breasts dry with a paper towel and put them skin-side facing downwards in a cold frying pan. Turn on the heat and cook on low heat—the skin will soon release its fat and then will brown (this should take about 10 minutes).

Turn the heat up to medium, turn the breasts over and cook for a further 2–3 minutes—the center of the breast should still be pink. If you have a meat thermometer, aim for 125°F (51°C) for rare duck meat and 140°F (61°C) for medium. Remove the breasts from the pan and leave them to rest for 5 minutes before cutting them into thick slices.

Pour off all but 1 tablespoon of the duck fat from the frying pan, then add the orange and ginger sauce and reheat. Divide the sauce among four serving plates and arrange the sliced duck breasts on top. Serve with boiled rice.

SLOW-COOKED LAMB WITH LENTILS Serves 6

I spent my childhood thinking that the best Indian food was made by my mom in England. It was the early 1970s and this recipe reminds me of gale-swept, wintry nights, the rain lashing down, while Mom's *dal gosht* simmered on the stove, leaving trails of condensation on the kitchen window. This is a rustic recipe where the lentils soften into the meaty masala, imparting a wonderful earthiness to the finished dish.

½ cup (100 g) red lentils (*masoor dal*)

⅔ cup (150 g) split Bengal gram (*chana dal*) or split yellow peas

8 garlic cloves, coarsely chopped

1½ oz (50 g) ginger root, peeled and coarsely chopped

scant ½ cup (75 g) ghee (see page 18), or ½ cup (120 ml) sunflower oil

2 Indian bay leaves (*tej patta*), or ¾ in (2 cm) cinnamon stick

1½ in (4 cm) cinnamon stick

2 large onions, finely sliced

3 green chiles, slit lengthways but still intact at the stem, most of the seeds removed

1 lb 12 oz (800 g) lamb neck fillet, cut into 1½ in (4 cm) pieces

1 tsp Kashmiri chile powder

¾ tsp ground turmeric

1 tsp garam masala (see page 19)

scant 1 cup (200 ml) full-fat Greek yogurt

1 tbsp chopped cilantro leaves

2 tbsp shredded mint leaves

sea salt

boiled rice or Indian flatbreads, to serve

Mix together the red and yellow lentils in a bowl and soak them in hot water, covered, for 1 hour.

Put the garlic and ginger in a small food processor, add enough water to barely cover, then process until smooth. (You can alternatively use a handheld immersion blender and a bowl for this or you could crush the garlic and finely grate the ginger.) Leave to one side.

Heat the ghee or oil in large, sturdy pot on medium-high heat, and add the bay leaves and cinnamon, followed by the onions. Season with salt and fry the onions for about 12–15 minutes, until browned. Add the ginger-garlic paste, then the chiles and, after 30 seconds, the lamb.

Fry until the lamb has evenly browned (about 15 minutes), adding a ladleful of water if the onions look like they are catching on the bottom of the pot. Drain the lentils from their soaking water and add them to the pot. Preheat the oven to 340°F (170°C).

Stir in the chile powder, turmeric, garam masala and half of the yogurt and cook for 2–3 minutes, stirring all the time. Add the remaining yogurt and cook for another 1 minute.

Pour over enough hot water to cover the meat by three-quarters and bring the masala to a simmer. Cover with foil and a lid and transfer the pot to the oven to cook for 1 hour 15 minutes, or until the lamb and lentils are tender. Scatter with cilantro and mint, then serve with boiled rice or Indian flatbreads.

KASHMIRI LAMB WITH SAFFRON, CARDAMOM & RED CHILES

Serves 4

My adaptation of this classic Kashmiri curry combines several recipes from the Muslim and Hindu communities. The dish is characterized by its mild chile flavor, which works well with the sweetness of locally grown saffron, ground fennel seeds and smoky-tasting cardamom. This dish tastes even better if you make it a day or two before you intend to serve.

¼ tsp saffron strands

2 tbsp hot water, plus extra to cover the meat

1 tbsp fennel seeds

4 brown cardamom pods

12 green cardamom pods

½ tsp sugar

scant ½ cup (75 g) ghee (see page 18), or ½ cup (125 ml) sunflower oil

pinch of asafoetida (*heeng*; optional)

6 cloves

1 lb 10 oz (750 g) boneless lamb shoulder, cut into 1½ in (4 cm) pieces

¾ cup (175 ml) full-fat Greek yogurt

1 tsp ground ginger

2 tsp Kashmiri chile powder

½ tsp ground turmeric

2 tsp roasted and ground coriander seeds

1 tsp ground cinnamon

¾ tsp coarsely ground black peppercorns

sea salt

boiled rice, to serve

Soak the saffron in the hot water, bruising the stems with the back of a teaspoon to release the flavor and color. Leave to one side.

Roast the fennel seeds in a small, dry frying pan on medium heat, stirring all the time, until they release their fragrance, about 1 minute. Transfer the seeds to a small bowl.

Split the brown and green cardamom pods with a sharp knife, removed the seeds and mix them with the roasted fennel seeds and sugar in a mortar (discard the pods). Pound the spices with the pestle to a coarse powder. Set aside.

Heat the ghee or oil in a large, sturdy pot on medium-high heat and add the asafoetida, if using. Add the cloves and swirl them around in the oil for a few seconds until they release their aroma. Add the lamb pieces and fry them for about 15 minutes, stirring frequently, until browned all over. Preheat the oven to 320°F (160°C).

A spoonful at a time, stir in the yogurt, and keep frying the meat for a few minutes between each addition. Turn the heat down to medium and add the ground ginger, chile, turmeric, coriander, cinnamon, black pepper and salt and cook for 1 minute, stirring all the time.

Pour over enough hot water to reach three-quarters of the way up the meat, and stir in the saffron and its soaking liquid. Cover the pot with a tight-fitting lid and transfer it to the oven for about 1 hour, or until the lamb is tender and the masala has thickened and cloaks the meat. Serve with boiled rice.

> Asafoetida is a resin that is often added to lentils, beans and lentils. Its sulphurous aroma mellows to sweetness on cooking, and it's believed to be an effective digestive.

HIMALAYAN BELT **LARGE PLATES** 177

BRAISED LAMB WITH ONION & ALMONDS

Serves 4–6

This simple yet elegant one-pot lamb curry is finished with caramelized onions, which infuse sweetness and richness into the masala. The meat isn't browned, but cooks slowly in the garlic-ginger yogurt until it almost falls apart. Make it the day before serving so that the flavors can mellow.

¼ cup (50 g) ghee (see page 18), or 6 tbsp sunflower oil

1 tsp cumin seeds

6 green cardamom pods, pierced

2 in (5 cm) cinnamon stick

4 Indian bay leaves (*tej patta*), or 1 in (3 cm) cinnamon stick

4 cloves

1 large onion, thinly sliced

8 garlic cloves, shredded

1 oz (30 g) ginger root, peeled and finely chopped

1 tsp coarsely ground black peppercorns

2 lb 3 oz (1 kg) lamb neck fillet, cut into 1½ in (4 cm) cubes

¾ cup (175 ml) full-fat Greek yogurt

sea salt

Indian flatbreads, to serve

TO FINISH

4 dried Kashmiri red chiles

3 tbsp ghee (see page 18), or 3½ tbsp sunflower oil

1 blade of mace

1 large onion, thinly sliced

1 tbsp almonds, blanched and shredded or 1 tbsp sliced almonds

2 tbsp chopped cilantro leaves

sea salt

Preheat the oven to 320°F (160°C). Heat the ghee or oil in a large, sturdy pot on medium-high heat and add the cumin, cardamom pods, cinnamon, bay leaves and cloves.

Sizzle the spices for 30 seconds, until aromatic, then add the onion, garlic, ginger and black pepper. Turn the heat down to medium and cook, stirring often, for 8–10 minutes, until the onion has softened but not browned.

Add the lamb and yogurt and bring the mixture to the simmer. Cover the pot, transfer it to the oven to cook for 1 hour 45 minutes, until the lamb is tender and the masala has thickened.

To finish, snip the tops off the chiles with scissors and shake out and discard most of the seeds. Heat the ghee or oil in a frying pan on medium-high heat and add the chiles, mace and, after a few seconds, the sliced onion. Season generously with salt, and fry for 10–12 minutes, until browned, then stir the onion mixture into the lamb. Scatter with the almonds and cilantro before serving. Serve with Indian flatbreads.

LAMB COOKED IN YOGURT WITH GINGER & ORANGE

Serves 8

I like to use lamb neck fillet for this elegant curry—it has a fair amount of fat, which keeps the meat tender and juicy as it slowly cooks in the citrussy masala. As the lamb is boneless, I add a little chicken stock to embolden the flavor, but you could make this with lamb shanks and use water instead.

- 1 lb 10 oz (750 g) lamb neck fillet, cut into 2½ in (6 cm) pieces
- ½ cup (120 ml) full-fat Greek yogurt
- 1 oz (30 g) ginger root, peeled, ½ oz (15 g) finely grated and ½ oz (15 g) cut into fine strips
- 1 tsp Kashmiri chile powder
- 1 tsp roasted and ground cumin seeds
- ¾ tsp ground turmeric
- ⅓ cup (60 g) ghee (see page 18), or 2 tbsp sunflower oil and 3 tbsp unsalted butter
- ⅔ cup (150 ml) chicken stock or water
- pared zest of ½ an orange, finely shredded, and the juice of 3 oranges
- juice of 1 small lemon
- 1 tbsp shredded mint leaves
- sea salt
- boiled rice or Indian flatbreads, to serve

Mix the lamb with the yogurt, grated ginger, chile powder, cumin and turmeric. Season with salt. Cover and refrigerate for 1 hour, or overnight if you have the time.

Heat the ghee or oil and butter in a large, sturdy pot on medium-high heat and fry the lamb along with any marinade for 10 minutes, until any moisture has evaporated and the meat has sealed—it doesn't need to brown. Add a splash of water if the yogurty masala catches on the bottom of the pot. Preheat the oven to 320°F (160°C).

Add half the stock to the pot. Scrape up any sediment with a metal spoon and reduce the volume by half, then add the remaining stock and reduce it again.

Add half the orange and half the lemon juice and reduce by half, then add the remainder. Cover the pot and cook the lamb in the oven for about 1 hour, or until the meat is tender.

For the topping, bring a small saucepan of water to a boil. Add the shredded orange zest and return the water to a boil for 10 seconds. Tip the shreds into a sieve and refresh with cold running water. Mix the orange shreds with the ginger strips and the mint and scatter the topping over the lamb before serving. Serve with boiled rice or Indian flatbreads.

COMMUNITY ROOTS
NORTHWEST

NAVED SHAFI, OLD DELHI

I've walked the gullies around Old Delhi's Jama Masjid mosque in Chandni Chowk many times. Built in the seventeenth century by the Mughal Emperor Shah Jahan, the mosque is one of the largest in India, and it's where thousands of Muslims gather every Friday for worship. Soaring sandstone walls, marble domes and towering minarets overlook the surrounding street level bazaars, many of which have been there almost as long as the mosque itself. The recent opening of an underground train station has meant that the old city is now better connected to the rest of Delhi but I find that little else has changed over the last few decades as I cross the narrow lanes of Chandni Chowk.

A tangle of trailing electric wires hangs low overhead as I step cautiously on the uneven ground, dodging hand carts, rickshaws and the crowds. In the hotchpotch of wholesale markets and workshops, shops and stalls, there's an established blueprint for designated trading spaces. Khari Baoli is the largest wholesale spice market in Asia—here the air hangs heavy with chile powder and catches my throat as I walk past. I might buy silver jewelry from another lane, Dariba Kalan, where the price is determined by weight and not workmanship. Then there are other areas for other interests—Chawri Bazaar for stationery, Nai Sarak for books, Kinari Bazaar for brocade, and there's even a market for multi-colored paper kites.

Each area has its go-to places to eat, and many of the restaurants, cafés and kiosks have been in business here for over a century. Most of the cooks replicate Mughal-style dishes—sometimes the curries are infused with *khara* masala, whole spice infusions, almost all will feature plenty of ghee, and, occasionally, there'll be a flourish of regal saffron and thin wisps of silver leaf. Meaty grills, flavored kulfis, cookies baked over charcoal—there's plenty to choose from. I'm on my way to meet Naved Shafi—he lives close to Karim's, one of the oldest and most famed restaurants in the area. I've enjoyed fragrant kormas, kebabs and rotis here many times, and may have walked past Naved's house without a second thought. But not today.

It's raining, the ground soon turns muddy, and I flag down a bicycle rickshaw. We pass welders repairing spare parts for cars as sparks fly off anvils and hammers dent sheet metal—it's noisy, hot, crowded and very humid. I'd have missed Naved's house if he hadn't been outside waiting for me. It's clear that my arrival has been clocked in the lane—everyone knows the Shafi family.

Suddenly there is calm. A heavy studded wooden door opens onto the main courtyard of Nawab House. Thick outer walls silence the mayhem outside, and only birdsong and an occasional call to prayer from the neighboring mosque filters through. Naved's great-great-grandfather was the nawab of

Sari shopping for the festive season in Delhi.

▶ Karnal, a ruler and aristocrat. He moved to Delhi in the 1880s and built this *haveli*, which is one of the few standing stately townhouses in the area. Many other heritage homes have long since been demolished, converted to warehouses or partitioned and sold off piecemeal.

We sit on the veranda overlooking one of three courtyards. The architecture reflects Mughal styling with ornamental arches and a geometrical designed mandala on the tiled marble floor. The sitting room has three wooden doorways, each topped with a glass-paned arch, where framed wedding photographs of Naved's parents are displayed on the mantlepiece. In its heyday, this room would have been bustling with relatives, many of them living in chambers on the first floor. Although its grandeur has faded, and much of the covered area is no longer in daily use, this is a home of distinction and historical value.

Naved was born here. After marrying, he worked across India in corporate business, but returned to the family home after his mother passed away. Now he looks after his elderly and frail father at home. Erudite and entertaining, he shares memories, smiling as he recollects his grandma, Amma Dadi, slipping him a few rupees after returning from school. The money was spent at Karim's restaurant on half a plate of korma and a *khamiri roti*. Karim's korma is tender goat meat, slow cooked in richly spiced yogurt-onion masala, and just right for serving with this soft yeasted flatbread.

Naved tells me that his mother was from Lucknow, and that her refined style of cooking had been shaped by the Mughals and passed down through generations. He talks about her delicate pulaos, embellished with the likes of saffron, sweet cardamom and mace, and kormas enriched with nut pastes. He admits that vegetables were usually cooked with meat. Favorite dishes included koftas, ground goat meatballs, cooked in poppy-seed masala with baby turnips and *chukandar gosht*—clove and brown cardamom-spiced meat, simmered in shredded beet and tomato broth. Red meat was cooked at home, and chicken looked down upon. If the cook was sent to the butcher to buy a bird, neighbors would come over and ask who was ill—poultry was considered fit only for invalids.

I'm introduced to Shenaz Begum, the current cook, who has been with the family for more than three decades. She's lively and confident and was trained by Naved's mother. We walk across the courtyard to the kitchen. Although slightly built, she's very much in charge of kitchen affairs.

Today, Shenaz is making *namak mirch*, "mutton," but made with goat meat, which is the norm in most of India. *Namak* means salt and *mirch*, chiles. Naved explains that back in the day, his relatives would hunt and shoot game, which was prepared on the spot and cooked on an outdoor wood fire. Only basic ingredients were carried on these trips—garlic, a *potli* (small bag) of chiles and a pot of yogurt. Shenaz is recreating this recipe today.

Garlic paste, lots of it, is frying in oil in the pressure cooker with Shenaz's metal spoon clanging against the pot as she lifts up any

▶ sediment. Next, a handful of broken, dried red chiles, followed by chopped meat, salt and then a big ladle of tart homemade yogurt. The curd she uses is thinner than the kind I buy in Western supermarkets and needs no water. After a couple of whistles under pressure, the pot is uncovered, and any yogurty liquid bubbled down and fried until the tender meat is cloaked in garlicky masala. She ladles everything into a glass bowl and it's brought to the table along with dry-cooked white *urad dal*, finished with browned onions, fat green chiles cooked with onions, and a colorful plate of salad.

I love the straight-up flavors of *namak mirch* "mutton" and the way in which the chiles, tempered with the tang of yogurt, contrast the caramelized garlic. Naved has ordered in some of the famous *nihari*, a rich slow-cooked goat dish, from Karim's next door and breads to accompany. This classic curry is delicious for its buttery, floral flavor and is topped with shredded ginger, green chiles and a thick layer of glistening spiced ghee. For many traditionalists, including my mother, some ghee or oil is a mark of quality—nowadays, modern home cooks prefer minimal amounts, but there is some sacrifice to the flavor.

The Mughals were famous for introducing rich, sweetly spiced bread varieties to royal palace kitchens and many remain popular both in five-star hotels and street food markets. Naved has bought a selection today, one of which is *sheermal*—a yeasted, sweetened flatbread, enriched with milk and ghee and scented with saffron. The dough is rolled into a thick disc and pierced before being slapped against the walls of a hot tandoor. And then there's my all-time favorite, *romali roti*, made on a curved griddle, which resembles an upturned karahi. *Romal* means handkerchief and these thin, soft, folded breads make a splendid partner with *namak mirch* meat.

Over lunch, Naved reflects on changing times, and how Chandni Chowk's food offering is shifting to accommodate the Punjabi preference for tomatoey, cream-laden curries.

I ask about where he shops for daily vegetables and he tells me that local vendors supply small quantities of the basics, but he enjoys visiting the *sabzi mandi* every ten days to buy at least 11 lb (5 kg) of onions and enough ginger, garlic, green chiles and cilantro to keep the kitchen ticking over. Otherwise, there's always delivery apps for groceries—during lockdown, this was the only way to ensure freshly cooked home dishes. Change, it seems, is inevitable.

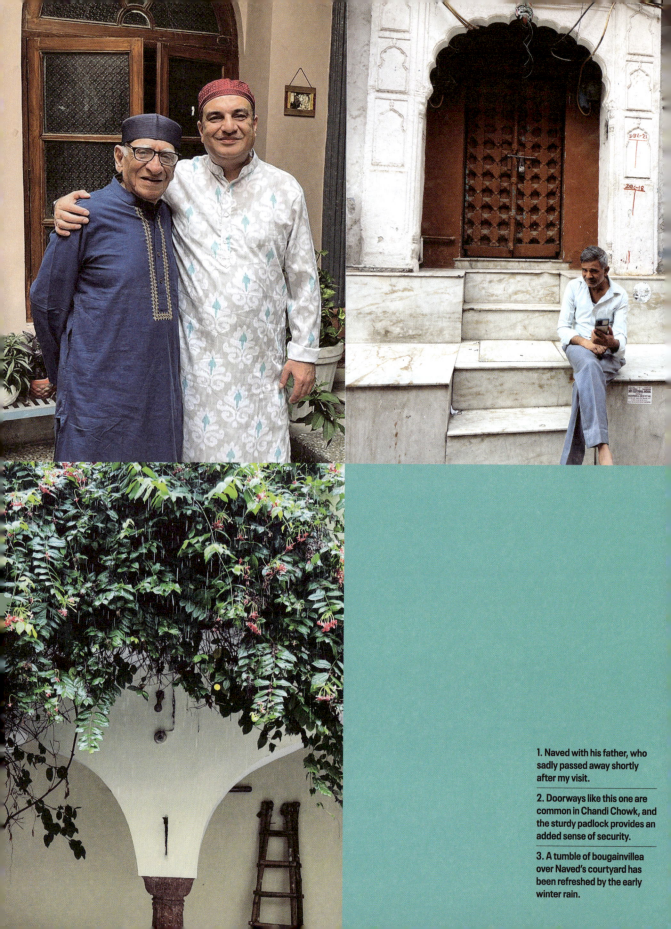

1. Naved with his father, who sadly passed away shortly after my visit.

2. Doorways like this one are common in Chandi Chowk, and the sturdy padlock provides an added sense of security.

3. A tumble of bougainvillea over Naved's courtyard has been refreshed by the early winter rain.

4. Close to Naved's *haveli* are crowded lanes, some of them dedicated to selling beautiful embroidered cloth, brocades and special-occasion outfits.

5. Naved in his drawing room.

6. A Mughal-style archway and entrance in Chandni Chowk market, where semi-precious stone inlay work has been replaced with paintwork.

1. Shenaz, Naved's home helper.
2. Naved's parents on their wedding day.
3. Broken red chiles for the lamb.

RED CHILE & GARLIC LAMB

Serves 6

NAVED SHAFI

This recipe is a beauty—the aromatic garlicky yogurt clings to the lamb and develops an almost caramelized sweetness as it browns, which takes the edge off the fiery red chiles. Ask your butcher to chop the lamb on the bone for this dish—that way it will make its own meaty stock in the yogurty masala as it simmers. Watching Naved Shafi's home helper, Shenaz, make this heritage family dish reminded me that classic recipes are often unsung heroes and don't need a raft of rare spice blends to make them stand out.

---

12 dried Kashmiri red chiles

2 large heads garlic, cloves separated, peeled and coarsely chopped

⅔ cup (120 g) ghee (see page 18), or ¾ cup (180 ml) sunflower oil

2 lb 3 oz (1 kg) lamb shoulder, chopped on the bone into 1½ in (4 cm) pieces

1 cup (250 ml) full-fat Greek yogurt

about ⅔ cup (150 ml) hot water

2 green chiles, coarsely chopped with seeds

sea salt

Indian flatbreads, to serve

Using scissors, snip the tops off 6 Kashmiri chiles and shake out and discard most of the seeds. Leave the seeds in the remaining ones. Roughly snip all the chiles into ½ in (1 cm) pieces.

Put the garlic in a small food processor. Pour over enough water to cover, and blend to a smooth paste. (You can alternatively use a handheld immersion blender and a bowl for this.)

Heat the ghee on medium-low heat in a large, sturdy Dutch oven and add the garlic paste. Cook for 4–5 minutes, stirring all the time, until it starts to pick up flecks of color. Add the Kashmiri chiles and fry for 1 minute.

Preheat the oven to 340°F (170°C). Add the lamb to the pot, stir, season generously with salt, and cook for 5–7 minutes, until sealed but not browned.

Spoon in half the yogurt and continue cooking for 2 minutes, then add the rest of the yogurt and cook for another 2 minutes. By now, the lamb will be evenly coated in the masala. Pour over enough of the hot water to cover the bottom of the pot by ¼ in (5 mm). Cover and transfer the pot to the oven and cook for 1 hour 15 minutes, or until the lamb is tender.

Uncover, stir in the green chiles and simmer on the stove for another 5–7 minutes, until the masala thickens and cloaks the meat. Serve with Indian flatbreads.

GROUND LAMB WITH TOMATOES & PEAS

Serves 4–6

Is there any greater show of love than a bowl of *keema* accompanied with glistening parathas? *Keema mattar* has no pretensions of grandeur—it's straight-down-the-line comfort food. For the best results, choose ground meat that isn't too lean—fat provides flavor and keeps the ground meat meltingly soft as it simmers in the garlicky tomato masala.

---

2 onions, coarsely chopped

¼ cup (50 g) ghee (see page 18), or 6 tbsp sunflower oil

1 tsp whole cumin seeds

2 brown cardamom pods, pierced

6 green cardamom pods, pierced

4 Indian bay leaves (*tej patta*), or 1 in (3 cm) cinnamon stick

1½ oz (50 g) ginger root, peeled and finely grated

6 large garlic cloves, crushed

1 x 14 oz (400 g) can of chopped tomatoes

¾ tsp ground turmeric

1 tsp garam masala (see page 19)

1 tsp Kashmiri chile powder

2 tsp ground coriander

1 lb 10 oz (750 g) ground lamb

2–3 green chiles, slit in half, along their length, seeds removed

½ cup (75 g) frozen or fresh peas

sea salt

Indian flatbreads, to serve

TO FINISH

juice of 1 lime, to taste

¾ tsp roasted and ground cumin seeds

2 tbsp chopped cilantro leaves

Put the onions in a small food processor, add enough water to barely cover them, and blend to a smooth paste. (You can alternatively use a handheld immersion blender or coarsely grate the onions.) Set aside.

Heat the ghee or oil in a sturdy Dutch oven on medium-high heat. Add the cumin, brown and green cardamom pods, and bay leaves or cinnamon stick. Swirl everything around for 30 seconds, or until the spices release their aroma.

Add the onions and fry for about 10 minutes, stirring all the time, until they start to brown. Stir in the ginger and garlic and cook for 1 minute.

Tip in the chopped tomatoes and add the turmeric, garam masala, chile powder and ground coriander. Cook for 5 minutes, or until the tomatoes have thickened and beads of oil appear around the side of the pot.

Add the ground meat and fry for 10 minutes, stirring all the time. You may need to add a splash of water if it sticks to the bottom of the pot. Once the ground meat has darkened, add the green chiles and pour over enough hot water to cover.

Turn the heat down to low and simmer uncovered for 20 minutes, until the lamb is tender. Stir in the peas and cook for a further 3–4 minutes, until tender. To finish, season with sea salt, add enough lime juice to sharpen and sprinkle with ground cumin and chopped cilantro before serving with Indian flatbreads.

BIHARI LAMB BROTH WITH DUMPLINGS Serves 6

Known as *akhti*, this Mughal-inspired curry originated in Central Asia and has evolved over the centuries to accommodate Indian tastes. Its miniature dumplings are made with chapati dough, and although they take time to shape, they provide a delicate contrast to the richness of cumin-scented broth. There are many versions of this dish—this one is from Bihar in eastern India, and is traditionally made by the Muslim community.

1 large onion, coarsely chopped

5 garlic cloves, coarsely chopped

1 tsp Kashmiri chile powder

1 tsp ground turmeric

1 tsp ground coriander

1 tsp roasted and ground cumin seeds

1 tsp garam masala (see page 19)

scant ½ cup (75 g) ghee (see page 18), or ½ cup (125 ml) sunflower oil, plus extra for oiling

4 large lamb shanks (about 9 oz/ 250 g each)

scant 1 cup (200 ml) full-fat Greek yogurt

juice of 1 lime

9½ cups (2.25 liters) chicken or lamb stock or water

sea salt

FOR THE TOPPING

1 large onion, thinly sliced, generously salted and left to one side for 1 hour

4 tbsp sunflower oil

2 tbsp chopped mint leaves

2 green chiles, deseeded and finely chopped

FOR THE DUMPLINGS

½ quantity chapati dough (see page 279)

192 INDIAN KITCHENS

Put the onion in a small food processor, add the garlic and pour over enough water to cover. Process until smooth. (You can alternatively use a handheld immersion blender and a bowl for this.) Transfer to a small bowl and add the chile powder, turmeric, coriander, cumin and garam masala and season with salt.

Heat the ghee or oil in a large Dutch oven or pot on medium-high heat. Add the spiced onion paste and fry for about 10 minutes, stirring often, until any water evaporates and the paste starts to brown.

Add the lamb shanks and continue frying for 10 minutes, turning, until the meat is sealed all over. Add a ladleful of water if the onions catch on the bottom of the pan and stir with a metal spoon to lift any sediment.

Lightly whisk the yogurt with the lime juice, add half to the pot and cook for 2-3 minutes before stirring in the remainder and cooking for 1 minute more. Preheat the oven to 340°F (170°C).

Pour over enough stock or water to cover the lamb by a depth of 2-2½ in (5-6 cm) and bring the liquid to the simmer. Cover the pot and cook in the oven for about 1 hour, until the meat is tender and almost falling off the bone. Alternatively, you can simmer the lamb on the stovetop on very gentle heat for the same amount of time.

Make the topping and dumplings while the lamb is cooking. Using your hands, squeeze and discard any excess liquid from the salted onion and pat the onion dry with paper towels.

Heat the oil in a frying pan on medium heat and fry the onion for about 12-15 minutes, until deep brown. Drain on paper towels and leave to cool before mixing with the chopped mint and green chiles. Leave to one side to add to the broth before serving.

For the dumplings, lightly oil the countertop and roll the chapati dough thinly into a large circle (about 2 mm thick). Using a small pastry cutter, stamp out about 36, 1 in (3 cm) diameter discs. Fold each disc in half and lightly pinch the middle together with your fingers. Push the opposite open edges together in the same way so that you have a flower shape with four petals (use the photograph as a guide). Set the dumplings on a baking sheet lined with parchment paper and cover with a second sheet of paper so that they don't dry out.

Once the lamb is tender, lift the shanks onto a plate. When they are cool enough to handle, strip the meat from the bones and roughly chop it into bite-sized pieces. Discard the bones, skim any oil from the surface of the broth, and return the lamb to the pot.

Bring the broth to a simmer, add the dumplings and cook uncovered on medium heat for about 10 minutes, until they rise to the surface. Ladle the lamb, dumplings and broth into deep bowls, scatter with the fried onion, mint and green chiles and serve straight away.

KASHMIRI LAMB PULAO Serves 4

This elegant pulao is studded with tender pieces of simmered lamb and flecked with golden fried onions. The main spice here is *shahi jeera*, also known as *kali jeera* or royal cumin, which is darker than regular cumin and has a lovely smoky flavor. You can use caraway seeds in its place.

⅓ cup (75 g) ghee, or 5 tbsp sunflower oil and 3 tbsp unsalted butter

6 cloves

1½ in (4 cm) cinnamon stick

3 brown cardamom pods, pierced

8 green cardamom pods, pierced

4 Indian bay leaves (*tej patta*), or 1 in (3 cm) cinnamon stick

2 large onions, thinly sliced

1½ oz (50 g) ginger root, peeled and finely chopped

6 garlic cloves, finely chopped

¾ tsp coarsely ground black peppercorns

1 tsp royal cumin seeds (*shai jeera*) or caraway seeds, or 1 tsp roasted and ground cumin seeds

1 lb 10 oz (750 g) boneless lamb shoulder, chopped into 1½ in (4 cm) pieces

1½ cups (375 ml) chicken or lamb stock, or water

1¼ cups (250 g) basmati rice

sea salt

full-fat Greek yogurt and kachumber (see page 288), to serve

Preheat the oven to 270°F (130°C).

Heat the ghee, or sunflower oil and butter, in a sturdy Dutch oven on medium-high heat and add the cloves, cinnamon, brown and green cardamom pods, and bay leaves (or cinnamon). Swirl everything around for about 30 seconds, until the spices release their fragrance, then turn down the heat to medium and add the onions.

Fry for about 10–12 minutes, until the onions are golden, stirring often. Add the chopped ginger and garlic, and after 1 minute, stir in the black pepper, royal cumin or caraway seeds or ground cumin, followed by the lamb. Season with salt and cook for 2–3 minutes, stirring all the time. Heat the stock or water, pour it over the lamb, and bring to a simmer.

Cover, transfer the pot to the oven and cook for about 1 hour, until the lamb is tender.

While the meat is in the oven, rinse the rice in a sieve under cold running water until the water runs clear. Tip the grains into a bowl and cover with fresh water and leave to one side for 30 minutes.

Transfer the pot to the stove and scoop the cooked lamb into a bowl. You should have about 2 cups (500 ml) of liquid left in the pot. Add extra water if it falls short or boil the stock to reduce its volume if you have too much. Return the meat to the pot.

Drain the soaked rice and add the grains to the hot stock. Cover with foil and a tight-fitting lid and cook on the stovetop on very gentle heat for 10 minutes, until the liquid has been absorbed and the grains are tender. Leave the pot undisturbed for 10 minutes before removing the lid. Serve with yogurt and kachumber on the side.

LAMB KOFTAS IN TOMATO & CINNAMON MASALA

Serves 4

Almost every country has its favorite way of cooking meatballs and this is the recipe I turn to when I'm looking for proper home food. The ground lamb mixture will benefit from a good beating and pummelling before being shaped into balls—this incorporates air and makes for a lighter, softer kofta. I'm particularly fond of the cinnamon spicing and how its sweetness contrasts with the astringency of ginger and the sharp green chiles. If you have an electric spice grinder, I recommend making your own powder from cinnamon sticks—it's so much more fragrant than buying it ground.

FOR THE KOFTAS

- 1 onion, finely chopped
- 1 oz (30 g) ginger root, peeled and finely grated
- 2 green chiles, deseeded and finely chopped
- 3 tbsp chopped cilantro
- ½ tsp ground cinnamon
- 1 lb (500 g) ground lamb
- 1 egg, lightly beaten

FOR THE MASALA

- ½ cup (120 ml) sunflower oil
- 1 onion, coarsely chopped
- 1 oz (30 g) ginger root, peeled and finely grated
- 1 tsp ground turmeric
- ¾ tsp garam masala (see page 19)
- 1 x 14 oz (400 g) can of chopped tomatoes
- 1⅔ cups (400 ml) hot water
- 1 tbsp chopped cilantro leaves to serve
- boiled rice or Indian flatbread to serve

Mix together all the kofta ingredients, and beat until well blended. I like to do this in an electric mixer.

Using wet hands, shape the mixture into meatballs—this quantity will make 20 koftas that are about 1½ in (4 cm) in diameter and 1 oz (30 g) each in weight. Arrange them on a tray and refrigerate for 30 minutes.

Once the meatballs have chilled, heat the oil for the masala in a large Dutch oven or ovenproof deep-sided frying pan, on medium-high heat—there should be enough oil to coat the base of the pan by ⅛ in (3 mm). Fry the meatballs in batches for 3-5 minutes, turning them once or twice during cooking, until browned all over. Scoop them out and set aside while you make the masala. Pour off and discard any excess oil from the pan, leaving behind about 4 tablespoons. Turn off the heat.

Put the onion in a small food processor, cover with water and blend to a paste. (You can alternatively use a handheld immersion blender and a bowl for this.)

Reheat the leftover oil from frying the koftas on medium heat. Add the onion paste and fry for about 10-12 minutes, stirring often, until golden.

Add the ginger, turmeric and garam masala and fry for 1 minute, then stir in the tomatoes. Pour over the hot water and bring the masala to a boil.

Turn down the heat to low, add the meatballs, along with any juices, and simmer, uncovered, for 20 minutes, until tender. Scatter with chopped cilantro and serve with boiled rice or Indian flatbreads.

LAMB SHANKS WITH KASHMIRI CHILES & GARLIC

Serves 4

I first tasted this dish, called *lal maas*, in Rajasthan when the temperature outside was edging north of 118°F (48°C). Slow-cooked meat, cloaked in a soft tangle of buttery chiles and garlicky onions, isn't for the faint hearted—but this rich and indulgent dish is utterly delicious and one of my all-time favorites. There are relatively few spices in this recipe because, historically, this dish was made on royal hunts in makeshift field kitchens. I've used Kashmiri chiles for their mild flavor, but you can swap them for regular dried ones if you fancy a kick of heat. Usually, the smaller and thinner the chile, the fierier will be the flavor. If you can, make the dish a day or two before you need it, so that the flavors have time to develop.

12-14 dried Kashmiri red chiles

1 cup (250 ml) full-fat Greek yogurt

juice of ½ lemon

¾ tsp ground turmeric

2 tsp roasted and ground coriander seeds

6 small lamb shanks (about 6 oz/ 170 g each)

⅔ cup (125 g) ghee (see page 18)

3 large onions, thinly sliced

4 brown cardamom pods, pierced

1 large head garlic, cloves separated, peeled and shredded

4 Indian bay leaves (*tej patta*), or 1 in (3 cm) cinnamon stick

sea salt

Indian flatbreads, to serve

Using scissors, snip the tops off the chiles and shake out and discard most of the seeds. Put them in a small bowl, cover with boiling water and leave to one side for 1 hour. Drain, reserving the soaking water, and roughly chop.

Mix the chiles with the yogurt, lemon juice, turmeric and ground coriander. Put the shanks in a shallow dish and coat with the chile yogurt. Leave to one side for at least 1 hour or, ideally, covered overnight in the fridge.

Heat the ghee in a large, sturdy Dutch oven on medium-high heat. Add the onions, season with salt and fry until golden. Stir in the cardamom pods, shredded garlic and bay leaves or cinnamon, and continue frying for another 5 minutes, until the garlic picks up flecks of color. Preheat the oven to 320°F (160°C).

Take the lamb out of its marinade, pat the shanks dry with paper towels and add to the onions in the pot. Fry the shanks on medium-high heat until any moisture evaporates and the meat starts to brown. Stir in any leftover yogurt marinade and continue frying until the masala turns a russet brown (about 20 minutes). Add a ladleful of the reserved chile soaking water if it looks like catching on the bottom of the pot. You might need to do this a couple of times.

Pour over enough water to barely come halfway up the shanks, cover the pot with a tight-fitting lid, and transfer it to the oven for about 1 hour 30 minutes, until the meat is almost falling off the bone. Serve piping hot with Indian flatbreads.

ROAST LAMB SHOULDER WITH GINGER & FRESH TURMERIC Serves 4–6

Ovens are a relatively new addition to many Indian kitchens—in Calcutta, this lamb shoulder would originally have been pot-roasted on the stove or cooked in a big pressure cooker. Fresh turmeric is the keynote spice here—it isn't as astringent as dried and ground turmeric and has a bright orange hue and citrussy flavor.

---

6 dried Kashmiri red chilies

2½ oz (75 g) ginger root, peeled and coarsely chopped

½ oz (15 g) turmeric root, peeled and coarsely chopped

4 tbsp sunflower oil

juice of 2 limes

2 tsp coarsely ground black peppercorns

2 tsp sea-salt flakes

2 tsp ground coriander

1 tsp roasted and ground cumin seeds

2 tsp sugar

2 lb 3 oz (1 kg) onions, thickly sliced

1 head garlic, cloves separated and peeled

4 Indian bay leaves (*tej patta*), or 1 in (3 cm) cinnamon stick

2 lb 3 oz (1 kg) bone-in lamb shoulder

scant 1 cup (200 ml) chicken stock or water

Snip the tops off the chiles with scissors, shake out and discard most of the seeds, and soak the chiles in enough hot water to cover for 1 hour. Drain, reserving 4 tablespoons of the soaking water. Preheat the oven to 425°F (220°C).

Put the ginger, turmeric and drained red chiles in a food processor and add the reserved soaking water, oil and lime juice. Process until smooth. (You can alternatively use a handheld immersion blender and a bowl for this.) Stir in the pepper, salt, coriander, cumin and sugar.

In a roasting pan large enough to hold the lamb, mix the onions, peeled garlic cloves and the bay leaves (or cinnamon) with a quarter of the spice paste. Put the lamb on top of the onion mixture and spread the remaining spice paste over the shoulder. It's a good idea to wear disposable gloves for this.

Roast, uncovered, in the oven for 30 minutes. Pour over the chicken stock or water, cover the pan with foil and lower the heat to 320°F (160°C). Continue cooking for 3 hours, until the lamb is so tender that it's almost falling off the bone.

PORK RIBS WITH MANGO, CHILE & GINGER GLAZE

Serves 4–6

This recipe is inspired by spices used in a Nagaland kitchen. It isn't a traditional dish by any measure, but my modern interpretation is a winner for its big, bold flavors. I've used Sichuan peppercorns instead of locally grown *timur*—both have a buzzy tongue-numbing flavor. These ribs are glazed with chile-flecked mango pulp, shot through with garlic and ginger and sharpened with vinegar, and they cook to a lovely sticky glaze in the oven. Any leftovers make a gold-star midnight snack when eaten straight from the fridge.

---

2 lb 12 oz (1.25 kg) baby pork ribs, cut into blocks of 4

1 large onion, quartered

6 star anise

4¼ cups (1 liter) dry hard cider

sea salt

green mango salad (see page 289) or kachumber (see page 288), to serve

FOR THE GLAZE

2 tbsp sunflower oil

1 tsp red chile flakes

1 tsp roasted and ground Sichuan peppercorns

1½ oz (40 g) ginger root, peeled and finely grated

5 large garlic cloves, crushed

1½ cups (350 ml) mango pulp (fresh or canned)

about ¾ oz (20 g) jaggery or light brown sugar

about ¼ cup (60 ml) red wine vinegar

Put the ribs in a large pot with the onion, star anise and salt to season. Pour over the cider and add enough water to submerge the ribs. Bring the liquid to a boil on medium heat, then skim any impurities from the surface. Half-cover the pot and simmer the ribs for about 2 hours, until tender. Remove them from the pot, discard the cooking liquid and leave the ribs to cool on a roasting pan.

For the glaze, heat the oil in a karahi or wok on medium-high heat and add the chile flakes and ground Sichuan pepper. Turn the heat down to medium and stir in the ginger and garlic, followed, after a few seconds, by the mango pulp. Bring the sauce to a boil, add the jaggery (or sugar) and vinegar and simmer, uncovered, for 5 minutes, until thickened and jam-like in consistency. Taste for sweetness—canned mango pulp often contains extra sugar, so you may need to add 1–2 teaspoons of vinegar to sharpen. Aim for a balanced sweet-sour flavor. Leave the glaze to one side to cool.

Arrange the ribs, meaty side upwards, in a foil-lined roasting pan and brush them with a thick layer of the mango glaze. Save any remaining glaze for cooking the ribs. Put the uncovered pan in the fridge for at least 1 hour, or covered overnight if you have the time.

Preheat the oven to 425°F (220°C). Roast the ribs for 30–40 minutes, spooning or brushing over more glaze every 10 minutes when the previous layer becomes sticky and starts to caramelize. Cut the blocks into single ribs and serve them with green mango salad or kachumber.

COMMUNITY ROOTS
SOUTH

SUMAN GANAPATHY, KARNATAKA

I first came across this hilly and remote region while reading Dervla Murphy's book, *On a Shoestring to Coorg*. Her writing depicts jungle landscapes of dense rain forests, colorful flora and fauna and occasional encounters with local wildlife, but it was her portrayal of local communities and their daily life that caught my attention. For many years, I'd wanted to learn more about the warrior *Kodava* clan, a small, dwindling group of hill people, who have lived off the land since antiquity. I waited three decades for the opportunity—and it came through a chance meeting on Instagram.

Kaveri Ponnapa is an anthropologist and a leading authority on Coorg culture. She writes a blog, *The Coorg Table*, and has documented a cultural study, *The Vanishing Kodavas*. I'm drawn to her social media posts, which include dishes that are quite unfamiliar to me: from the spiral curl of fiddlehead ferns, quick-fried with onions, garlic and chiles, or tender-cooked bamboo shoots speckled with mustard seeds, to dried jackfruit seeds pounded into chutney. Although game such as wild boar is no longer hunted, pork is one of the most popular meats to cook with. We chat over the phone, make plans to meet and I book flights to Coorg, which is also known by the new name of Kodagu.

The taxi picks me up from Kannur airport in northern Kerala, and we soon cross the border into Karnataka and start the ascent to southwest Coorg. There's been heavy rainfall and landslips and the road is bumpy as we drive alongside densely forested slopes, their ridges and peaks swathed in mist. Looking over the precipice, I can see waterfalls and streams, paddy fields and ravines.

It's a four-hour drive to the hotel and the last two hours are in darkness. The car's headlamps spotlight a snake as it crosses the road in front of us. We pass signs on hairpin bends asking drivers to watch out for the perils of wild elephant herds. The hotel lights twinkle on a nearby hill, but looks are deceptive, and it takes 45 minutes to reach the main entrance. I'm driven in a golf cart along a path to a stilt-mounted wooden cottage, jutting from the hillside. The rain has held off and the sound of crickets and cicadas reverberate around the hillside. The next morning, the sky is blue, the sun bright and blue jays and mynahs provide a cheery wake-up call. My view from the balcony is spectacular. It's a beautiful setting, surrounded by thick rain forest and acres of cardamom and coffee plantations, interspersed with bamboo thickets, banana and nutmeg trees, ferns and grasslands.

The next day, I wait at the village post office for Kaveri, who is driving from Bangalore to meet me. There's a European tourist waiting for a bus across the road. We're not sure how to react in this isolated paradise, so we nod in recognition of a shared awkwardness. Luckily Kaveri's car soon pulls up. ▶

Palms near Suman's home in Kakkabe, southwest Coorg.

▶ We're going to meet her friend Suman, who has invited us for lunch and lives in the nearby hamlet of Kakkabe.

Kaveri is dressed in a stunning pink silk sari, tied in the typical Kodava style, with pleats neatly folded at the back, and the *pallu*, a short length of cloth draped over the shoulder and secured with a brooch in front of her. She tells me about the Kodava cooking tradition and how folklore is intertwined with daily life. She remembers workers on her grandmother's coffee plantation foraging for wild mushrooms in the monsoon season. They would fill baskets with different varieties and bring them home to scent the air with earthy dampness. After cooking, her aunt would plunge the heated blade of a knife into the bubbling mushrooms to chase away forest spirits, and only then did she bring the curry to the table. It's stories like this that Kaveri fears won't be passed on to the next generation. She reflects that youngsters from the area are migrating to cities in droves, and because of this, time-honored culinary skills are disappearing.

We travel along a tract to Suman's family home. Their main ancestral house, *ain mane*, is a few miles away but Suman, her husband, Sagar, their two teenage sons and her mother-in-law, the 86-year-old matriarch, live in an easier-to-maintain bungalow. It's built on a plinth and surrounded by colorful flowering plants—inside, the concrete floors are traditionally painted with red oxide. The kitchen is spacious and next to the modern stove is a crackling open fire, its smoke wafting into a blackened chimney. The family own coffee plantations and an adventure tourism destination for trekkers and kayakers. Suman also finds time to study for law exams.

This is a warrior clan, which worships its ancestors and not deities—its collective identity is inexorably linked to the land. There's a sacred brass lamp hanging near the main entrance, in front of which daily prayers are offered and blessings from ancestors invoked. Kaveri points out a sheaf of rice threaded through one of the chain's links— it's from the first harvest of the year and a symbol of gratitude for nature's abundance.

This family traces its lineage to the sixteenth century. Later, Sagar takes me to their eighteenth-century ancestral home—it's a beautiful building, decorated with ornate dark wood and stone carvings and fronted by a large portico. I ask about the hooks on pillars—they're for hanging swords. Inside, there's a spacious area with a central opening in the roof for ventilation and a chimney. There would be eight or nine families living in this house and, although each cooked on their own wood-fired stove, everyone came together for shared meals. Gradually, as families grew, clusters of smaller houses were built around the main house, one of which Suman and family now stay in.

We return to Suman and Kaveri. In the kitchen, the fermented juice from a variety of kokum has been boiling on a wood fire for 17 hours, ably stirred by their home helper, Putta Gouri. Its honeyed hue becomes treacle-like in color and consistency as it approaches readiness. This potent vinegar, *kachampuli*, has an intensely fruity, smoky flavor, and is a key ingredient in Kodava cooking, adding sharpness to dishes. Suman's mother-in-law sits on a chair in the kitchen and has a ringside view of Suman as she makes *pandi* pork for lunch. This is the region's best-known dish, notable for its

▶ vinegary flavor and dark *pandi* spice mix, made from roasted and ground peppercorns, curry leaves, cumin and astringent aromatics. Her mother-in-law shares tips and techniques, helpfully translated for me by Kaveri and Suman. Peppercorns grow wild on twisted vines here and are called *kartha paun*—black gold.

Chopped fatty pork with bones and some of the skin has already been marinated with turmeric and chile powder. It's all tipped in the pan and heated until the fat is released. Suman spoons over fresh cilantro and curry leaf paste, blended with onions, ginger and garlic. She looks at *mavi* (the generic name for mother-in-law in Kodagu), and smiles, "This is her recipe, and we don't mix this paste with the pork until the meat is tender—it would spoil the flavor." Her mother-in-law nods. Traditionally, this dish would have been cooked in a mud pot on a wooden fire and stirred with a ladle fashioned from a wooden handle tied to a halved empty coconut shell. Some concessions have been made to modernity—after 20 minutes in a pressure cooker, the pork is ready, the herby paste is stirred in, and the spice added. The transformation is dramatic as it turns into a dark masala, deepened with the addition of glossy black vinegar. Oil from the pork glistens; it is part of the dish's appeal and soaks lusciously into rice.

It's brought to the table with several more regional dishes. Today, we're feasting on delights that include Kaveri's deliciously coconutty chicken curry. There's also *kaad mangae*, whole wild mango curry sweetened with jaggery and seasoned with *pandi* spices. Chile heat isn't the predominant flavor here—there's more emphasis on the warmth of black pepper. Herbs are used as a main ingredient and not as a finishing flourish.

Rice is a staple, and a locally grown, short-grain variety is often ground or broken before being boiled or made into breads and dumplings. *Kadambuttus*, steamed rice dumplings, enriched with ghee are a splendid partner to both the chicken and *pandi* pork. There are also *paputtu*, steamed rice cakes, made with milk and coconut, and *akki otti*—unleavened rice flatbreads made from boiled rice and rice flour.

Over lunch, I ask Suman about her day. It starts at 6:30 am with milky coffee brewed with homegrown beans, sweetened with jaggery. Three rice-based cooked meals are made every day, because work here isn't desk-based, but strenuous manual graft. Breakfast is the main meal and served around 8 am, perhaps rice dumplings served with egg curry, and kidney beans cooked with green bananas. Lunch is rice, dal cooked with vegetables, and perhaps a chicken curry followed by a teatime snack of battered jackfruit or banana fritters, flecked with sesame seeds. Dinner would be in a similar vein with more freshly made dishes.

She tells me that the children's school is 25 miles (40 km) away, where the family owns a small apartment—so during the week they stay there, returning to Kakkabe at the weekend. What about daily challenges? Surely it can't be easy studying for law exams, while bringing up two children, running a home and a business and managing the coffee plantation? Suman replies, "Ah yes, we do have our moments—the main problem is herds of wild elephants trampling our crops and flattening boundary fences."

1. Kaveri with Suman's mother-in-law, with a pan filled with *atti otti*—flatbreads made from boiled rice and rice flour.

2. I treated myself to a stay at The Tamara Coorg, near Suman's home. The bungalow boasted a stupendous vista over the surrounding jungle.

3. The big sky landscape of this area is particularly striking.

4. Breakfasts at the hotel included plenty of fresh fruit; a healthy start to a day, which would soon call for feasting on tasty specialties from across the Coorg region.

5. Locally grown fiddlehead ferns are cooked as a vegetable here.

6. Suman and Sagar run a campsite close to their home, which is located by the Kakkabe river and surrounded by woodland. This image features the main dining area.

1. Suman with her *pandi* curry.

2. Low hanging cloud and rolling mist on a rainy afternoon in Coorg. It reminded me of my childhood in England.

3. Onions in India, even larger ones, tend to be sweeter and less pungent than Western varieties. Suman's "black masala" is in the background, alongside leafy cilantro and curry leaves for her masala.

PANDI PORK CURRY   Serves 6

SUMAN GANAPATHY

This is one of the most famous dishes from Kodava. I met Suman there and watched as she cooked a spectacular lunch for family and friends. The blend of spices is close to black with pounded peppercorns—and the masala is further darkened with a thick vinegar called *kachampuli*, made from a variety of fermented kokum fruit. I've approximated but not replicated its flavor with a little soy sauce and vinegar.

---

1 lb (500 g) boneless pork belly, chopped into 1½ in (4 cm) pieces

1 lb (500 g) pork shoulder, chopped on the bone into 1½ in (4 cm) pieces

1 tsp sea salt

1 tsp ground turmeric

1 tsp Kashmiri chile powder

FOR THE CILANTRO AND CURRY LEAF PASTE

1 large onion, coarsely chopped

1½ oz (50 g) ginger root, peeled and coarsely chopped

1 head garlic, cloves separated, peeled and coarsely chopped

about 15 fresh curry leaves

1 large handful of cilantro, leaves and stems coarsely chopped

FOR THE FINISHING SPICES

about 15 fresh curry leaves

1 rounded tsp black peppercorns

1 tsp cumin seeds

½ tsp fenugreek seeds

1 tsp brown mustard seeds

1 tsp coriander seeds

1 tsp garam masala (see page 19)

1-2 tbsp malt or black rice vinegar

1 tbsp dark soy sauce

Put all the pork in a mixing bowl and add the salt, turmeric and chile powder. Massage the spices into the meat (I use gloves to do this) and refrigerate for 2–3 hours, or covered overnight if you have the time.

Make the cilantro and curry leaf paste. Put the onion, ginger, garlic, curry leaves and cilantro in a food processor or blender and add 3½ tablespoons of water. Process to a coarse paste. (You can alternatively use a handheld immersion blender and a bowl for this.) Leave to one side.

Add the marinated pork to a cold, heavy-bottomed pot, then put it on medium heat. Cook, stirring often, until the pork releases fat and is sealed but not browned—this should take 10–12 minutes. Preheat the oven to 320°F (160°C).

Spoon the cilantro and curry leaf paste over the pork, but don't stir it in. Add ⅓ cup (75 ml) of water and bring to a simmer. Cover, transfer the pot to the oven and cook for about 1½ hours, until the pork is tender.

While the pork is in the oven, prepare the finishing spices. Heat a small, sturdy frying pan on medium-low heat and add the curry leaves, peppercorns, cumin, fenugreek, mustard and coriander seeds. Cook, stirring, until aromatic—this should take about 2 minutes. Tip the spices onto a plate so that they don't continue to cook in the heat of the pan, then grind them to a powder in a spice grinder or in a mortar with the pestle. Mix the ground spices with the garam masala. Leave the finishing spices to one side.

When the pork is cooked, the masala will have thickened and coated the meat and the oil risen to the surface of the curry. Most people don't bother spooning off the excess oil as it has so much meaty flavor, although I usually skim some of it off at this stage.

Return the uncovered pot to the stovetop, add the ground finishing spices and cook, uncovered, for 3–4 minutes on medium heat. Taste for seasoning and add enough vinegar and soy sauce to sharpen. Simmer the curry for another 5 minutes to warm through.

POT ROAST BEEF WITH VEGETABLES   Serves 4

I love how a plainly cooked British "pot roast" has been embraced by the Anglo-Indian community, but adapted here with black pepper, red chile powder, cinnamon and the tang of wine vinegar. Food writer Bridget White Kumar has kindly shared her recipe with me—I've played around with the ingredients and added garlic cloves, but you can leave them out if you prefer.

---

2 tsp sea-salt flakes, plus extra to season

1 tsp coarsely ground black peppercorns, plus extra to season

1 tsp Kashmiri chile powder

2 tbsp red wine vinegar

2 lb 14 oz (1.3 kg) beef brisket, rolled

scant ½ cup (100 ml) sunflower oil

2 large onions, sliced

2 in (5 cm) cinnamon stick

1 large garlic head, cloves separated and peeled

1 lb 5 oz (600 g) starchy potatoes (such as Russets), peeled, then halved or quartered

3 cups (750 ml) hot chicken or beef stock

2 tbsp unsalted butter

7 oz (200 g) baby carrots

7 oz (200 g) green beans

Mix the salt, pepper, chile powder and vinegar in a small bowl. Put the beef in a mixing bowl and rub the spice mixture all over it. Cover and leave the beef in the fridge overnight.

Heat the oil in a large, sturdy Dutch oven on medium-high heat. Pat the beef dry with paper towels, then seal it on all sides in the hot oil, turning it often—this should take about 7–10 minutes. Lift the brisket out of the pot and onto a plate and leave it to one side.

Pour off most of the oil, leaving behind about 3 tablespoons. Turn the heat down to low, add the onions, cinnamon and salt to season. Cover the pot and cook for 20 minutes, stirring occasionally, until the onions are meltingly soft.

Add the garlic cloves and continue cooking, with the lid on, for another 10 minutes. Preheat the oven to 320°F (160°C).

Uncover the pot, turn the heat up to medium, and fry the softened onions and garlic for a further 7–10 minutes, until browned. Return the beef to the pot and add the potatoes followed by enough hot stock to come two-thirds of the way up the beef. Bring the liquid to a simmer, cover the pot, and transfer it to the oven. Cook for 3½–4 hours, until the meat is tender and the potatoes are soft and starting to crumble at the edges.

While the beef is in the oven, heat the butter in a frying pan on low heat. Add the carrots and season with salt and black pepper. Cover and cook for about 10 minutes, shaking the carrots every few minutes, until they are just tender.

Bring a large pot of salted water to a boil, add the beans and blanch them for 2 minutes—they should still have a bite to them. Drain them in a colander, refresh with cold running water, then leave them to one side.

Lift the brisket and potatoes onto a serving plate and snip off any strings tied around the meat. Discard the cinnamon stick, bring the sauce to a simmer, then add the carrots and beans and reheat for 1–2 minutes. Arrange the vegetables around the brisket, then ladle over a little sauce. Serve any extra in a jug.

GOAN SHORT RIBS IN TAMARIND MASALA
Serves 4

Make this dish the day before you need it, so that the spices can mellow and the chiles meld into the meaty masala. I love how the tender beef needs just a gentle nudge to fall off the bone into the peppery tamarind sauce. All you need with it is a heap of rice or chunky wedges of crusty bread.

4½ lb (2 kg) beef short ribs (6-8 ribs)

FOR THE SPICE PASTE

15 dried Kashmiri red chiles (1½ oz/ 40 g)

1⅔ cups (400 ml) hot water

1 large head garlic, cloves separated, peeled and coarsely chopped

2½ oz (75 g) ginger root, peeled and coarsely chopped

1 tsp ground cinnamon

1 tsp roasted and ground cumin seeds

½ tsp cloves

2 tsp black peppercorns

¾ tsp ground turmeric

3 tbsp red wine vinegar

FOR THE MASALA

⅓ cup (75 ml) melted coconut oil or sunflower oil

2 large onions, diced

1 cup (250 ml) tomato passata

2 green chiles, slit, with seeds

1 tbsp jaggery or light brown sugar

about 30 fresh curry leaves

1 lb (500 g) starchy potatoes (such as Russets), peeled and halved

1½ cups (350 ml) chicken stock

1-2 tbsp tamarind pulp (see page 21), to taste

Make the spice paste. Using scissors, snip the tops off the chiles and shake out and discard most of the seeds. Put them in a small heatproof bowl, cover with the hot water, and leave them aside for 30 minutes.

Put the chiles in a small food processor, reserving the soaking water. Add the garlic, ginger, cinnamon, cumin, cloves, pepper, turmeric and vinegar. Pour over ⅓ cup (75 ml) of the chile soaking water (reserve the remainder), then blend everything to a smooth paste and set aside.

For the masala, heat the oil in a large sturdy Dutch oven on medium-high heat and fry the beef ribs for about 7-10 minutes, turning, until they are sealed and browned all over. Transfer the ribs to a plate and set them aside. Preheat the oven to 320°F (160°C).

Turn the heat down to medium, add the onions to the same pot and fry until browned—this should take about 10-12 minutes. Stir in the spice paste and continue frying for 5 minutes, until it has darkened. Add the passata, green chiles, jaggery (or sugar) and curry leaves and cook for 10 minutes, until the masala has thickened to a coating consistency.

Return the ribs to the pot and cook for 5 minutes. Add a ladleful of the remaining chile soaking water if the masala starts to catch on the bottom of the pot.

Add the potatoes and stock and bring the curry to a simmer. Cover, transfer the pot to the oven and cook for about 1¼ hours, or until the meat is tender and almost falling off the bone and the sauce has reduced to a coating consistency.

Stir in enough tamarind pulp to sharpen the masala and return the beef to the oven for 15 minutes before serving. I like to skim any extra oil from the masala at this stage, although most home cooks in India wouldn't bother.

VEGETABLE

SIDES

BABY ZUCCHINI IN TOMATO SAUCE Serves 4

This is a lovely dish to make at the height of summer when tomatoes are ripe and zucchini are in season. While living in Delhi, I'd use a variety of summer squash known as *tinda*. The best *tinda* are about the size of a golf ball and have a pale green skin. Their neutral flavor marries well with the mango spicing in this tomato-based masala. I've used baby zucchini here because they're easier to find.

---

1 tsp Kashmiri chile powder

1 tsp mango powder (*amchoor*)

½ tsp ground turmeric

1 tsp sea salt

14 oz (400 g) baby zucchini

½ cup (125 ml) hot water

Indian flatbreads or boiled rice, to serve

plain yogurt, to serve

FOR THE MASALA

1 onion, coarsely chopped

3 garlic cloves, chopped

¾ oz (20 g) ginger root, peeled and coarsely chopped

3–4 tbsp sunflower oil

1 tsp cumin seeds

1 x 14 oz (400 g) can of chopped tomatoes

1 tsp tomato paste

2 tsp sugar

½ tsp garam masala (see page 19)

Mix the chile powder, mango powder, turmeric and salt in a small bowl. Using a sharp knife, make an incision along the length of each zucchini, not quite all the way through—they should still be held together at the top. Put the zucchini on a tray and sprinkle ¼ teaspoon of the spice mixture inside each slit—some of it will fall onto the tray below, which is okay. Leave to one side while you make the masala.

Put the chopped onion in a small food processor, cover it with water, then blend to a smooth, slack paste. (You can alternatively do this in a bowl with a handheld immersion blender.) Tip the paste into a small bowl. Blend the garlic and ginger with enough water to cover in the same way.

Heat the oil in a karahi or wok on medium-high heat, then add the cumin seeds—they should sizzle straight away. Swirl the seeds around for about 20 seconds until they release their aroma.

Turn the heat down to medium, add the onion paste and fry for around 7–10 minutes, stirring, until the water evaporates and the paste is golden. Stir in the garlic and ginger paste and continue cooking for 2–3 minutes, until any water has evaporated.

Add the tomatoes, tomato paste, sugar and garam masala and cook uncovered for 3–4 minutes, until the masala thickens to a coating consistency.

Turn the heat down to medium-low and add the zucchini, along with any spices that have fallen onto the tray. Add the hot water and simmer the curry, uncovered, for 5–7 minutes, until the zucchini are just tender but still hold their shape. Serve with flatbreads (such as chapatis) or boiled rice, and yogurt on the side.

NORTHWEST INDIA — VEGETABLE SIDES

MIXED VEGETABLES WITH GROUND CORIANDER & GARAM MASALA

Serves 4

This dish is a harvest festival of vegetables and open to interpretation. You could swap the potatoes for butternut squash or substitute carrots for parsnips—use whatever vegetables you have lying around. Simply spiced with coriander, chile powder and garam masala—this is a quick dish to cook and makes a satisfying light lunch with chapatis.

---

4 tbsp sunflower oil

2 onions, diced

2 starchy potatoes (such as Russets), peeled and cut into ¾ in (2 cm) pieces

2 carrots, diced

1 small cauliflower, cut into small florets

2 tsp ground coriander

¾ tsp Kashmiri chile powder

½ tsp garam masala (see page 19)

1 cup (125 g) frozen peas, blanched in boiling water for 2 minutes and drained

2 tbsp chopped cilantro leaves

sea salt

Heat the oil in a karahi or wok on medium-low heat and fry the onions for 8–10 minutes, until softened and turning golden at the edges.

Add the potatoes, carrots and cauliflower, followed by the ground coriander, chile powder and garam masala. Season with salt and cook, uncovered, for 5 minutes, stirring occasionally.

Turn the heat down to low, cover the pan and continue cooking for about 10 minutes, until the vegetables are tender but still hold their shape. Remove the lid, add the blanched peas and warm through for 1–2 minutes. Stir in the chopped cilantro just before serving.

CUMIN POTATOES   Serves 4

Speckled with nutty-tasting cumin seeds and spiced with ginger, these turmeric-hued potatoes are a mainstay of Punjabi picnics and long train journeys—and they're also popular as a school tiffin snack. Serve them warm or at room temperature with puris, chapatis or parathas, and a little pickle on the side.

---

6 tbsp sunflower oil

2 tsp cumin seeds

¾ tsp ground turmeric

½ tsp Kashmiri chile powder

1 oz (30 g) ginger root, peeled and finely chopped

1 lb 10 oz (750 g) starchy potatoes (such as Russets), peeled and cut into ¾ in (2 cm) pieces

sea salt

Indian flatbreads, to serve

Heat the oil in a karahi or wok on medium heat. Add the cumin seeds and swirl them around for 20 seconds until aromatic. Stir in the turmeric, chile powder and ginger and fry for a further 20 seconds.

Add the potatoes, season with salt, and cook for 10 minutes on medium heat, stirring often. Turn the heat down to low, cover the pan and cook for another 10–15 minutes, until the potatoes are tender and starting to crumble around the edges. Stir the potatoes occasionally during this time so that they don't catch on the bottom of the pan. Serve with Indian flatbreads.

POTATO, ONION & TOMATO MASALA

Serves 4–6

These potatoes are often served as a weekend brunch. They're simmered in a thin, broth-like masala, which is well suited for mopping up with lentil puris (see page 281). The cooked potatoes are crushed and simmered in garlicky vegetable stock and seasoned with warming cumin, astringent coriander and a light touch of chiles. Every home cook has their own spin on this recipe, and this is mine.

---

4 ripe tomatoes

1 lb (500 g) starchy potatoes (such as Russets), peeled and quartered or halved

2 onions, diced

4 garlic cloves

4 tbsp sunflower oil

1½ tsp cumin seeds

4 Indian bay leaves (*tej patta*) or 1 in (3 cm) cinnamon stick

½ tsp ground turmeric

½ tsp Kashmiri chile powder

1 tsp ground coriander

2 tbsp chopped cilantro leaves

sea salt

lentil puris, to serve (see page 281)

Bring a pot of water to a boil, then turn off the heat and plunge in the tomatoes. After about 30 seconds, scoop them out of the water with a slotted spoon and transfer them to a bowl filled with water. Once they are cool enough to handle, peel off the skin and roughly chop the flesh along with the seeds. Leave to one side.

Tip the potatoes into a pot with the chopped tomatoes, onions and whole garlic cloves. Pour over enough water to cover by 1 in (3 cm), half-cover the pot with a lid and bring the water to a boil on medium heat. Boil until the potatoes are tender when pierced with a sharp knife (how long this takes will depend on the size of your potatoes).

Scoop the potatoes out of the pot and onto a plate and lightly crush them with a fork while they are still hot—aim to keep the texture quite chunky. Strain the cooking liquid through a sieve and into a jug. Reserve the liquid and also the onion-tomato mixture left behind in the sieve.

Heat the oil in a karahi or wok on medium-high heat, add the cumin seeds and bay leaves (or cinnamon stick) and sizzle for 20 seconds, until the cumin releases its aroma.

Turn the heat down to medium-low, add the onion-tomato-garlic mixture from the sieve, season with salt and fry for 8–10 minutes, stirring often, until it has darkened and thickened and beads of oil appear around the side of the pan. Add the turmeric, chile powder and ground coriander and cook for 1 minute, stirring all the time.

Pour in the reserved cooking liquid from the jug and bring to a boil. Add the potatoes and simmer, uncovered, for 5 minutes, until warmed through. Turn off the heat and stir in the chopped cilantro. Cover the pan and leave the flavors to mellow for 10 minutes, then serve with lentil puris.

POTATOES & PEA SHOOTS Serves 3–4

I'd be hard pushed to find another country with so many regional variations on cooking potatoes. In this recipe they are made Bengali style, with spices that lend a sweet, chile and astringent flavor. I wait to add the pea shoots at the end of cooking, and I love the way they wilt in the warmth of the potatoes.

4–6 tbsp mustard oil, blended mustard oil or sunflower oil

1 tsp *panch phoran* (see page 20)

1 dried Kashmiri red chile

4 Indian bay leaves (*tej patta*), or 1 in (3 cm) cinnamon stick

1 large onion, sliced

1 lb (500 g) starchy potatoes (such as Russets), peeled and cut into 1 in (3 cm) pieces

½ tsp Kashmiri chile powder

½ tsp ground turmeric

½ tsp garam masala (see page 19)

1 tsp sugar

2 green chiles, deseeded and finely shredded

1 large handful of pea shoots

sea salt

Heat the oil in a karahi or wok on medium-high heat and add the *panch phoran*, whole red chile and bay leaves or cinnamon—the spices should sizzle in the oil straight away. Swirl them around for about 30 seconds, until they release their aroma.

Turn the heat down to medium-low, add the onion, season with salt and fry for about 10 minutes, until softened. Tip in the potatoes and stir in the chile powder, turmeric, garam masala and sugar. Cover the pan and cook for a further 10 minutes, stirring often, until the potatoes are tender.

Uncover the pan, add the green chiles and pea shoots and turn the heat up to medium. Cook for about 20 seconds, until the pea shoots have wilted. Serve straight away.

Mustard oil is the cooking oil of choice for most Bengalis. Much loved for its characteristic wasabi-like flavor, it has been used in the region for centuries. However, food agencies in many parts of the world have banned its use in cooking because of health concerns. Blended mustard oil is now available in the West for cooking with, or you can use sunflower oil in its place, although your final dish will lose the punchy mustardy flavor.

CABBAGE WITH MUSTARD SEEDS & CURRY LEAVES

Serves 4

Shredded cabbage, speckled with pungent mustard seeds, chile flakes and peppery-tasting curry leaves, marries well with melting onions and baby potatoes. In Delhi, I had a lovely home helper who lived with our family for over a decade. Lakshmi brought her South Indian style of cooking to our North Indian table and this was a regular lunch dish. The credit for this recipe is all hers.

3-4 tbsp sunflower oil

1 tsp brown mustard seeds

about 15 fresh curry leaves

½ tsp dried red chile flakes

2 large onions, thinly sliced

1 oz (30 g) ginger root, peeled and finely chopped

10½ oz (300 g) baby new potatoes, halved

1 white cabbage (about 1 lb 5 oz/ 600 g), finely shredded

¾ cup (200 g) cherry tomatoes, halved

sea salt

Heat the oil in a karahi or wok on medium-high heat, then add the mustard seeds—they should start sizzling straight away. Add the curry leaves and chile flakes (they will splutter, so stand back). Swirl everything around for about 30 seconds, until the curry leaves stop crackling.

Add the onions, season with salt and fry on medium heat, stirring often for 10-12 minutes, until the onions are golden. Add the ginger, followed, after a few seconds, by the potatoes and cook for 5 minutes with the lid on. Uncover, stir in the cabbage and continue cooking for 10-12 minutes, stirring every few minutes, until the potatoes are tender. Add the cherry tomatoes just before serving.

CAULIFLOWER WITH GINGER, TURMERIC & ORANGE

Serves 4

Turmeric-yellow cauliflower florets make a marvelous marriage with cardamom-spiced orange juice, while green chiles and sharp-tasting ginger bring lightness and piquancy to this classic Bengali dish.

FOR THE CAULIFLOWER

½ tsp ground turmeric

2 tsp sea salt

2 cups (500 ml) sunflower oil, for deep-frying

1 cauliflower, cut into florets

FOR THE MASALA

4 green cardamom pods, pierced

1 in (3 cm) cinnamon stick

4 cloves

2 Indian bay leaves (*tej patta*), or ¾ in (2 cm) cinnamon stick

1 onion, diced

¾ oz (20 g) ginger root, peeled and finely grated

½ tsp ground turmeric

½ tsp Kashmiri red chile powder

½ tsp roasted and ground cumin seeds, plus extra for sprinkling

1 green chile, deseeded and finely chopped

1 tsp sugar

3 large oranges (juice of 2, and 1 segmented)

2 tbsp shredded mint leaves

Mix the turmeric and salt in a big bowl with 2 tablespoons of the sunflower oil. Add the cauliflower florets and use your hands to turn them to coat them evenly with the turmeric paste. (I use disposable gloves for this so that I don't stain my fingers.)

Heat the remaining oil in a karahi or wok on medium heat. The oil is ready for frying when it reaches 350°F (180°C) on a food thermometer, or when a cube of bread dropped into the oil browns in 30 seconds.

Deep-fry the cauliflower in batches for 7–10 minutes each time, until the florets are golden, then drain them on paper towels and set aside.

Leave the oil to cool, then pour off most of it, leaving behind 4–6 tablespoons in the pan.

Make the masala. Reheat the oil in the pan on medium-high heat and fry the cardamom, cinnamon, cloves and bay leaves (or cinnamon) for 30 seconds, until fragrant. Turn the heat to medium, add the onion and fry until golden, stirring often.

Add the ginger to the pan, followed, a few seconds later by the turmeric, chile powder, cumin, green chile and sugar. Fry the spices for 1 minute, then return the cauliflower florets to the pan and cook, uncovered, for 5 minutes, stirring often.

Add the juice of the 2 oranges and simmer the liquid, uncovered, for 5–7 minutes, until most of the juice has evaporated and the cauliflower is tender but still holds its shape. Stir in the orange segments and mint and sprinkle with a generous pinch of ground cumin before serving.

BENGALI-STYLE BUTTERNUT SQUASH

Serves 3–4

Sticky, glazed butternut squash, sharpened with fiery bursts of chile flakes, this is one of my favorite dishes to cook for a crowd. To save time, I buy ready-cubed butternut squash from the supermarket and keep a batch of tamarind pulp in the freezer—I freeze mine in deep ice cube trays for easy access.

4–6 tbsp mustard oil, blended mustard oil, or sunflower oil

1 tsp *panch phoran* (see page 20)

¾ tsp dried red chile flakes

1 oz (25 g) ginger root, peeled and finely chopped

1 lb 8 oz (700 g) cubed butternut squash

1 tbsp jaggery or light brown sugar

1 tbsp tamarind pulp (see page 21), or to taste

sea salt

Heat the oil in a karahi or wok on medium-high heat and add the *panch phoran* and chile flakes—the spices should sizzle straight away. Swirl them around for 30 seconds, until fragrant, then add the ginger and fry for another 30 seconds.

Add the butternut squash and cook for 3–4 minutes, stirring often. Turn the heat to medium-low, cover the pan and cook for around 10–15 minutes, until tender.

Uncover, turn down the heat to high, add the jaggery or sugar, season with salt and fry the squash, stirring often, until it starts to caramelize. Add in enough tamarind to sharpen and then heat the dish through for 1 minute before serving.

OYSTER MUSHROOMS WITH GINGER, BLACK PEPPER & CURRY LEAVES

Serves 3–4

Wild mushrooms thrive in the rainy season and are harvested on the hilly slopes of Kodagu, in Karnataka. I've used cultivated oyster mushrooms here, but you could make this dish with any edible variety. The fresh-tasting burst of popped mustard seeds, ginger and sizzling curry leaves is immensely satisfying and provides a splendid contrast to the earthiness of mushrooms.

---

3 tbsp sunflower oil

1 tsp brown mustard seeds

15 fresh curry leaves

½ tsp dried red chile flakes

¾ oz (20 g) ginger root, peeled and finely chopped

½ tsp cracked black peppercorns

1 red onion, thickly sliced

12 oz (350 g) oyster mushrooms, halved or thickly sliced if large

2 tbsp chopped cilantro leaves

juice of 1 lime, to taste

sea salt

Heat the oil in a wok or karahi on medium-high heat. Add the mustard seeds and swirl them around for 30 seconds, and when the popping quietens, add the curry leaves and chile flakes and fry for another 30 seconds.

Turn down the heat to medium and stir in the ginger, cracked peppercorns and onion. Fry for around 7–10 minutes, until the onion has softened, then add the mushrooms and continue cooking for 2–3 minutes, until just tender. Stir in the chopped cilantro, sharpen with lime juice and season with salt just before serving.

COMMUNITY ROOTS
HIMALAYAN BELT

ANITA & UMESH MATTOO, HARYANA

Originally from Goa, on the west coast of India, Anita moved to Delhi as a teenager and found work in the room-service department of a large hotel. While there, she met Umesh, a young chef, born and brought up in the Kashmir Valley. Their backgrounds couldn't have been more contrasting—the sandy beaches of Goa, with tropical sunshine and tourist resorts, were a world away from Umesh's childhood home among snow-capped Himalayan ranges and dense forests.

I met Umesh and Anita in northwest London, where they were visiting Umesh's relatives, who live in the UK. The occasion was a family wedding, and Anita had just made a home-style Kashmiri meal, which everyone loved and appreciated for its emotive resonance with "back home." Umesh laughs and tells me that everyone recognizes that Anita is the best Kashmiri cook in the family. She smiles and says, "Well, we've been married 32 years, so I must be doing something right!" Her childhood dishes of coconut-based fish curries, Goan chorizo and garlicky pork vindaloo would have had little in common with Umesh's daily meals. I was curious to find out how a young woman from Goa adopted Kashmiri cooking and made it her own, so a couple of months later, I visited them in India.

Home for Anita and Umesh is in Gurgaon, also known as Gurugram—a relatively new and affluent city in Haryana. Umesh is from the Kashmiri Pundit community—*pundit* in this context refers to a "priestly, Brahmin class." His family's cooking is steeped in centuries of Hindu tradition, later honed by the Mughals and also by Central Asian influences. Unlike most other Brahmins, who tend to be vegetarian, Kashmiri Pundits eat meat, but lamb and mutton rather than goat. Onions and garlic are given a wide berth, though, because they are believed to be impure.

Anita tells me that in the early 1990s, shortly after she and Umesh were married, many of her husband's relatives left Kashmir because of religious conflict, seeking a safer and secure future in Delhi. There would often be eight to twelve people to look after at home. Juggling a full-time job while running a kitchen was daunting, especially as Umesh's mother didn't speak English, and their local languages were quite different. But Anita persevered, and with a common bond in the kitchen, she found herself a quick learner. Of course, Umesh was also keen to share his knowledge of regional Kashmiri cooking.

I'm here to find out about day-to-day cooking in the Mattoo household. But first, tea. I join Anita in her spacious kitchen where she's making *kong kahwa*— Kashmiri green tea. On the stove, a pot of water has come to a boil. She adds cardamom pods, cinnamon sticks and then a spoonful of green tea leaves and a little sugar. Almonds are roughly pounded in a weighty stone

Wooded slopes in Kashmir.

▶ mortar, sprinkled into three cups, and the brew poured over. Although she strains the tea today, the leaves are normally left to be chewed for an extra boost of flavor. Outside, the late summer heat is spent and there's a hint of cooler days ahead. It's raining and the tea, grassy and fresh, feels an appropriate way to mark the change of season.

Umesh tells me that his mother would never accept tea from a china cup because she regarded it as containing animal bone ash, which would be unholy. He shows me her brass drinking bowl and their samovar. Embossed with a decorative design, the samovar has a funnel in the middle for hot charcoal to brew the tea and keep it hot all day—as it would in the long, cold winters of Kashmir. Although they live in the plains, hundreds of miles from Kashmir, these well-used vessels remain an emotional link to the family's heritage.

I ask about seasonings used in Kashmiri Pundit cooking. She opens a large glass jar filled with dark brown granular discs. This is *ver*, a version of Kashmiri garam masala, made from pounded asafoetida and spices, which include ground fennel, brown cardamom, cloves and cinnamon. It's moistened with mustard oil and bound with ground lentils before being shaped and dried outdoors. The discs are often crumbled over dishes at the end of cooking and lend depth of flavor. Until recently, Umesh's aunt would make batches of *ver* for the family, but she's now old and infirm, and Anita has bought these ones from a Kashmiri shop in Delhi. But it's clear from her expression that they don't measure up. There are two main varieties of *ver*—Muslim cooks add dried onions and garlic to theirs and leave out the asafoetida.

For Umesh's birthday, the day before, Anita made several party dishes, one of which was *mutsch*—cylindrical lamb koftas. Each piece of meat had been laboriously pounded until the fibers became paste-like. I asked if she would consider buying ground meat to save time but was given short shrift. Seasoned with ground fennel seeds, dried ginger and smoky brown cardamom, they had been poached in a tart yogurt masala and warmed with mild Kashmiri chiles, and had a meltingly soft, ricotta-like texture. I'm aware that feasting is a serious business in this part of the world, and these delicious and delicate meatballs provided a taster of Kashmiri "fine dining."

Even for everyday meals, Muslim and Hindu cultures have commonalities and differences in their approaches to cooking. Often dishes with the same name will have distinguishing features. Muslim communities tend to favor meaty stocks infused with onion and garlic, while Hindu families like Umesh's prefer yogurt-based masalas, sometimes spiced with turmeric.

Today, on my request, we're going back to basics, and Anita is making a simple staple of *monja* for lunch. It's a comforting, broth-like vegetable dish with kohlrabi. Rather than chop the garlic on a board, Anita cradles the bulb in her hand, cutting it into uneven chunks, which she says makes for a more interesting texture. A generous glug of golden *kachi ghani*—cold-pressed mustard oil—goes into the pressure cooker. As it heats, I'm struck by how refined it is compared to the eye-wateringly pungent variety I'm familiar with.

▶ She breaks off a small piece of pastel-colored paste and lightly softens it with her fingers. This is asafoetida (*heeng*), a resin with a mildly sulphurous aroma and umami flavor. She drops it into hot oil and it mellows to sweetness within seconds. The flavor, layered and nuanced, plays an important role in compensating for the absence of onions and garlic. The asafoetida I buy in Britain is rock-hard and has little resemblance to the variety Anita cooks with. She tells me that, even in India, *heeng* is often mixed with flour to extend its shelf life, and much of its subtlety is lost in the process.

Next, kohlrabi is tumbled in and fried over a fierce heat, followed by its trimmed tops and leaves. She warms a couple of green chiles in her palm, snaps them with her thumb to extract maximum flavor and throws them in. Water is added, lots of it, and her sturdy pressure cooker is then put to good use.

Returning to the sitting room, we continue chatting over more hot tea. Umesh tells me that during the summer, home cooks in Kashmir will dry seasonal fruit and vegetables outdoors in the sunshine—perhaps bottle gourd, zucchini, eggplants, apples and quince. In winter, when fresh produce is in short supply, these will be cooked either on their own or with meat or fish, which has also been dried. Despite the year-round availability of ingredients in Gurgaon, Anita continues to promote preserving in this traditional way. She's even taught Kashmiri kitchen techniques to local youngsters, some of whom are now chefs in restaurant kitchens.

The whistle blows on the pressure cooker and the kohlrabi is ready. It's had 5 minutes under pressure, and Anita is clear that any longer and the dish will lose its fresh flavor and the leaves their green color. A puff of mustardy steam scents the air as she lifts off the lid, and I ladle tender, translucent kohlrabi and wilted leafy greens over a heap of hot rice. The clear broth runs down in rivulets, settling in a shallow moat on the plate. Kohlrabi, with its faintly turnip-like taste, makes for such a simple and satisfying dish, and although I appreciate the complexity of formal Kashmiri dining, there's comfort in enjoying a dish that has been made with just four ingredients.

1. The finished kohlrabi in its broth.

2. Anita with an earthenware cooking pot.

3. Anita and husband Umesh at home, with their family samovar.

KOHLRABI COOKED IN MUSTARD OIL WITH GREEN CHILES

Serves 4–6

ANITA MATTOO

This bowl of goodness is a broth-like staple in Kashmir and makes a warming meal with boiled rice. There are just a few spices in this dish and its distinctive flavor comes mainly from the slight bitterness of kohlrabi and the mustardy sweetness of the oil it's cooked in. Anita Mattoo cooked this for me, and like so many home cooks in India, the pressure cooker is a key tool in her kitchen, where cooking time is measured in whistles rather than minutes. I've made this comforting dish in a regular pot, but you could use a pressure cooker if you prefer, in which case the kohlrabi will cook in one whistle (if you have an old-fashioned cooker with weights on the top) or in about 10 minutes, under pressure.

- 1 lb 10 oz (750 g) kohlrabi, ideally with leaves attached
- 7 oz (200 g) collard greens or chard if the kohlrabi doesn't have leaves
- ½ cup (120 ml) mustard oil or blended mustard oil
- generous pinch of asafoetida
- 2 green chiles, snapped in half horizontally, with seeds
- sea salt
- boiled rice, to serve

If the kohlrabi hasn't already been trimmed, strip the leaves from the long stems, discard the stems, and tear the larger leaves into rough pieces, so that they are about the size of a smallish spinach leaf.

Peel the kohlrabi and slice it into ½ in (1 cm) thick rounds. Cut each slice into quarters so that you have bite-sized pieces.

If the kohlrabi doesn't have its leaves attached, roughly chop the collard greens or chard with their stems and leave to one side.

Heat the oil in a karahi, wok or pot on medium-high heat. Add the asafoetida followed, after a few seconds, by the kohlrabi and green chiles. Fry for about 3–4 minutes, stirring often, until it starts to soften but doesn't color.

Pour over enough hot water to cover by a depth of 1 in (3 cm), season with salt and bring to a boil. Turn down the heat to medium-low, half-cover the pot and cook for 15–20 minutes, until the kohlrabi is tender but still holds its shape. Stir in the leaves and cook, uncovered, for 4–5 minutes, until tender. Serve straight away with boiled rice.

BABY PEPPERS WITH COCONUT, TAMARIND & SESAME SEEDS

Serves 6–8

This rich, regal dish from Hyderabad is best made in advance so that the lovely, tart tamarind and toasted coconut masala can mellow and take on the sweetness from the peppers. This is traditionally made with fat green chiles, which you could use instead of the baby peppers. If you do use chiles, remember to remove any seeds—otherwise the fiery heat level will be off the scale.

FOR THE COCONUT PASTE

⅓ cup (50 g) unsalted peanuts, skinned

3 tbsp white sesame seeds

¼ cup (25 g) desiccated coconut

¼ tsp fenugreek seeds

6 garlic cloves, coarsely chopped

1 oz (30 g) ginger root, peeled and coarsely chopped

2 tsp ground coriander

1 tsp roasted and ground cumin seeds

2 tbsp tamarind pulp (see page 21)

2 rounded tsp jaggery or light brown sugar

Indian flatbreads or boiled rice, to serve

FOR THE MASALA

1 lb (500 g) baby sweet peppers

⅓ cup (75 ml) sunflower oil

about 15 fresh curry leaves

2 large onions, thinly sliced

¼ tsp ground turmeric

¾ tsp Kashmiri chile powder

2 cups (500 ml) hot water

sea salt

Heat a small dry, frying pan on medium heat and roast the peanuts until they start to pick up flecks of color. Add the sesame seeds, coconut and fenugreek seeds and continue cooking, stirring all the time, until the coconut turns golden. Tip everything onto a plate and leave to cool.

Transfer this mixture into a small food processor and add the garlic, ginger, coriander, cumin, tamarind pulp and jaggery or sugar. Pour in 1 cup (225 ml) of water, then grind until smooth. Spoon the paste into a small bowl and leave to one side.

For the masala, make an incision along the length of each pepper, keeping it intact at the top, then remove the seeds with a small knife. Heat the oil in a karahi or wok on high heat and fry the peppers for 5–7 minutes, turning them, until the skin starts to blister, then scoop them out onto a tray, leaving the oil in the pan.

Turn down the heat to medium-high. Add the curry leaves—they will splutter, so step back as they hit the oil, then, after a few seconds, add the onions and season with salt. Fry for 10–12 minutes, until the onions are golden.

Turn down the heat to medium and stir in the turmeric and chile powder, followed by the coconut paste. Fry for 5–7 minutes, until the paste has darkened and small droplets of oil appear around the side of the pan.

Return the peppers to the pan and pour in the hot water. Continue cooking, without a lid, for 3–4 minutes, until the peppers are just tender. Serve with Indian flatbreads or boiled rice.

PEAS SIMMERED IN FRESH CILANTRO & PEANUT MASALA Serves 4

As green as a bowling lawn, this herby masala is enriched with peanuts, studded with peas, and sharpened with green chiles. It's a popular, rustic dish, made in villages across the state of Maharashtra, and served with crisp-cooked flatbread and sliced red onion on the side. Boiled rice works particularly well, too.

½ cup (75 g) unsalted peanuts, skinned

3 garlic cloves

1 large handful cilantro leaves with stems

2 green chiles, chopped, with seeds

4 tbsp sunflower oil

about 15 fresh curry leaves

1 small red onion, finely diced

about 1⅔ cups (400 ml) hot water

1½ cups (200 g) frozen peas

sea salt

Indian flatbreads or boiled rice, to serve

Put the peanuts, garlic, cilantro and green chiles in a small food processor, add enough water to barely cover, then blend everything to a paste. (You can alternatively use a handheld immersion blender and a bowl for this.) Leave to one side.

Heat the oil in a karahi or wok on medium-high heat, add the curry leaves and fry them for about 20 seconds, until the crackling quietens. Turn down the heat to medium, stir in the onion and fry, stirring often, until golden.

Add the peanut and herb paste and cook for 2 minutes, stirring constantly, then pour over the hot water (use enough to make a thin, soupy consistency). Season with salt, add the peas and simmer uncovered for 2–3 minutes, until tender. Serve with Indian flatbreads or boiled rice.

CRUSHED ZUCCHINI WITH TAMARIND & JAGGERY

Serves 4

My cousin's wife, Shama, brings joy to the family dining table with her outstanding Punjabi cooking. On my last visit, she served puffed lentil puris (*bedmis*) for breakfast with spiced *petha*, a type of squash also known as ash gourd or winter melon. Instead of ash gourd, I've used zucchini here, which are softened, crushed and sharpened with tamarind, sweetened with jaggery and seasoned with cumin seeds. You could serve this as an accompaniment vegetable, or team it with potato, onion & tomato masala (see page 221) or lentil puris (see page 281).

¼ cup (50 g) ghee (see page 18)

1 tsp cumin seeds

1 lb 8 oz (700 g) zucchini, peeled and diced

¼ tsp ground turmeric

1 tsp ground coriander

3 whole green chiles

1 tbsp tamarind pulp (see page 21)

1 tbsp jaggery or light brown sugar

sea salt

Heat the ghee in a karahi, wok or pot on medium-high heat. Add the cumin seeds and sizzle for about 20 seconds, until they release a nutty aroma. Stir in the zucchini, turmeric, coriander and green chiles, and season with salt.

Turn down the heat to medium-low, cover the pan and simmer for about 20 minutes, until the zucchini are soft and translucent. Roughly crush them with a potato masher and stir in enough tamarind pulp to sharpen and add enough jaggery or sugar to sweeten. Simmer uncovered for 2–3 minutes, until any excess liquid has evaporated. Serve piping hot.

SPINACH WITH GARLIC, CHILE & GINGER

Serves 4

I have eaten many lovely spinach dishes, but this recipe, with its short cooking time and simple ginger-garlic-chile seasoning, is one of the best side dishes ever.

---

11 oz (320 g) baby spinach leaves

2 large garlic cloves, very thinly sliced

½ tsp dried red chile flakes

2 tbsp cooled melted ghee (see page 18) or sunflower oil

1 large banana shallot, thinly sliced

¾ oz (20 g) ginger root, peeled and finely grated

sea salt

Heat a sturdy dry pan on medium-high heat. Add the spinach and cook, stirring all the time, for 1 minute, until it starts to wilt. Transfer the leaves to a colander set over a bowl and leave to cool. Using the palms of your hands, when the spinach is cool enough to handle, squeeze any water from the spinach and leave to one side.

Put the garlic and chile flakes in a karahi or wok with the melted ghee or oil. Season with salt and cook on very gentle heat for 5-7 minutes, stirring occasionally, until the garlic is translucent. Add the shallot and ginger and continue cooking for 2-3 minutes.

Turn up the heat to medium-high, add the spinach and reheat, stirring all the time, for 30-40 seconds, and serve straight away.

DALS & PULSES

CHANA DAL WITH SPINACH

Serves 4

It's usual to use *chana dal* for this dish, but you could also make it with split yellow peas. Both have a robust, almost meaty flavor, which stands up well to leafy green vegetables. Add the softened spinach at the last minute, so that it retains its fresh grassy-green color. This dal is finished with a fried *tarka* flourish, made with sizzling spices, garlic, ginger and the sharpness of green chiles.

---

1 cup (200 g) split Bengal gram (*chana dal*), washed and soaked in hot water for 2–3 hours

¼ tsp ground turmeric

12 oz (350 g) baby spinach leaves

juice of ½ lime

sea salt

FOR THE TARKA

¼ cup (50 g) ghee (see page 18), or 5 tbsp sunflower oil

1 tsp cumin seeds

1 dried Kashmiri red chile

4 garlic cloves, finely chopped

1 oz (30 g) ginger root, peeled and finely grated

2 green chiles, deseeded and chopped

1 tomato, diced

Discard the soaking water from the Bengal gram and transfer the dal to a pressure cooker. Cover with water by a depth of 1½ in (4 cm). Add the turmeric and cook under pressure for 30 minutes, until the gram is soft and has broken down. Roughly crush the dal with a potato masher against the side of the pot. Aim for the consistency of thick soup. If it looks a bit watery, boil the dal for a few more minutes without any pressure.

Alternatively, put the Bengal gram and turmeric in a medium pot and cover with water by a depth of 1½ in (4 cm). Half-cover the pot and cook the dal on medium heat for 1½–2 hours, until completely tender, adding extra water if needed to prevent it from becoming too thick. Roughly crush the dal in the same way with a potato masher. Keep the dal warm.

Heat a sturdy, dry pan on high heat and add the spinach. Cook, stirring all the time, until the leaves start to wilt—this should take 1 minute. (You may need to do this in batches.) Scoop the leaves into a colander set over a bowl and leave to cool. When the spinach is cool enough to handle, squeeze any excess liquid out of the leaves with the palms of your hands, then roughly chop them. Leave to one side.

For the *tarka*, heat the ghee or oil in a small pan on medium-high heat and add the cumin seeds and Kashmiri chile. Swirl everything around for about 20 seconds, until the cumin releases its nutty fragrance and the chile swells and becomes darker.

Turn down the heat to medium and add the garlic, ginger and green chiles and fry for 1 minute. Stir in the diced tomato and cook for another 2 minutes, until softened. Tip this *tarka* into the hot dal, season generously with salt, then stir in the chopped spinach. Reheat and finish with the lime juice before serving straight away.

BROWN CHICKPEAS WITH GINGER & MANGO POWDER

Serves 6

This is an especially popular dish with the Jain community, who don't eat onions and garlic for religious reasons. Instead, it boasts a big, bold spice blend to compensate. Dark brown chickpeas are smaller than the regular beige variety, have a deep nutty flavor and remain firm after cooking. I love how the fruity, gingery, astringent masala cloaks them. This is traditionally served with puris.

FOR THE SPICE MIX

1 tsp dried fenugreek leaves (*kasuri methi*)

¼ tsp carom seeds (*ajwain*)

1 tsp roasted and ground cumin seeds

2 tsp ground coriander

2 tsp mango powder (*amchoor*)

1 tsp ground ginger

1 tsp Kashmiri chile powder

FOR THE CHICKPEAS

4 tbsp sunflower oil

1 tsp cumin seeds

¾ oz (20 g) ginger root, peeled and finely grated

2 green chiles, deseeded and coarsely chopped

2 x 14 oz (400 g) cans of brown chickpeas (*kala chana*), drained and rinsed

1 cup (250 ml) hot water

juice of 1 lime

sea salt

FOR THE TOPPING

1 red onion, sliced into thin rings

2 tbsp ghee (see page 18), or 2-3 tbsp sunflower oil

1 tbsp chopped cilantro leaves

For the spice mix, dry-roast the fenugreek leaves in a small pan on medium heat, stirring all the time, until they release a toasted aroma—this only takes a few seconds. Transfer the leaves to a plate and leave to cool. Using your fingers, crumble them to a powder and mix with the carom seeds, ground cumin, coriander, mango powder, ground ginger and Kashmiri chile powder. Add a scant ½ cup (100 ml) of water and make a slack paste.

For the chickpeas, heat the oil in a karahi or wok on medium-high heat, add the cumin seeds and swirl them around for 30 seconds, until they release their aroma. Stir in the ginger and green chiles, followed, after a few seconds, by the spice paste. Cook, stirring all the time, for 1-2 minutes, until the water evaporates and the spices are fragrant.

Turn down the heat to low and add the chickpeas and the hot water. Season with salt, half-cover and simmer for about 7-10 minutes, until the water has evaporated.

Turn off the heat, stir in the lime juice, then transfer the chickpeas to a heatproof serving dish and scatter with the onion rings. Heat the ghee or oil in a small pan on medium heat, until it starts to smoke, then quickly pour it over the hot chickpeas. Scatter the dish with chopped cilantro and serve straight away.

COMMUNITY ROOTS
WEST

RASILA SHAH, GUJARAT

Dabasang is not a tourist destination. It is a remote village located about an hour's drive from Jamnagar and is several kilometers away from the nearest main road. On this late October morning, the sky is blue and cloudless. The taxi shows the temperature nudging north of 95°F (35°C). The view from our car is of unremarkable scrubland, interspersed with crops of cotton, soybean and peanuts.

I'm traveling to Dabasang with my London-based friend, Madhu Colwill. Her father was born here and left India as a young man in the 1940s to join recently settled Gujarati traders and businessmen in Mombasa, Kenya. The family later returned to India for a year—it's in this ancestral village where Madhu spent much time as a child and retains close ties with her extended family.

Our driver drops us outside the village shop—from here the road narrows into a dusty lane barely wide enough for a car, so we make our way on foot for the final yards to our destination. Electricity and running water are relatively recent additions, but this is not a poor village by Indian standards—a small school, temple, shop and surrounding farmland make for a largely self-sufficient community.

Madhu heads through a pair of open, turquoise-painted wooden doors, where Rasila is waiting. Any nervousness I feel about gate-crashing this family reunion evaporates with the warm welcome we get from her, along with visiting relatives and curious neighbors. We step onto a veranda, slip off our sandals and line them up with everyone's *chappals* and flip flops. We're facing an open courtyard, surrounded on two sides by compact, corrugated iron-roofed rooms with small window frames ribbed with iron-rod grilles.

Rasila is in her late fifties and carries the assurance that comes from years of hard work and providing for others. She's wearing a printed blue sari, folded in the traditional Gujarati style, with the cloth pulled tight over her left shoulder and folded sling-style in front of her chest. She is married to Vasant and has three grown-up, married children settled in Mumbai and Jamnagar. She looks after her husband's 92-year-old mother, and both husband and wife also run the family farm.

A few relatives are already relaxing on *charpoys*, woven rope-like beds stretched taut across a wooden frame. White plastic "garden" chairs are drawn close, and space made for about a dozen people under the breeze of the ceiling fan. It's a traditional community and the atmosphere is boisterous and playground-like. There's color, chatter and genuine camaraderie, and the men hang back, happy to let the women take center stage. Neighbors stop by ▶

Rasila, my dear friend Madhu's cousin.

▶ and make themselves at home, introducing themselves as Madhu's *bhai* or *ben*, "brother or sister," which is commonplace across Gujarat.

The rough-finished concrete ground is warm under foot, and the courtyard has been swept clean of any dust from the lane outside. An outdoor fire has already been lit and is fueled by wood and dried cow-dung cakes. Its flames are fanned by the practiced hand of Rasila's mother-in-law, who squats comfortably in front of a weathered, once white-washed wall, oblivious to the intense heat. I'm trying hard to join this kitchen activity, but streams of sweat sting my eyes and I soon step away.

Rasila takes me indoors to her simple, practical kitchen. Every pot has a purpose, and there are few concessions to modern gadgets. Meals are made fresh every day and with careful planning; there's no need for a fridge. A pail hangs from a sturdy nail on the wall for the buffalo milk from their nearby farm.

Earthenware vessels keep drinking water cool and are also used to set homemade yogurt. Fermented pickles mature and ripen in glazed stone and glass jars in Rasila's larder, and large, tightly lidded steel and occasional plastic containers accommodate other storage needs. A wooden stick with a grooved end is used for churning *chaas*, which is like a lighter version of *lassi*—this cooling drink accompanies every meal. Rasila tells me that her mother-in-law used to cook with copper pans, but they were too time-consuming to maintain so she opts for steel and aluminum.

There are two gas burners attached to a gas cylinder, which help speed things up when cooking for a crowd, but the main hub of activity is the outdoor fire. Even at this early stage of our acquaintance, it's clear that Rasila is in charge and she's as comfortable cooking for twelve people as she is overseeing community events for 200. Supervising others is a well-earned boon that comes with her advancing seniority within the extended family. Steel thalis and metal glasses shine on the open shelves and although the sparsely furnished dining area, kitchen and spacious larder are functional, the rooms lack for nothing.

The lentils have already been cooked in a pressure cooker indoors and are taken outside to be finished with dry spices and fresh, homegrown curry leaves. Vasant crouches next to the wood fire, waiting for Rasila to give him the nod so he can drop the mustard seeds into hot oil. This is unusual—most men in this conservative community would stay well away from the kitchen. Within seconds, the chile stains the oil red, and the turmeric transforms it to auburn. The soupy dal is tipped into the sizzling spices and he stirs as it bubbles in the pan. Lunch is almost ready—it's the main meal of the day and is made from scratch every morning to serve just before noon.

The entire village is vegetarian—many are from the Jain community and don't eat onion or garlic for religious reasons. Eggs aren't on the menu either and Rasila doesn't cook green leafy vegetables in the monsoon season, just in case any insects nestling in the leaves are inadvertently killed.

▶ She turns her attention to kneading unleavened millet dough for flatbreads, known as *bajra rotla*. All grain is ground by hand in small batches, between two heavy stones, just as it has been for the last two centuries. The dough into portions, she rolls out smooth *rotlas*, and flips each one between her palms, before slapping it on to a hot iron griddle. Within seconds the bread releases a nutty, toasted aroma, imbued with woody smoke from the open fire. Next, she makes a stack of *rotli* with chapati flour—each one glistening with melted homemade ghee.

We're led to the indoor dining area next to the kitchen and most family members, including her 89-year-old aunt, squat or sit cross-legged comfortably on the floor. I managed to get to the ground easily enough, but years spent slouching on sofas have done me no favors as I struggle to get up afterwards.

The rice is ready in a covered pot, and Rasila passes *dhosa ladoos* around. Densely textured, these are made from chapati flour dough, cooked until hard in the embers of a fire. The dough is then pounded to fine crumbs and kneaded with ghee, butterscotch-like jaggery, nutmeg and cardamom before being reshaped into soft balls. There's a tradition in Gujarat of serving sweet dishes with savory, and these *ladoos* will partner the dal she has just made. Crushed turmeric-hued potatoes, lemony shredded cabbage salad, dal and crisp green chiles are finished with tart and salty *chaas* in small steel bowls. Desserts aren't usually served unless there's a festival or an auspicious occasion. Instead, Rasila's nephew shares his haul of cellophane-wrapped morsels of sweet, sticky and slightly fibrous tamarind. They're delicious and a lot healthier than the hard candies of my childhood.

Afterwards, metal plates are clattered together and taken to the cemented outdoor washing area—there's a faucet in the wall at one end of the courtyard, and this is where dishes will pile up after lunch. Almost everyone melts away for an hour-long siesta on *charpoys* under the fan. Rasila stays behind to clear up. A cow quizzically pops its head around the open front door for the second time in an hour. Rasila laughs and tips any peelings and scrapings into a metal bucket and takes it outdoors for the cow. This happens every day—nothing goes to waste here.

In the stillness of the afternoon, I ask about Rasila's family life and she's happy to oblige. "The first time I met my husband was at the engagement party arranged by our families when I was 22 years old. After we married, my main responsibility was to look after his family and to be respectful to my in-laws. It hasn't always been easy, especially as I was cooking for, and looking after, at least twelve people every day." Ever positive, she quickly adds, "I learned how to make the most out of my day and manage my in-laws' needs, and after the younger brothers were married, I learned how to delegate. But they moved to Mumbai, and I've managed everything ever since."

"My day starts around 6am, when I knead dough, make *bajra rotlas* [millet flatbread] and boil tea for breakfast. When I was younger, I'd carry clothes for washing to ▶

▶ a lake where rainwater was harvested, which was more than an hour's walk away. But that's changed since we now have tap water at home."

"In my early married life, I drew drinking water from the well and carried it back on my head in a pot. Its taste was so much sweeter than water from the tap." After a pause, she adds, "I don't miss the walk or the weighty urn on my head, but I do miss the mid-morning gossip sessions."

By now the heat of the day has dissipated and we join the family as they head to their 35-acre farm, 2 miles (3 km) away. Vasant walks the distance several times a day and Rasila sometimes joins him, although not as often, because they have recently appointed a farm manager, Sonaben, who takes care of much of the day-to-day management. Today, seven of us squash into a taxi and we reach there in minutes. The soybeans are already piled high in a brightly colored trailer, but there are vegetables to be harvested, papayas to be picked, cumin seeds and chiles to gather, and peanuts and cotton to be tended. Rasila remarks that when the monsoon rains replenish the earth, there is enough food for everyone in the village—this is a community that remains largely dependent on nature.

In winter, Rasila collects cow dung for shaping into flat discs and slaps each one on the ground to dry. The dung cakes are then loaded onto a bullock-drawn wooden cart and brought back to the village to use as fuel.

Until recently, Rasila was responsible for milking the buffaloes. It's a role now taken up by Sonaben, and I watch as she fills a large steel bucket to the brim with warm, creamy milk. Now that there's milk, the tea can be made. It's poured, traditional style, from an aluminum kettle directly into saucers rather than cups, and it's very, very sweet. We stand, some of us squat, around glowing embers on the ground, snacking on roasting peanuts picked out from the ash. The sun has set, and the stars are sparkling. Rasila tells me that her mother-in-law used to look to the night sky and note the placement of stars to gauge the passing of seasons; I notice that none of the local women in this group are wearing watches.

I'm glad that it's a generous harvest from a less than bountiful land—Rasila smiles and comments, "Most of our produce is grown for those in our village, but when the monsoons are good, we will sell any surplus in the market. We may not have much, but we are happy."

1. Sonaben, the Shah family's farm manager, has a home on-site and her kitchen is a beauty!

2. Members of Madhu's hospitable family: Kasturben (left) and Manisha.

3. Milk for our tea came from this buffalo.

1. Sunset on the farm.

2. Madhu's lovely aunt, Kanku.

3. Rasila's husband, Vasant, with peanuts plucked minutes before I took this photo.

4. Rasila rolling out rotis made with their own home-grown grain.

5. Sonaben, just before milking time for the buffalo.

6. Maize, grown on the farm.

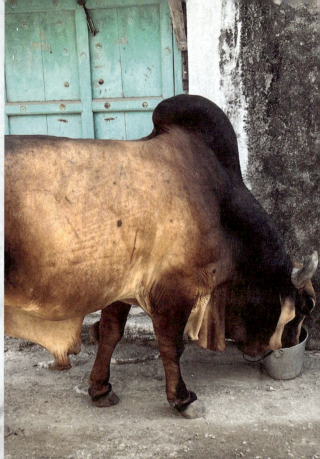

1. Rasila with her pot of comforting dal.

2. This local cow has waited patiently for the leftovers from our lunch.

3. Houses in this region are built to protect rooms from the intensity of the summer heat.

MIXED LENTIL DAL

Serves 3–4

RASILA SHAH

This homey dal is finished with a sizzling *tarka* of mustard seeds, curry leaves and ground spices and was made for me by Rasila at her home in rural Gujarat. Cooked outdoors on an open fire, her dal bubbled in a weathered aluminum pot, its earthy aroma carried in plumes of steam, before being lost in the afternoon breeze. The blend of dals used here lend a nutty flavor, which works well with the astringent finishing spices. Although green gram and black lentils aren't as well known in the West as yellow lentils, they are cheap to buy from South Asian grocery stores or you can order them online.

½ cup (100 g) whole black lentils (*sabut urad dal*)

1 oz (25 g) whole green gram (*sabut moong dal*)

2 tbsp split Bengal gram (*chana dal*) or split yellow peas

4 tbsp sunflower oil

1 tsp brown mustard seeds

generous pinch of ground asafoetida (*heeng*)

¾ tsp ground turmeric

about 15 fresh curry leaves

1 rounded tsp ground coriander

1 rounded tsp Kashmiri chile powder

2 tbsp chopped cilantro leaves

sea salt

boiled rice, to serve

Mix together the three varieties of dal and wash them in a colander under cold, running water, then transfer to a large heatproof bowl. Cover them with hot water and leave to soak overnight.

Drain and discard the soaking water and tip the dal into a pressure cooker. Cover with water by a depth of 1 in (3 cm). Cook under pressure for 40 minutes, then turn off the heat. Leave the pressure to release naturally before opening the lid.

The dal should be fully cooked and broken down—if it's not quite ready, cook under pressure for another 10 minutes. Alternatively you can simmer the dal in a sturdy pot for about 2 hours. Remember to top up the water level as it cooks.

Heat the oil in a large pot over medium-high heat. Add the mustard seeds—they should sizzle straight away. Swirl them around for about 15 seconds and when the popping quietens, add the asafoetida, turmeric, curry leaves, ground coriander and chile powder. Fry everything for 20 seconds, or until the the curry leaves stop crackling, then add the dal and its cooking liquid and season generously with salt.

Aim for a thin, soupy consistency; you may need to add more hot water if it is too thick. Bring the dal to a boil, then reduce the heat and simmer, stirring occasionally, for 5 minutes. Add the chopped cilantro before serving, then serve with boiled rice.

MOONG DAL   Serves 4

This lightly flavored dal is seasoned with fried cumin and given a lift with refreshing ginger and browned onions. I sometimes float a heaped teaspoon of butter on top before serving, just to impart a little indulgence.

---

1 cup (200 g) split yellow moong beans (*moong dal*), washed and soaked in hot water for 1 hour

½ tsp ground turmeric

4 tbsp sunflower oil

1½ tsp cumin seeds

1 onion, diced

1 oz (25 g) ginger root, peeled and finely chopped

½ tsp Kashmiri chile powder

¾ tsp garam masala (see page 19)

sea salt

Indian flatbreads or boiled rice, to serve

Drain the dal from its soaking water and tip it into a sturdy Dutch oven or pot. Cover with water by a depth of 1½ in (4 cm) and add the turmeric. Bring to a boil, then reduce the heat and simmer for about 30 minutes, until it has completely broken down and is soft and soupy in consistency. You may need to add more water as it cooks.

Heat the oil in a small frying pan on medium-high heat. Add the cumin seeds and let them sizzle for about 30 seconds, until aromatic.

Stir in the onion and ginger and fry for about 7-10 minutes, until the onion has browned. Add the chile powder and garam masala, and after a few seconds, tip this *tarka* into the hot dal. Season with salt, cover and leave the lentils for 20 minutes or longer before reheating and serving with Indian flatbreads or boiled rice.

RED LENTIL & TAMARIND DAL

Serves 4–6

My mother kept her lentils and pulses in tall glass jars that had been donated by the corner shop in our village. Some of the containers still had labels for classic British candies like lemon bon bons, sherbet pips and pear drops stuck to them. I pretty much took these staples for granted—they were cheap, filling and life-affirming. It was only when I lived in India that I realized the reach and versatility of the humble lentil. This dal is made with red lentils, which are quick to cook and mild in flavor. It reminds me of Lakshmi, our home helper in India, who was from Chennai, and dressed-up her daily dal with popped mustard seeds, crackling curry leaves and a big dollop of tart tamarind. I've recreated it here.

---

2 ripe tomatoes

1½ cups (275 g) red lentils (*lal masoor*), washed and soaked in hot water for 20 minutes

½ tsp ground turmeric

3 tbsp sunflower oil

1 tsp brown mustard seeds

about 15 fresh curry leaves

1 onion, finely diced

1 oz (25 g) ginger root, peeled and finely chopped

2 garlic cloves, thinly sliced

½ tsp Kashmiri chile powder

1 green chile, deseeded and finely chopped

1-2 tbsp tamarind pulp (see page 21), to taste

sea salt

Bring a pot of water to a boil, then turn off the heat. Add the tomatoes, and after about 30 seconds, scoop them out with a slotted spoon into a bowl of water. When they are cool enough to handle, peel off the skin and roughly chop the flesh with the seeds.

Drain the lentils in a sieve, transfer them to a pot, and cover with water by a depth of 1½ in (4 cm). Add the turmeric and chopped tomatoes and season with salt. Bring to a simmer, then half-cover and cook for about 40 minutes, until the lentils are completely soft and are soupy in consistency. You may need to top up the water as it cooks.

For the *tarka*, heat the oil in a small sturdy pan on medium-high heat, add the mustard seeds and sizzle for about 30 seconds, until the popping quietens. Stir in the curry leaves and fry for another 20 seconds, until they stop crackling.

Turn down the heat to medium, add the onion and fry for around 7-10 minutes, until golden. Stir in the ginger and garlic, followed after 1 minute by the chile powder and green chile. Tip the *tarka* into the hot lentils and stir well. Add enough tamarind pulp to sharpen and simmer the dal for 5 minutes before serving.

SOUTH INDIA

BLACK-EYED PEAS IN GARLIC TOMATO MASALA Serves 6

My Punjabi mother, like many women in India during the 1960s, was given a pressure cooker at her wedding. As a child in England, I remember returning from school to the sound of it blasting steam all over the kitchen. She was militant in pre-soaking and cooking lentils and pulses from scratch, and only canned baked beans made it into the house, served "English-style" for Sunday breakfast. I feel quite rebellious in admitting that I always use canned black-eyed peas for this recipe—they are affordable, and there's little danger of overcooking them. This is a dish that benefits from being made a day before serving. Mom would often fry 9 oz (250 g) of sliced cremini mushrooms in butter and add them to the cooked beans before bringing them to the table.

---

2 tsp dried fenugreek leaves (*kasuri methi*)

4-6 tbsp sunflower oil

¾ tsp cumin seeds

1½ in (4 cm) cinnamon stick

1 large onion, diced

1 oz (25 g) ginger root, peeled and finely chopped

5 garlic cloves, peeled and finely chopped

1 x 14 oz (400 g) can of chopped tomatoes

¾ tsp ground turmeric

1 tsp Kashmiri chile powder

1 tsp garam masala (see page 19)

2 x 14 oz (400 g) cans of black-eyed peas, drained and rinsed

1⅔ cups (400 ml) hot water

juice of 1 lime, to taste

2 tbsp chopped cilantro leaves

1 tbsp shredded mint leaves

sea salt

Dry-roast the fenugreek leaves in a small pan on medium heat, stirring all the time, until they release a toasted aroma—this only takes a few seconds. Transfer the leaves to a plate and leave them to cool. Using your fingers, crumble them to a powder and leave to one side.

Heat the oil in a karahi or wok on medium-high heat, then add the cumin seeds and cinnamon stick and sizzle for 20 seconds, until fragrant. Add the onion, season with salt, and fry for 7-10 minutes, until golden.

Stir in the ginger and garlic, and after 1 minute, add the tomatoes, turmeric, chile powder, garam masala and crumbled fenugreek leaves. Cook for about 5 minutes, stirring often, until lightly thickened to a soupy consistency.

Add the rinsed black-eyed peas and the hot water. Simmer, uncovered, for 15 minutes, or until the masala reduces to a coating consistency. You may need to add more water if it becomes too thick. Sharpen the black-eyed peas with lime juice, stir in the cilantro and mint and serve with chapatis or boiled rice.

> The bitter flavor of dried fenugreek leaves mellows when roasted and crumbled. Used mainly in North Indian masalas and marinades, a little goes a long way, and the leaves will keep for over a year in a sealed jar.

DRY-COOKED MOONG DAL WITH DILL Serves 4

This dal is from the state of Maharashtra—it's made with skinned and split yellow beans, which are tiny and cook in minutes. The dill is usually lightly cooked rather than used raw, and it will add grassy freshness and color to the finished dish. Indian dill has a stronger flavor than the European variety and is sold in big bunches in South Asian grocery stores.

---

4 tbsp sunflower oil

1½ tsp brown mustard seeds

1 tsp cumin seeds

1 onion, diced

5 garlic cloves, finely chopped

2 green chiles, deseeded and finely chopped

½ tsp ground turmeric

1½ cups (300 g) split yellow moong beans (*moong dal*), washed and soaked in hot water for 1 hour

1 large bunch of dill (about 2½ oz/75 g), leaves stripped from the bigger stems and finely chopped

juice of 1 lime, to taste

Indian flatbreads or boiled rice, to serve

sea salt

Heat the oil in a pot on medium-high heat. Add the mustard seeds and swirl them around for about 30 seconds, until they stop popping. Add the cumin seeds and sizzle for 20 seconds, until aromatic. Turn down the heat to medium, stir in the onion and fry for about 10 minutes, until softened but not browned.

Add the garlic and green chiles and fry for 1 minute, then drain the *moong dal* and add it to the pot with the turmeric. Pour over enough water to half-cover the dal and bring to a boil.

Turn the heat down to low, cover the pot and simmer for 15–20 minutes, adding a little more water if needed as the lentils cook. Aim for a dry texture rather than a soupy consistency. Stir in the chopped dill and cook, uncovered, for 1 minute. Sharpen with lime juice, season with salt, fluff the dal with a fork and serve with Indian breads or rice.

WEST INDIA

MOONG DAL WITH GREEN MANGOES

Serves 4–6

Pairing soothing lentils with tart mangoes is unusual but delicious. In this dish, the fruit provides texture and little bursts of sunshine flavor, a little jaggery provides a hint of sweetness, while fried nigella seeds bring a lightly pickled flavor to this special dal.

- 1¼ cups (250 g) split yellow moong beans (*moong dal*), washed and soaked in hot water for 1 hour
- ½ tsp ground turmeric
- ¾ tsp Kashmiri chile powder
- 1 lb 5 oz (600 g) green, unripe mangoes
- 1 tsp sea-salt flakes, plus extra to taste
- 1 tbsp jaggery or light brown sugar, plus extra to taste
- 3 tbsp sunflower oil
- ½ tsp nigella seeds
- 2 green chiles, deseeded and finely chopped
- boiled rice, to serve

Drain the dal and transfer to a sturdy pot. Add the turmeric and chile powder, and cover with water by a depth of 1½ in (4 cm). Bring to a boil, then skim any impurities from the surface. Turn down the heat to medium-low and cook, half-covered with a lid, for about 30 minutes, until the lentils are soft and have broken down. If they start to catch on the bottom of the pot or if they become too thick, add more hot water to the pot. The consistency should be broth-like when fully cooked.

While the dal is cooking, peel the mangoes and discard the pits. Chop the flesh into ¾ in (2 cm) cubes and transfer to a bowl. Add the salt and the jaggery or sugar and mix well.

Heat the oil in a sturdy frying pan on medium-high heat and add the nigella seeds. After 15 seconds, add the mangoes. Fry for about 5–7 minutes, stirring frequently, until the sugar caramelizes, then add the fruit to the hot dal.

Swirl a ladleful of the cooked lentils into the frying pan, so that it picks up all the caramelized flavor from the mangoes and tip it back into the pot. Stir in the chopped green chiles and adjust the seasoning by adding more salt or jaggery—aim for a fruity, sweet-sour flavor. Cover, and leave to one side for 10 minutes for the flavors to infuse, then serve with boiled rice.

TOMATO DAL WITH MUSTARD SEEDS & CURRY LEAVES

Serves 4–6

This dal comes from Andhra Pradesh and is eye-wateringly hot when made with locally grown *guntur* chiles. I've opted for milder Kashmiri chiles here, and I serve this dish with pungent red chile chutney for extra heat. *Toor* lentils are sold in South Asian grocery stores, but yellow split peas or split Bengal gram (*chana dal*) will work well, too.

---

1 cup (200 g) split pigeon peas (*toor dal*), washed and soaked in boiling water for 1–2 hours

1 large onion, diced

1 x 14 oz (400 g) can of chopped tomatoes

2 green chiles, chopped with seeds

½ tsp ground turmeric

1 tsp sunflower oil

FOR TEMPERING

¼ cup (50 g) ghee (see page 18), or 5 tbsp sunflower oil

1 tsp brown mustard seeds

about 15 fresh curry leaves

1 dried Kashmiri red chile, broken in half, deseeded

1 tsp cumin seeds

¼ tsp ground asafoetida (*heeng*; optional)

3 garlic cloves, thinly sliced

½ tsp Kashmiri chile powder

½–1 tbsp tamarind pulp (see page 21), to taste

sea salt

boiled rice, to serve

fresh red chile chutney (see page 285), to serve

Drain the dal and transfer to a pressure cooker. Add the onion, tomatoes, green chiles, turmeric and the oil. Cover the lentils with water by a depth of 1½ in (4 cm) and cook under pressure for 30 minutes, until they are soft and starting to lose their shape. Alternatively, put the lentils in a sturdy pot with the onion, tomatoes, green chiles, turmeric and oil and cover with water by 1½ in (4 cm). Half-cover the pot with a lid, and cook on medium heat for 1–2 hours. You may need to add extra water if it looks too thick. Aim for a soupy consistency.

To temper, heat the ghee or oil in a small frying pan on medium-high heat. Add the mustard seeds and swirl them around for 30 seconds, until they stop popping. Stir in the curry leaves, broken red chile, cumin seeds and asafoetida, if using, and fry for another 30 seconds, stirring all the time, until the leaves stop spluttering and the red chile darkens. Turn the heat to low, add the garlic and chile powder and continue frying for 1 minute.

Tip this *tarka* into the hot dal and stir in enough tamarind pulp to provide a little sharpness. Cover the dal and leave it on one side for 10 minutes so that the flavors can mingle and mellow. Serve with boiled rice and red chile chutney on the side.

SOUTH INDIA

COMMUNITY ROOTS
CENTRAL

BHAVNA SINGH, RAJASTHAN

As my taxi leaves Udaipur, the urban landmarks give way to desert-like scrub, broken with occasional villages set among low-rise hills. The traffic is sparse, aside from colorful trucks. I admire their hand-painted artwork—many are embellished with buxom village women balancing pots on their heads, and emblazoned with "Horn Ok Please." My driver obliges, keeping his hand firmly on the horn as we overtake at speed.

We're on our way to Deogarh, a village of medieval times, sited midway between Udaipur and Jodhpur in Rajasthan. The driver pulls over at a roadside chai stop, decorated in similar style to the trucks we have just passed. The "caff" is a glorious pastiche of swipe-clean tables, plastic chairs and massive murals depicting elaborate rural idylls. In contrast to the pantomime set surroundings, my *chai wallah* looks bored as he bruises chopped ginger in a mortar, fires up a kerosene stove and boils the no-frills brew to within a split second of spilling over the counter. Sweet, milky tea is strained into clay tumblers and handed to me without a word.

After a three-hour drive, we're now in Rajasthan's rural interior, and the car drops a gear as we follow a bullock cart for a few miles. The landscape changes and a beautifully kept lawn stretches in front of us. I've booked a room at Bhavna and Shatranjai Singh's home, Dev Shree, for two nights. The house, although recently built, is shaped by the majesty of Mughal-style architecture with rows of symmetrical arches, stone pillars and ornate carvings. Bhavna is married into a regal Rajput family and retains the stately traditions of that lineage, while also striking out as an independent entrepreneur.

Bhavna welcomes me at the entrance. She's standing at the top of a flight of stairs and wearing a beautiful pink chiffon sari, draped elegantly over her head. We walk through the reception area into a sunlit Moroccan-style courtyard, flanked on two sides by an arched walkway and eight rooms—one of which is mine. The curtains are drawn in my room to soften the intense sunshine, a ceiling fan paddles through the air, and I settle in for an afternoon siesta.

Later in the evening, I'm sitting in a rattan chair on the veranda with the rhythmic hum of crickets as a nightly chorus. A bearer walks around the house carrying a metal goblet that disperses a trail of scented smoke. It's called *gugal dhoop*, and Bhavna tells me that this is a daily ritual where fragrant resin, lit with charcoal, is believed to banish negative energy.

Dev Shree is a home open to guests and not a hotel. Bhavna's staff has been with the family for years and new recruits from the village are trained onsite. There isn't an à la carte menu or room service, and dishes served in the dining ▶

Deogarh, Rajasthan. Fragrant marigolds for prayer offerings, garlands and decorating homes.

room are drawn from the family's repertoire of mainly Rajasthani recipes that go back five generations. She shows me her collection of vintage cooking equipment, which include weighty karahis, steamers and brass utensils. There are also her mother's handwritten notebooks, featuring recipes for classic Indian dishes alongside banana fritters and chocolate nut caramels.

That night, Bhavna and Shatranjai host dinner for about twelve guests, and it's clear that they both enjoy socializing and entertaining. Magnificent silver thalis are arranged down the length of the dining table, each with six small bowls around the edge. We help ourselves to the likes of crisp-fried okra, light gingery dal and delicately spiced rice. Mithu, the head cook, and Shatranjai have cooked *champaran* "mutton." Mithu has been with the family for 21 years, starting off as a dishwasher. Over time, he started helping in the kitchen, and with the help of YouTube videos, found a flair for cooking even though he couldn't read or write.

Across much of India, meat dishes are made with goat, even though most recipes will refer to them as lamb or mutton. *Champaran* "mutton," originally from Bihar, is simmered in a sealed earthenware pot with whole garlic heads, pungent local *mathania* chiles, and fried onions, ginger and garlic. Despite its chile heat, the flavor is mellow, the meat tender and imbued with lovely caramelly garlic and onions. Unlike Mughal royal cooking, meaty Rajput dishes aren't reliant on complex spice blends. There's an earthy appeal about dipping bread into a pool of masala enriched with homemade ghee and infused with chiles.

I meet Rukmini and Bhaiji, staff from Deogarh, who are making cornmeal, *baat cheet* popadums on the veranda, which has been repurposed as a field kitchen. It's laborious work—decades ago, women gathered and gossiped as portions of thickened paste were patted into discs and dried in the sun until crisp. The saying "I have made many *papad* in my life" is commonly used for repetitive and tiresome daily chores.

Both women are married to men in the village and dressed in gorgeous, vibrant colors. Rukmini's head and face is in *purdah*, while Bhaiji covers only her head. Bhavna tells me that if a wife is not originally from the village, she is generally required to be more restricted in her dress and demeanor to show her good standing in the community. In respect of such tradition, even Bhavna keeps her head covered in public, because she's a daughter-in-law of the Singh family. All married women are encouraged to wear bright colors and bangles to denote their status, while widows dress in muted shades and don't wear a bindi on their forehead or decorative anklets.

While they prepare popadums, Bhavna and I chat about how nature can be a harsh provider. Although there are numerous small lakes in the area, once summer hits its stride, landscapes become parched, and the temperature hovers around 122°F (50°C) for weeks without respite. Fresh, locally grown produce is scarce during these months, but Rajasthani home cooks have always been resourceful. For daily meals, ground lentils might be mixed with green chiles, fresh cilantro and ginger, and shaped into droplets. These *moongadi* are then sun-dried

▶ until crisp and cooked in a yogurty masala with chopped gourd. Hot-weather produce, such as watermelons, make a refreshing change when lightly cooked with mint and green chiles, and the rind put to good use in mustardy pickles.

Today, Bhavna and Mithu are making a local specialty with regular, store-bought popadums, which have been roasted over an open flame until crisp and smoky. For the masala, cumin seeds are sizzled in hot oil, and then a slack onion paste hits the oil with a whoosh, followed by garlic and ginger and it's vigorously stirred until browned. Next in, pale yellow turmeric yogurt, spiked with red chile and ground coriander, followed by a jug of water. Once it reaches a rolling boil, the pace slows—shards of popadum are slipped into the masala and they soften within seconds to a pasta-like texture. I love the simplicity of this dish—all it needs is a heap of boiled rice and Shatranjai's homemade mango pickle to complete my lunch.

Despite the challenges of arid summers, Bhavna's kitchen garden thrives, and this year's harvest includes guavas, three varieties of limes, chiles and an array of herbs. Last winter she planted broccoli, lettuce and rocket, but the peacocks ate the lot. The family also own farmland, but this year's maize harvest benefitted only the antelope that feasted on much of it.

In the night I hear beating of drums and raucous singing in the village. It's the festival of Dusshera, a time when towering effigies of demons filled with firecrackers are burned. The next day, there's an air of anticipation as I walk through the village. Diwali is just three weeks away, potters are shaping and drying clay lamps, shops are well stocked with brightly colored fabrics, flowers are piled high on carts and vegetables haggled over. The season has turned, and the sting of summer's relentless heat is on its way out. Now is the time for matchmaking, weddings and feasting.

Deoghar village life.

1. Bhavna with her finished dish.

2. Bhavna and Shatranjai's shaded swimming pool at Dev Shree.

3. Bhaji (left) and Rukmini both live in Deogarh and often help with the cooking at Dev Shree.

POPADUM CURRY Serves 4

BHAVNA SINGH

This Rajasthani dish was traditionally made with homemade popadums, prepared from pounded ground lentils. It's a laborious process so most people now use store-bought varieties. The yogurt and turmeric lend a pleasing tartness to the masala—I'm especially taken by the way in which the crisp popadums soften in the masala until they have the texture of cooked pasta. This is Bhavna Singh's family recipe, and it's one that celebrates the creativity of home cooks living in a region where fresh vegetables may not always be easy to find.

---

1 large onion, coarsely chopped

1 oz (25 g) ginger root, peeled and coarsely chopped

6 garlic cloves, coarsely chopped

⅔ cup (150 ml) full-fat Greek yogurt

½ tsp ground turmeric

¾ tsp Kashmiri chile powder

1 tsp ground coriander

4 tbsp sunflower oil

1 tsp cumin seeds

2 cups (500 ml) hot water

2 tbsp chopped cilantro leaves

5 plain popadums, ready-to-eat

sea salt

Indian flatbreads or boiled rice, and a pickle, such as eggplant pickle (see page 287), to serve

Put the onion in a small food processor and pour over enough water to cover. Process until it resembles a slack paste. (You can alternatively use a handheld immersion blender and a bowl for this.) Transfer the paste to a small bowl and leave to one side.

Put the ginger and garlic in the food processor, cover with water and blend in the same way and set aside.

Mix the yogurt with the turmeric, chile powder and ground coriander, and season with salt.

Heat the oil in a karahi or wok on medium-high heat, add the cumin seeds and swirl them around in the hot oil for 30 seconds, until they release a nutty aroma. Add the onion paste and fry for 8–10 minutes, stirring often, until the water has evaporated and the onion is golden.

Turn down the heat to medium, add the ginger-garlic paste and fry for 2 minutes, stirring all the time, until any water has evaporated and it starts to brown. Spoon in half the spiced yogurt, cook for 1 minute, stirring, then add the rest. Continue cooking for 3–4 minutes, until the masala darkens and beads of oil appear around the side of the pan.

Pour over the hot water, add the chopped cilantro and simmer uncovered for 3–4 minutes—the masala should be thin and broth-like in consistency. Break the crisp popadums into large pieces and add them to the pan. Turn off the heat, cover the pan and leave the popadum pieces for 5 minutes, until they have softened. Serve with Indian flatbreads or boiled rice, and eggplant pickle.

ACCOMPA

ANIMENTS

CORNMEAL FLATBREADS

Makes 16

This popular Punjabi bread is cooked on a griddle and served with lots of melted butter. It's a classic partner to ginger-spiced greens (see page 31). Use *makki ka atta* (very finely ground Indian cornmeal) for this recipe, rather than the coarser-grained "fine cornmeal" that you'll find in supermarkets. *Makki ka atta* is available from South Asian grocery stores.

1⅔ cups (250 g) finely ground Indian cornmeal (*makki ka atta*)

⅔ cup (70 g) chapati flour or wholewheat flour

½ rounded tsp carom seeds (*ajwain*; optional)

1 tsp Kashmiri chile powder

1 tsp sea salt

⅓ cup (70 g) ghee (see page 18)

5 tbsp (70 g) unsalted butter

Sift the cornmeal into a bowl and mix it with the chapati flour, carom seeds (if using), chile powder and salt. Add about ¾ cup (180 ml) of warm water, or enough to make a soft but not sticky dough and firmly knead it in the bowl until smooth. Cover with a cloth or an upturned plate and leave to one side for 20–30 minutes to rest.

Divide the dough into 16 x 1 oz (30 g) portions and shape each one into balls with your hands. Cover them with a cloth to stop them from drying out.

I find it easier to roll this dough between two sheets of plastic (an opened-up freezer bag works well) or parchment paper. Dust one side of the plastic sheet or parchment paper with cornmeal. Put a dough ball on it and lightly dust with more flour. Cover with another plastic sheet or more parchment paper and roll the dough to a 4 in (11 cm) diameter circle, about ⅛ in (3 mm) thick. You can neaten any frayed edges with your fingers.

Heat a sturdy griddle or frying pan on medium heat and, when it's hot, add a teaspoon of ghee. Carefully lift the cornmeal disc from the plastic sheet or parchment paper onto the griddle and cook on one side for 2–3 minutes, until it starts to color.

Flip the bread over with a spatula and dot another teaspoon of ghee around the roti's edge and cook for 2–3 more minutes until it turns a speckled deep golden. Repeat this process with the remaining dough, keeping the rotis warm between the folds of a tea towel. Spread them with the butter and serve straight away.

CHAPATIS Makes 12

Home-cooked chapatis are usually thin and soft and cooked on a griddle, but across Punjab and the north, the raw dough might be taken to a communal clay oven (tandoor) to be cooked. These rotis will be thicker and more substantial. Either way, they're a much-loved staple.

2¼ cups (250 g) chapati flour (*chapati atta*), or 1 cup (125 g) wholewheat flour mixed with 1 cup (125 g) all-purpose flour, plus extra for dusting and rolling

1 tsp sunflower oil

½ tsp sea salt

Mix the flour, oil and salt in a mixing bowl. Gradually add enough water (about ½ cup/120 ml) to make a firm dough. Turn it out onto a floured surface and knead it well for 7–10 minutes, until smooth. Return the dough to a clean, dry bowl, cover with an upturned plate or dry cloth and leave it to rest for 30 minutes.

Add a little more chapati or all-purpose flour if the dough looks sticky, then divide it into 12 equal-sized balls. Sprinkle each one with flour.

Heat a dry griddle on medium heat. Put 3 tablespoons of extra flour in a small bowl. Using the palms of your hands, flatten one of the dough balls into a disc and dip both sides in the flour. Now roll it into a circle, about ⅛ in (2.5 mm) thickness and 5–5½ in (12–14 cm) in diameter.

Slap the dough disc onto the hot griddle and cook it for 1 minute, or until small air pockets appear on the surface. Turn the chapati over with your fingers (take care) or with a palette knife or tongs and continue cooking for about a further 1½ minutes, until the chapati picks up flecks of color.

Gently press the bread with a clean cloth as it cooks on the griddle— the chapati should swell with hot air. Keep turning the bread as it cooks. Home cooks will usually finish their chapatis on an open gas flame for a few seconds, which will make them puff—it does take practice though. Repeat for the remaining dough balls, keeping the cooked chapatis warm by wrapping them in a cloth or in foil.

ACCOMPANIMENTS

LAYERED MINT PARATHAS Makes 6

Lachha roughly translates as "layers," of which these parathas have many! They take time to make, but the results make the extra effort worthwhile.

---

1 cup (125 g) all-purpose flour

½ tsp sea salt

1 cup (125 g) chapati flour or wholewheat flour, plus extra for rolling

2 tbsp melted ghee (see page 18), plus about 6 tbsp extra for layering and cooking

½ oz (15 g) mint leaves, shredded

plain yogurt and pickle, such as eggplant pickle (see page 287), to serve

FOR THE SPICE MIX

1 small handful mint leaves

2 tsp roasted and ground cumin seeds

1½ tsp roasted and ground fennel seeds

2 tsp mango powder (*amchoor*)

½ tsp coarsely ground black pepper

½ tsp Kashmiri chile powder

1 tsp sea-salt flakes

Sift the flour and salt into a mixing bowl and add the chapati or wholewheat flour, the melted ghee and shredded mint. Add a scant ½ cup (100 ml) of water, or enough to make a soft but not sticky dough and firmly knead it in the bowl until smooth. Cover with a cloth and leave to one side for 30 minutes to rest.

For the spice mix, heat a sturdy, small frying pan on low heat. Add the whole mint leaves and cook, stirring all the time, until they are dry and crisp. Tip them into a small bowl, then crumble to a powder with your fingers.

Add the ground cumin, ground fennel, mango powder, pepper, chile powder and salt and leave to one side.

Divide the dough into 6 equal portions and shape each one with your hands into a ball. Keep the dough balls covered with a cloth so that they don't dry out.

Flatten one of the balls on your palm into a 2½ in (6 cm) diameter disc, about ¾ in (2 cm) thick. Dip both sides in chapati or wholewheat flour. Roll out the dough on a work surface to a 7½ in (19 cm) diameter circle, about ⅛ in (3 mm) thick. Brush the disc with melted ghee, then sprinkle with 2 teaspoons of the spice mix.

Fold in one side of the circle by ½ in (1 cm), then fold back by ½ in (1 cm). Keep folding forwards and backwards, in the same way as you would for a paper fan, until you have a strip of layered dough.

Using your fingers, coil the strip of dough into a spiral—like a pinwheel. Put the coil on a floured surface and roll it out again to a 5½ in (14 cm) diameter circle. Repeat this process with the remaining dough balls.

Heat a sturdy griddle on medium-high heat and add 1 teaspoon of ghee. Using a spatula, lift the paratha onto the griddle and cook it on one side for about 2–3 minutes, until it turns a speckled golden.

Flip the paratha over and spread it with another teaspoon of ghee. Cook for another 2–3 minutes until golden. Serve piping hot. Repeat for the remaining parathas. Serve them with creamy yogurt and eggplant pickle on the side.

LENTIL PURIS Makes 14–16

Most often made in Uttar Pradesh and Rajasthan, *bedmis* are a fried bread enriched with ground lentils cut through with green chiles and seasoned with spices, which include ginger, tangy mango powder and ground fennel seeds. Serve them with potato, onion & tomato masala (see page 221) and crushed zucchini with tamarind & jaggery (see page 239).

---

1 cup (125 g) chapati flour (*chapati atta*) or wholewheat flour

1 cup (125 g) all-purpose flour

½ tsp Kashmiri chile powder

2 tsp mango powder (*amchoor*)

1 tsp ground coriander

1 tsp roasted and ground fennel seeds

½ tsp roasted and ground cumin seeds

¼ tsp ground asafoetida (*heeng*; optional)

FOR THE LENTILS

⅓ cup (75 g) skinned, white urad lentils (*dhuli urad dal*) or split yellow moong beans (*moong dal*), soaked in hot water for 3 hours

¾ oz (20 g) ginger root, peeled and coarsely chopped

2 green chiles, deseeded and coarsely chopped

1 tsp sea salt

scant ½ cup (100 ml) warm water, plus extra if needed

2 tbsp sunflower oil, plus 2 cups (500 ml) for oiling and deep-frying

Mix both the flours with the chile powder, mango powder, coriander, fennel, cumin and asafoetida (if using).

For the lentils, drain the soaked lentils in a colander and transfer them to a food processor with the ginger, green chiles and salt. Add the scant ½ cup (100 ml) of warm water and blend to a paste.

Make a well in the flour mixture and add the lentil paste and the 2 tablespoons of oil. Firmly knead everything to a firm dough. You may need to add a couple of tablespoons of warm water if the dough is too dry.

Lightly oil your worktop and knead the dough with the heel of your hand until smooth. Cover it with an upturned plate or cloth and leave the dough to rest at room temperature for at least 30 minutes.

Knead the dough again and divide it into 16 balls, each about the size of a golf ball. Keep the balls covered with a cloth to prevent them from drying out.

Slightly flatten the top of each ball into a disc and roll it out on a lightly oiled surface to a 5 in (13 cm) diameter circle, about ⅛ in (3 mm) thick. You can flip the dough over a couple of times as you roll it.

To deep-fry, fill a large wide, sturdy pot no more than two-thirds full with oil. The oil is ready for frying when it reaches 350°F (180°C) on a food thermometer, or when a cube of bread dropped into the oil browns in 30 seconds.

Carefully slide a *bedmi* into the oil and, using a spatula, gently press on the top so that it puffs as it cooks. After about 30 seconds, flip the bread over and cook for a further 15 seconds. Drain the bread on paper towels and repeat for the remaining dough. *Bedmi* are best served straight away, but they can be made in advance and enjoyed at room temperature too.

LUCHIS Makes 18–20

Popular in West Bengal, *luchis* are deep-fried and similar to puris, but made with all-purpose flour instead of chapati flour. I like to serve them with classic Bengali dishes, such as shrimp in coconut masala (see page 110) or cauliflower with ginger, turmeric & orange (see page 224).

---

2 cups (250 g) all-purpose flour

½ tsp sea salt

2 tbsp sunflower oil, plus extra for oiling and about 2 cups (500 ml) for deep-frying

Sift the flour and salt in a bowl, work in the oil with your fingers, then add ⅓-a scant ½ cup (80–100 ml) of cold water, or enough to make a firm dough—its texture should be stiffer than for shortcrust pastry.

Firmly knead the dough in the bowl for about 5 minutes until smooth, then shape it into a ball and transfer to a clean, lightly oiled bowl. Cover with a cloth or upturned plate and leave to one side for 30 minutes to rest. Then, knead the dough again for 2–3 minutes and divide the dough into 18–20 balls, each about 1½ in (4 cm) in diameter.

Slightly flatten the top of each ball and roll it out on an oiled surface to a 4 in (11 cm) diameter circle, about ⅛ in (3 mm) thick. You can flip the dough over a couple of times as you roll it. Repeat the process with the remaining dough balls.

To deep-fry, fill a large, wide, sturdy pot no more than two-thirds full with oil. The oil is ready for frying when it reaches 350°F (180°C) on a food thermometer, or when a cube of bread dropped into the oil browns in 30 seconds. Lower a *luchi* gently into the oil—it will sizzle and rise up to the top within a few seconds. Using a spatula, lightly press on the top of the *luchi* so that it puffs as it cooks. Flip the *luchi* over after about 30 seconds and fry for another 30 seconds—it should barely be tinged golden when cooked. Drain on paper towels and repeat the process with the remaining dough balls. *Luchis*, like puris, are best served straight away, but can be made in advance and enjoyed at room temperature too.

TOMATO-CHILE SAUCE
Makes 2 cups (500 ml) (8–10 servings)

3 dried Kashmiri red chiles

4 tbsp sunflower oil

1½ in (4 cm) cinnamon stick

1 large onion, chopped

8 large garlic cloves, peeled

1½ oz (50 g) ginger root, peeled and finely grated

2 lb 3 oz (1 kg) tomatoes, coarsely chopped

1 tsp Kashmiri chile powder

1 tsp garam masala (see page 19)

⅔ cup (125 g) sugar

⅔ cup (150 ml) white wine vinegar

1½ cups (350 ml) hot water

sea salt

Using scissors, snip the tops off the chiles and shake out most of the seeds.

Heat the oil in a large pot set over a medium-high heat and fry the chiles and cinnamon stick for 30 seconds, until the chiles swell and darken. Turn the heat to medium-low, add the onion and soften without browning for about 10 minutes.

Add the whole garlic cloves and grated ginger and fry for 1 minute, then stir in the chopped tomatoes, chile powder, garam masala, sugar, vinegar and hot water. Season with salt and simmer, uncovered, for about 45 minutes, stirring occasionally, until most of the liquid has evaporated and the tomatoes have thickened and reduced to a pulp.

Turn off the heat, discard the cinnamon stick and leave the tomatoes to cool before transferring them to a blender. Blend the sauce until smooth, then pass it through a sieve to remove any seeds and skin. Adjust the seasoning and add more sugar if it's too tart. It will keep for 3–5 days in the fridge, and will freeze well too. Serve warm or at room temperature.

PEANUT & COCONUT CRUMBS
Serves 6

3 tbsp unsalted peanuts, skinned

3 large garlic cloves, peeled

1 tsp white sesame seeds

2 tbsp desiccated coconut

½ tsp roasted and ground cumin seeds

½ tsp Kashmiri chile powder

sea salt

Heat a sturdy frying pan over medium heat and roast the peanuts for 4–5 minutes, stirring all the time, until they pick up flecks of color.

Turn the heat to low, add the peeled garlic cloves and cook until they are also flecked with color. Stir in the sesame seeds and desiccated coconut and continue cooking, stirring all the time, for 1–2 minutes, until golden.

Take the pan off the heat and add the cumin and chile powder and season with salt. Leave to one side to cool, then grind everything in a small food processor to a coarse powder. Store in a lidded jar—it will keep for 3–4 weeks at room temperature.

ACCOMPANIMENTS

FRESH CILANTRO & MINT RELISH Serves 6

1 large handful of cilantro, leaves and stems coarsely chopped

2 tbsp chopped mint leaves

1 small green pepper, deseeded and coarsely chopped

2 tsp sugar, plus extra if needed

1 tsp roasted and ground cumin seeds

¾ oz (20 g) ginger root, peeled and coarsely chopped

2 large garlic cloves, coarsely chopped

1 green chile, coarsely chopped

juice of 1 large lime, plus extra if needed

sea salt

Blend all the ingredients in a blender with and a small ladleful of water until smooth. Season with salt and aim for a sweet and tangy flavor—you may need to add more sugar or lime juice to get the balance right. Transfer the relish to a bowl, cover and keep it in the fridge until you're ready to serve. This relish tastes best on the day you make it.

TAMARIND & DATE SAUCE Makes 1¼ cups (300 ml) (4–6 servings)

5½ oz (150 g) wet, seedless tamarind

4½ oz (125 g) pitted dates

6 oz (175 g) jaggery or light brown sugar, plus extra to taste if needed

1 tsp ground ginger

½ tsp garam masala (see page 19)

1 tsp roasted and ground cumin seeds

sea salt

Break up the tamarind and put it in a saucepan with the dates, jaggery or sugar and enough water to cover—about 2 cups (500 ml). Bring the sauce to a simmer and cook for 20–30 minutes, adding extra water if the sauce looks like catching, until the tamarind and dates are really soft and pulpy.

Remove the pan from the heat and push the sauce through a sieve to remove any fibers.

Stir in the ginger, garam masala and cumin, and season with salt. Taste the sauce—it should have a sweet-and-sour flavor. Add more jaggery or sugar if it isn't sweet enough. The sauce will keep for 2–3 days in the fridge or 3–4 months in the freezer. Serve chilled.

FRESH RED CHILE CHUTNEY   Serves 6–8

3½ oz (100 g) fresh red chiles, deseeded and coarsely chopped

1 tsp fine sea salt, plus extra to season

¼ tsp fenugreek seeds, coarsely ground in a mortar with a pestle

3½ tbsp hot water

2 tbsp sunflower oil

½ tsp brown mustard seeds

1 dried Kashmiri red chile

¼ tsp ground turmeric

1 tsp sugar

2 tsp tamarind pulp (see page 21)

sea salt

Put the chopped red chiles in a small food processor and add the salt, fenugreek and hot water, then blend everything to a coarse paste. You can alternatively use a handheld immersion blender and a bowl for this.

Heat the oil in a small frying pan over medium-high heat, add the mustard seeds and fry for about 30 seconds, until they stop popping, then add the whole chile and fry for another 30 seconds, until it darkens. Turn off the heat and stir in the turmeric, sugar and tamarind pulp, followed by the red chile paste. Season with salt. Leave to one side to cool before serving at room temperature. This chutney will keep covered in the fridge for 2-3 days.

SESAME & GREEN CHILE CHUTNEY   Serves 4–6

1 tbsp white sesame seeds

3 green chiles, deseeded and chopped

2 tbsp coarsely chopped mint leaves

1 red onion, coarsely chopped

2 garlic cloves, coarsely chopped

1 rounded tsp sugar

sea salt

Roast the sesame seeds in a dry pan over medium heat, stirring all the time, until golden. Transfer them to a small food processor or blender and add the green chiles, mint, onion, garlic, sugar and salt to season. Add a splash of water and blend until smooth. This chutney is best enjoyed on the day it is made.

COCONUT, CILANTRO & PEANUT CHUTNEY

Serves 6–8

¾ cup (100 g) unsalted peanuts, skinned

½ cup (100 g) frozen grated coconut, defrosted

1 oz (25 g) ginger root, peeled and coarsely chopped

1 green chile, coarsely chopped with seeds

1 large handful of cilantro, leaves and stems coarsely chopped

1 tbsp tamarind pulp (see page 21), or to taste

sea salt

FOR TEMPERING

2 tbsp sunflower oil

1 tsp brown mustard seeds

½ tsp skinned white urad lentils (*dhuli urad dal*; optional)

about 15 fresh curry leaves

1 dried Kashmiri red chile

Heat a dry, sturdy frying pan over medium heat, add the peanuts and cook, stirring all the time, for about 5 minutes, until they pick up flecks of color. Transfer them to a plate and leave to cool.

Put the peanuts, coconut, ginger, green chile and cilantro in a blender. Pour in ⅔ cup (150 ml) of water and blend to a paste. You might need a little extra water to help break down the ingredients. Tip the paste into a heatproof bowl and stir in enough tamarind pulp to sharpen. Season with salt.

For tempering, heat the oil in a small frying pan over a medium-high heat and add the mustard seeds—they should start popping straight away. After 30 seconds, or when the popping subsides, add the lentils, if using, the curry leaves and whole red chile, and stir and fry for another 30 seconds, until the spices are fragrant and the lentils are golden.

Tip everything, including the oil, into the coconut chutney and stir to combine. Serve at room temperature. This chutney will keep covered in the fridge for 2–3 days.

EGGPLANT PICKLE

Makes 1 lb 5 oz (600 g)

2 round eggplants, cut into 1 in (3 cm) pieces

2 tbsp sea salt

2 cups (500 ml) sunflower oil for deep-frying, plus extra for sealing

6 garlic cloves, thinly sliced

1½ oz (50 g) ginger root, peeled and finely grated

scant ½ cup (100 ml) white wine vinegar

FOR THE MASALA

1 tsp brown mustard seeds

1 tsp fennel seeds

1 tsp roasted and ground cumin seeds

¼ tsp fenugreek seeds

¾ tsp ground turmeric

1 tsp Kashmiri chile powder

about 30 fresh curry leaves

2 tbsp tamarind pulp (see page 21)

2 tbsp jaggery or light brown sugar

Mix the eggplants with the salt and transfer them to a large colander with a shallow tray underneath to catch any juices. Leave for 6 hours, or overnight if you have the time.

Drain and discard any liquid, and using your hands, squeeze the eggplant pieces to extract as much moisture as possible. Pat them dry with paper towels.

To deep-fry, fill a wok or karahi no more than two-thirds full with oil. The oil is ready for frying when it reaches 350°F (180°C) on a food thermometer, or when a cube of bread dropped into the oil browns in 30 seconds. Fry the eggplants over medium heat for 3-4 minutes, until golden, then drain them on paper towels and leave the oil to cool. You may need to do this in batches.

Meanwhile, make the masala. Heat a sturdy frying pan or griddle and roast the mustard, fennel, cumin and fenugreek seeds for about 30 seconds, until they take on a lovely, warm aroma. In a mortar, using a pestle, grind the spices to a powder and stir in the turmeric and chile powder.

Once the oil from deep-frying the eggplants has cooled, measure ⅔ cup (150 ml) and heat it in a pot over a medium-high heat. Add the curry leaves and fry them for 30 seconds—they will splutter and crackle, so step back as they hit the oil.

To finish the pickle, turn the heat to medium, add the garlic and ginger and fry for 1 minute. Pour in the vinegar and bubble for 5-7 minutes, until most of it has evaporated, leaving behind 2 tablespoons. Turn down the heat to low and stir in the ground spices, followed by the tamarind and jaggery or sugar.

Return the eggplants to the pot, stir well and spoon the pickle into a sterilized jar, leaving a ¾ in (2 cm) gap at the top.

Once the pickle has cooled, pour a ½ in (1 cm) depth of sunflower oil over the eggplants—the pieces should be submerged in oil. This pickle tastes best if left to mature for 3-4 days before opening, and it will keep for 6 months in the refrigerator.

TOMATO & MINT RAITA Serves 4

1⅓ cups (300 g) full-fat Greek yogurt

3 scallions, green and white parts finely chopped

¾ cup (125 g) cherry tomatoes, quartered

1 small garlic clove, crushed

squeeze of lime

1 tsp sugar

1 tbsp chopped mint leaves

¾ tsp roasted and ground cumin seeds

sea salt and freshly ground black pepper

Mix all the ingredients and season with salt and pepper. Serve chilled.

KACHUMBER Serves 4–6

1 cucumber, halved lengthways, deseeded and diced

3 tomatoes, quartered, deseeded and chopped

1 red onion, finely chopped

juice of 2 limes

¾ tsp roasted and ground cumin seeds

1 red or green chile, deseeded and finely chopped

½ tsp freshly ground black peppercorns

2 tsp sugar

3 tbsp chopped cilantro leaves

sea salt

Combine the diced cucumber, tomato and onion in a bowl.

In a separate bowl, mix the lime juice with the ground cumin, red or green chile, pepper, sugar and cilantro and pour this over the salad. Stir well to coat the ingredients and leave to steep for 15 minutes so that the flavors mellow. Season with salt just before serving.

CARROT SALAD Serves 4

2 carrots, coarsely grated

1 tomato, chopped

1 banana shallot, finely sliced

2 tbsp chopped mint leaves

1 tbsp chopped cilantro leaves

1 green chile, deseeded and finely chopped

½ tsp roasted and ground cumin seeds

½ tsp freshly ground black peppercorns

2 tsp sugar, plus extra to taste, if needed

juice of 1 large lime, plus extra to taste, if needed

sea salt

Mix all the ingredients and season with salt. Aim for a sweet-sour flavor, adding more sugar or lime juice if needed. Serve chilled.

GREEN MANGO SALAD Serves 6

10½ oz (300 g) green, underripe mangoes, peeled, pitted and diced

1 small red onion, finely chopped

1 green chile, deseeded and finely chopped

¼ tsp Kashmiri chile powder

½ tsp roasted and ground cumin seeds

1–2 tbsp jaggery or brown sugar

2 tbsp chopped cilantro leaves

sea salt

Using your hands, mix the diced mangoes with all the ingredients apart from the chopped cilantro and season with salt. Leave the salad to one side to steep for 1 hour and then stir in the cilantro just before serving.

ACCOMPANIMENTS 289

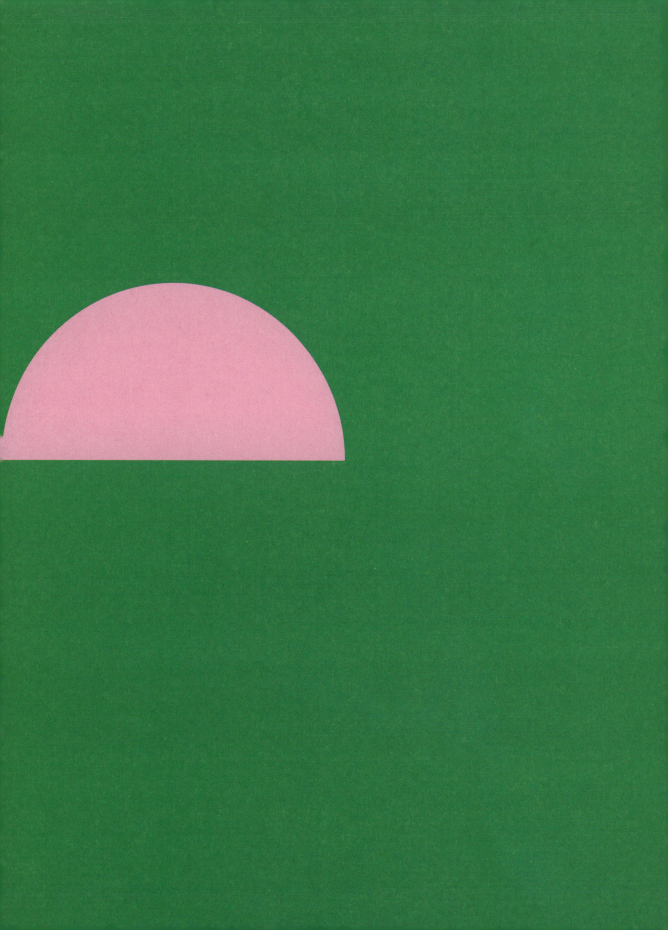

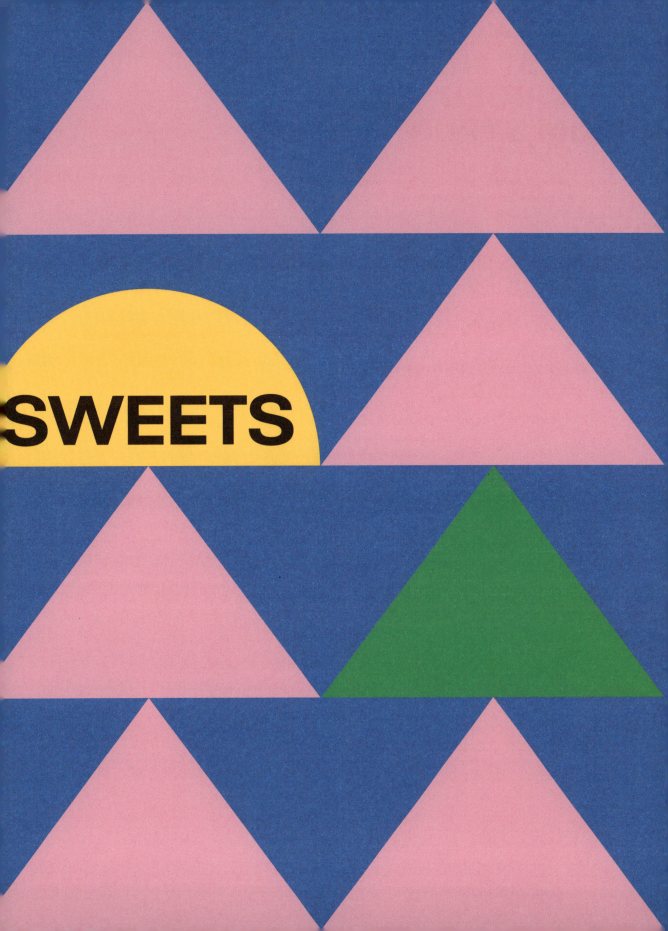

ROAST FIGS IN SPICED RUM SYRUP

Serves 4–6

I was sent to Pune in 1997 by the Taj Hotel for a management training course. The program included meditation, sports and even dream-analysis sessions. Hosted in a beautiful heritage home, surrounded by tended lawns, I've rarely been as relaxed, just sitting in the veranda under a slow-whirring ceiling fan with the sunshine warming my back. This is where I first tasted this delicious dessert. From my vantage point, I watched the chef pluck plump figs from a nearby tree and carry them a few yards to the kitchen. There, they gently bubbled in cinnamon-spiced rum, sweetened with toffee-like jaggery and were served warm, enrobed in a cloak of chilled cream. There are few desserts as restorative as this one.

½ cup (125 ml) golden or dark rum

2½ oz (75 g) jaggery or light brown sugar

2 star anise

1 in (3 cm) cinnamon stick

4 green cardamom pods, pierced

1 strip of pared orange zest

6 large figs

crème fraîche or light cream, to serve

Pour the rum and ½ cup (125 ml) of water into a saucepan and add the jaggery or sugar. Dissolve the jaggery or sugar on low heat, then add the star anise, cinnamon, cardamom and orange zest. Boil, uncovered, until the syrup has reduced and thickened to a coating consistency—this should take about 15 minutes.

Trim and discard the tips of the figs and stand the fruit in a small roasting pan or heatproof dish. Preheat the oven to 340°F (170°C).

Pour the hot syrup over the figs, transfer the pan to the oven and cook for about 20 minutes, spooning over the juices every 10 minutes. The figs are ready when they are tender but still hold their shape.

Divide the fruit amog six dessert bowls. Strain the syrup through a sieve, discard the spices and orange zest, and spoon the warm syrup equally over the figs. Serve warm with crème fraîche or a drizzle of cream.

PANEER, CARDAMOM & ROSEWATER SWEETMEAT

Serves 8–10

This Indian sweetmeat, known as *kalakand,* is enjoyed across the country and, unlike many traditional offerings, it's quick to make. Condensed milk is a magic, time-saving ingredient, and the slightly tart flavor of paneer takes the edge off its sweetness. I recommend using homemade, rather than store-bought paneer—its spongy, crumbly texture will ensure that the *kalakand* remains soft.

---

6 green cardamom pods, seeds removed

1 tsp sugar

9 oz (250 g) homemade paneer (see page 20), roughly crumbled

1 x 14 oz (400 g) can of condensed milk

few drops of rose water

3 tbsp chopped pistachios

In a mortar, using the pestle, grind the cardamom seeds with the sugar to a coarse powder. Leave to one side.

Heat the paneer, condensed milk and ground cardamom in a karahi or wok set on medium heat, stirring often to prevent sticking, until the liquid comes to a boil. Turn the heat to low and cook, stirring all the time, for 5–7 minutes, until the mixture thickens and leaves the sides of the pan. Aim for a soft dropping consistency with a grainy texture. Turn off the heat and add just enough rose water to lend a subtle flavor. Leave the *kalakand* to cool and thicken in the pan for 10 minutes.

Line a baking sheet with parchment paper and spread the sweetmeat into a rectangle, about ¾ in (2 cm) thick. Evenly press the chopped pistachios onto the surface and leave the sweetmeat to cool before chilling it in the fridge for 2–3 hours.

Once the *kalakand* is firm, cut it into 1 in (3 cm) squares. It will keep for 3–4 days in the fridge in an airtight box and is best served at room temperature.

PISTACHIO & CARDAMOM COOKIES

Makes 18–20

Even today, street hawkers in the old quarter of many cities will carry or push makeshift charcoal ovens fashioned out of tin drums. Cookies such as *nan khatai* are baked on the go in these ovens and sold while still warm in paper bags. I've added semolina to this dough for crunch and a little chickpea (gram) flour to provide toasty flavor and crumbly texture.

---

3 tbsp pistachios

⅓ cup (40 g) self-rising flour, sifted

¼ cup (25 g) chickpea (gram) flour, sifted

2 tbsp fine semolina

½ tsp baking powder

pinch of sea salt

6 green cardamom pods, seeds removed

⅓ cup (40 g) confectioners' sugar, sifted

7 tbsp (100 g) unsalted butter, softened

FOR THE TOPPING

1 tbsp pistachios, coarsely chopped

1 tsp granulated sugar

Put the pistachios in a food processor with the flour, chickpea flour, semolina, baking powder and salt and process until the nuts are finely ground.

In a mortar, using the pestle, grind the cardamom seeds with 1 teaspoon of the confectioners' sugar to a powder. Leave to one side.

Beat the butter, remaining confectioners' sugar and the ground cardamom until creamy, then stir in the dry ingredients, gently bringing everything together with your hands to a soft dough.

Using your hands, divide and shape the dough into 1 in (3 cm) diameter balls and arrange them on baking sheets lined with parchment paper, leaving room for the cookies to spread as they bake.

Slightly flatten the top of each ball with your fingers and press a few chopped pistachios in the middle, then sprinkle with sugar. Put the pans in the fridge for 20 minutes. Preheat the oven to 320°F (160°C).

Bake the cookies for 20–25 minutes, until golden, then leave them on the pans for 5 minutes to firm up before transferring them to a cooling rack. Once they are completely cooled, store in an airtight container.

HOT RUM PUNCH Serves 4–6

Making punch is an annual ritual in our house. Most people associate this drink with boisterous parties, but for me, the first mugful calls for a moment of private reflection. I remember past Christmases—the heady alcoholic vapors wafting from a cavernous pot; a quiet drink shared with my friend Geeta, and the unmistakable flavor of rum, spice and citrus.

9½ fl oz (275 ml) dark rum, plus extra to taste

1½ cups (350 ml) fresh orange juice, plus extra to taste

1 small red-skinned apple, quartered, cored and thickly sliced (skin-on)

6 cloves

½ oz (15 g) ginger, peeled and thinly sliced

1 blade of mace

6 green cardamom pods, pierced

1 star anise

2½ in (6 cm) cinnamon stick

2 strips of pared lemon zest

2 strips of pared orange zest

1½ oz (50 g) jaggery or light brown sugar, plus extra to taste

1 orange, segmented

Pour the rum, orange juice and ⅔ cup (150 ml) of water into a pot. Stud six apple slices with a clove each and put all the slices in the pot with the ginger, mace, cardamom pods, star anise and cinnamon. Add the lemon and orange zest and jaggery or sugar and bring the liquid to the boil. Turn down the heat to low, half-cover the pot and simmer for 10 minutes. Taste for sweetness, adding more sugar, rum or orange juice as necessary to get the balance right.

Ladle the punch into heatproof glasses or cups and add an apple slice and orange segment to each one. Serve hot.

BUTTERNUT SQUASH HALWA

Serves 6

Indian *halwa* is usually soft, rich with ghee, and eaten with a spoon. It's quite different from the firm-textured halvah made in Middle Eastern countries and doesn't include tahini. It's a versatile dessert and home cooks across South Asia make it with various grains, lentils and vegetables, and even with fruit such as papaya and watermelon. Pumpkins and squash make fabulous *halwa*—I love how they cook down, darken and caramelize in the pan.

---

2 lb 3 oz (1 kg) butternut squash halved lengthways, seeds and membrane removed

½ cup (100 g) ghee (see page 18)

8 green cardamom pods, seeds removed

1 tsp sugar

generous pinch of finely grated nutmeg

1 cup (250 ml) whole milk

2½ oz (75 g) jaggery or light brown sugar

2 tbsp blanched and shredded almonds

⅓ cup (50 g) raisins, soaked in hot water for 15 minutes

crème fraîche, to serve

Preheat the oven to 425°F (220°C). Put the butternut squash on a roasting pan lined with parchment paper and dot with 2 tablespoons of the ghee. Turn the squash over, so that the cut side faces downwards and cover the pan with foil. Roast for 1 hour, or until tender when pierced with a knife. Using a tablespoon, scoop out the flesh and mash it with a fork until smooth. Leave to one side.

In a mortar, using the pestle, grind the cardamom seeds with the sugar to a coarse powder. Leave to one side.

Heat the remaining ghee in a karahi or wok on medium heat. Add the squash, ground cardamom and nutmeg and pour over the milk. Cook, without a lid, stirring often, until the squash loses its milky appearance and has darkened. This should take about 20 minutes.

Add the jaggery or sugar and continue cooking for 10 minutes, stirring all the time, until droplets of ghee appear around the side of the pan and the halwa has a soft, dropping consistency.

Stir in half the almonds and half the drained raisins. Spoon the halwa into 6 small bowls and scatter with the remaining nuts and raisins. Serve piping hot with crème fraîche.

NORTHWEST INDIA

COCONUT, LIME & BUTTERMILK ICE CREAM

Makes 3 cups (750 ml)

This cooling ice cream with its sherbet-like texture is just the ticket for an Indian summer, and is complemented with the tropical flavors of lime, cardamom and coconut. Thanks to my friend Diana Henry for inspiring me to make this egg-free no-cook ice cream.

---

10 green cardamom pods, seeds removed

⅓ cup (125 g) superfine sugar

1¼ cups (300 ml) buttermilk

½ cup (125 ml) sour cream

1 cup (250 ml) coconut cream

3 limes, grated zest of 2 and juice of 3

¼ cup (25 g) desiccated coconut, roasted

In a mortar, using a pestle, grind the cardamom seeds with 1 teaspoon of the sugar to a coarse powder. Leave to one side.

Whisk the remaining sugar with the buttermilk, sour cream, coconut cream and lime zest and juice. Once blended, churn the mixture in an ice cream maker. When it is half set, add the desiccated coconut and continue churning until set. Transfer the ice cream to a freezer-proof container and put it in the freezer to store. Take it out of the freezer 15 minutes before serving, to soften.

If you don't have an ice-cream maker, put the mixture in a freezer-proof container and place it in the freezer, whisking every 2 hours to break up any ice crystals, until smooth and set. Remove from the freezer 15 minutes before serving, as before.

COMMUNITY ROOTS
WEST

JASMINE MARKER, DELHI

I'm in Delhi, it's a few days before Diwali, and the city is in a celebratory mood. This is Jasmine's busiest time of year. She's a home-based baker and caterer and has just delivered dozens of cupcakes for her daughter's Diwali school fête. I go upstairs to their second-floor apartment in upmarket South Delhi—the landing smells of melted chocolate, vanilla and toasting nuts. Inside, a pan of brownies is cooling on Jasmine's dining table, much to the excitement of her two children, who have just returned from school. The balcony at the front of the house is filled with leafy ferns, pots of greenery and hanging baskets. As the sun sets, I catch the heady smell from tiny blooms on the *saptaparni* tree, which also goes by the unfortunate name of devil's tree. I love this fragrance, although many don't—it signifies change, the ebbing of summer, and the start of the festive season.

Jasmine is from the Parsi community, a group that fled persecution in Persia, probably around the eighth and tenth centuries, and settled in Gujarat, in West India. They follow the Zoroastrian faith, one of the world's oldest religions. At its core is a belief that within each person is an ongoing battle between the forces of light and darkness. Followers are encouraged to focus on "good thoughts, good words and good deeds." Over time, the Parsi community adapted to the local Gujarati culture—and later, under British rule, they rose through the ranks to senior positions, often within the civil service. Today, most Parsis still live in and around Mumbai, and theirs is a story of success. A strong entrepreneurial spirit has brought financial reward—although the community is small, their contribution to industry, commerce and the arts is substantial.

Jasmine has just completed her final Diwali party order and looks relaxed as we chat over chai in her sitting room. Parsi cooking has been influenced by various communities, but still retains its roots in the tradition of ancient Persian kitchens. Over the centuries, locally grown ingredients from Gujarat and around Mumbai—coconut, tamarind, jaggery, chiles and spice blends—were incorporated into many recipes, so that flavors today reflect both a Persian and Indian heritage. In a nod to their Gujarati background, masalas often include herby pastes in dishes like *patrani macchi*—pomfret fillets, spread with a fresh chutney made from pounded coconut, cilantro, garlic and green chiles. Each fillet is wrapped in a banana leaf and steamed, and the package unleashes a puff of coconutty mist as it's opened at the table.

Jasmine tells me that certain Parsi dishes have a more direct link to Persia, such as meat cooked with dried fruits—as in *jardaloo*, a goat or chicken curry simmered with apricots. Then there's *dhansak*, for which Jasmine receives many catering orders. Here, assorted lentils are cooked with goat meat, vegetables and lots of spices, until the lentils break down and meld into

Diwali decorations for sale in a city market shop.

▶ the masala. Most home cooks add their own flourish—perhaps a spoonful of tamarind, a little jaggery and maybe more or fewer lentils.

Making *dhansak* isn't an exact science—it's a rich and time-consuming dish to prepare and is usually served for Sunday lunch. The accompaniments are traditional—an obligatory bowl of caramelized rice, a simple dal and salad. And chilled beer, followed by a much-needed siesta. Although a weekend favorite, *dhansak* is also made on the fourth day of mourning after someone dies, and for this reason, is never served at weddings or auspicious occasions. There are only around 700 Parsis in Delhi, and Jasmine's cooking provides a sense of connection, comfort and joy for this tiny community.

I'm interested in her curiosity, enthusiasm and flair for cooking European recipes. Historically, it wasn't uncommon for affluent Parsi families to have several cooks, each with a different culinary expertise. During the nineteenth and twentieth centuries, such delights as gratins, custards, cakes and pastries were regular features of Parsi party spreads. Jasmine often makes cutlets, *pattice*, with ground goat meat, bound with crushed potatoes, ginger, chopped cilantro, cumin and garam masala. They're shaped into round patties, crumbed, and fried— these ones sound a lot more fun than the potato patties I bought as a teenager from the corner shop in England.

She tells me that her mother and aunts were all good cooks but weren't that keen on baking. Because so few homes had ovens in the early 1980s, Jasmine, at twelve years old, baked her cakes in a portable substitute. It looks like a large, covered aluminum plant pot with holes in the top for the steam to escape. The magic happens in the bottom compartment—this is where the mud goes before it's heated on the stovetop. Next, a deep, ring-shaped metal mold is put over it, and the cake mixture spooned in. Once covered, the pot is returned to the stove and the cake bakes in heat from the mud. She laughs and says, "Even though I now use a modern electric oven, I could never part with this metal treasure—it will always have a home in my kitchen."

The cupcakes made for her daughter's school fête include *mawa* and were popularized by Irani bakeries in Mumbai more than a hundred years ago. They're made from cardamom-spiced Victoria sponge cake batter, enriched with crumbled *mawa*, which in India is also known as *khoya*. *Mawa* is milk that has been boiled until all the liquid has evaporated and only solids remain—it's also a key ingredient in Indian sweetmeats, such as fudgy blocks of *barfi*. Mine has a lovely, spiced Madeira cake quality, with just a hint of caramel.

I ask about the Parsi fondness for eggs. "We love eggs in all their guises, especially when they're cooked with vegetables—pretty much anything goes, and there are few dishes that can't be improved by them!" *Akoori*, Parsi-style scrambled eggs, are the family's Sunday morning favorite. Onions are fried until golden, and garlic-ginger paste and a little chopped tomato added, followed by ground coriander, cumin, turmeric and chile powder. Beaten eggs are folded in, and cooked until creamy, and then piled onto

▶ buttered toast. Home cooks will also make eggs frittata-style with spiced potatoes, or break them into a frying pan—like a shakshuka—with sliced, crisp-fried okra, onions, ginger and chopped tomatoes.

In the kitchen, Jasmine is cracking eggs into a bowl and making *lagan nu custard*. *Lagan* means wedding and if ever there is a special occasion custard, this is it. She smiles and says that there are two main events in a Parsi's life—the *navjote*, a coming-of-age ceremony, and marriage, and this pudding is often served at both.

She whisks eggs with sugar, and then pours in creamy warm milk, followed by caramelized condensed milk, grated nutmeg and a little vanilla. The custard is transferred to an ovenproof dish, slid into the oven and baked until almost set. She sprinkles sliced almonds over the top and then browns the custard under a hot broiler. I've rarely tasted an Indian dessert or sweetmeat without cardamom and have a feeling that the vanilla and nutmeg spicing here could be a throwback to the popularity of British baked custard back in the day.

Once it's ready, Jasmine carefully brings her dessert to the table to cool. We drink tea, Rohin, her husband, joins us, and the two children emerge from their bedrooms. All eyes are on the custard—it's simple to make, rich and creamy to taste, and although served at special occasions, it also ranks as the ultimate in childhood nursery desserts.

1. Jasmine with her baked *lagan nu* custard.

2. Caramelized top of *lagan nu* custard.

3. Although these diyas (clay lamps) aren't normally associated with the Parsis, they are often used to decorate homes during Diwali.

LAGAN NU CUSTARD Serves 6

JASMINE MARKER

Any sweet dish made with condensed milk is a winner for me. Jasmine made this creamy Parsi classic for me at her home in Delhi, and it's one of the best custards to sink a spoon into. She spiced her pudding with nutmeg, which works really well, but you could use ground cardamom instead and a little rose water if you fancy. The Parsi community are renowned for their love of eggs in both sweet and savory dishes—this custard is especially popular with children and often served at celebrations and auspicious events.

4¼ cups (1 liter) whole milk

4 eggs

1½ tbsp sugar

1 x 14 oz (400 g) can of caramelized condensed milk

½ tsp finely grated nutmeg

½ tsp vanilla extract

4 tbsp sliced almonds

1 tbsp confectioners' sugar

Bring the milk to a simmer in a wok or karahi and reduce its volume by half, which should take 20–30 minutes. Leave it to cool until lukewarm.

Preheat the oven to 340°F (170°C). Lightly whisk the eggs with the sugar until combined and add the warm milk, condensed milk, nutmeg and vanilla. Whisk to combine again.

Pour the custard into a shallow 4 cup (1 liter) baking dish, the sides of which should be about 1½ in (4 cm) high. Bake for about 30 minutes, until just set. Heat the broiler to its hottest setting.

Carefully take the custard out of the oven, scatter with sliced almonds and sift a thin layer of confectioners' sugar over the surface. Brown the top of the custard under the broiler, until speckled and caramelized. Leave to cool, then transfer the custard to the fridge and serve chilled.

MANGO, WHITE CHOCOLATE & PASSION FRUIT POTS

Serves 6–8

I like to serve these creamy mango pots with pistachio & cardamom cookies (see page 295), but you could layer the fruity cream with crushed amaretti cookies or gingernuts instead. Alphonso mangoes are noted for their floral flavor and I use them when in season. You can use canned pulp if you can't get hold of fresh, although it will need an extra squeeze of lime to cut the sweetness. Thanks to chef Justin Hammett for sharing this wonderful recipe when we worked together at the Royal Opera House in London.

---

9 oz (250 g) white chocolate, chopped

1¾ cups (400 g) mascarpone, lightly beaten

1¼ cups (300 ml) alphonso mango purée

juice of ½ lime, or to taste

3 ripe, wrinkled passion fruit

Pistachio and cardamom coookies (see page 295)

Melt the chocolate in a bowl set over a pan of simmering water, stirring from time to time—the bottom of the bowl should not touch the water. Leave to one side to cool but not set.

Beat the cooled, melted chocolate into the mascarpone, then stir in the mango purée and sharpen with lime juice to taste.

Spoon the mixture into ramekins or small glasses and transfer them to the fridge for at least 1 hour, or overnight if you have the time.

Halve the passionfruit, scoop out the pulp and spoon a little over the mango and white chocolate in each ramekin. Serve with the pistachio and cardamom cookies on the side.

CHERRY & PISTACHIO PUDDING
Serves 4

When my daughters were young, we'd escape Delhi's 45-degree summer heat and head to the Himalayan foothills. As we ascended, the tropical fruits of mangoes, lychees and melons would be replaced gradually with freshly plucked cherries, plums and apricots. We often stayed with friends in a village outside Shimla and it was in their kitchen that I baked this Indian-inspired riff on a clafoutis. Made without a weighing scale or measuring jug, and baked to perfection in an ancient Baby Belling oven with no functioning thermostat, this dessert is nothing less than a life-affirming triumph.

---

8 green cardamom pods, seeds removed

½ cup (100 g) sugar

3 tbsp unsalted butter, melted

1 lb (500 g) cherries, pitted

3 tbsp self-rising flour, sifted

⅔ cup (75 g) pistachios

2 eggs

2 egg yolks

1 cup (250 ml) whipping cream

1 tsp confectioners' sugar, for dusting

In a mortar, using the pestle, grind the cardamom seeds with 1 teaspoon of the sugar to a coarse powder. Leave to one side.

Preheat the oven to 350°F (180°C). Brush half the melted butter over the base and sides of a 4 cup (1 liter) capacity shallow baking dish and reserve the rest for the batter. Scatter the cherries over the bottom of the dish.

Put the flour, ground cardamom and pistachios in a food processor and pulse until the nuts are very finely chopped. Transfer everything to a mixing bowl.

In a large jug, lightly whisk the whole eggs and yolks with the remaining sugar, whipping cream and remaining melted butter. Gradually add the liquid to the dry ingredients and whisk until smooth.

Pour the batter over the cherries and bake in the oven for about 30 minutes, until the custard has just set but still has a slight wobble in the middle. Leave to cool for 10–15 minutes before dusting with confectioners' sugar. Serve warm.

ALMOND & SAFFRON BARFI

Makes 20 pieces (serves 6)

Fudgy in texture and marzipan-like in flavor, *barfi* is usually bought from neighborhood "*halwais*" (Indian confectioners) and served at festivals and auspicious events. Making your own takes a little effort, but the result will be far superior to most commercially produced varieties. I recommend using a karahi or wok to reduce the volume of milk rather than a heavy-based pot—the milk will evaporate more quickly and there's less chance of it catching on the bottom of the pot.

---

6 green cardamom pods, seeds removed

⅓ cup (75 g) sugar

4¼ cups (1 liter) whole milk

scant 1 cup (75 g) ground almonds

1-2 drops almond extract

¼ tsp saffron strands, soaked in 1 tbsp of warm milk for 1 hour

silver leaf, to decorate (optional)

In a mortar, using the pestle, grind the cardamom seeds with 1 teaspoon of the sugar to a coarse powder. Leave to one side.

Heat the milk in a large wok or karahi on medium heat and boil, stirring all the time, until it reduces to a thick cream. I like to use a metal spoon for this. Keep the heat on medium—you want the milk to reduce rapidly so that it retains its creamy color without browning. Keep scraping down the sides of the pan to prevent scorching.

After about 20-30 minutes, the milk will have thickened and left the sides of the pan and should have the consistency of scrambled eggs. Spoon this thick paste into a bowl and leave it to cool before chilling it for 2-3 hours. You should now have 8-9 oz (225-250 g) of reduced milk solids, which is known as "*khoya.*"

Coarsely grate the *khoya* using a box grater and transfer it to a sturdy pot or wok. Add the ground cardamom seeds and remaining sugar and cook on gentle heat, stirring all the time, for 10 minutes, until the sugar has dissolved and the mixture has thickened.

Turn off the heat and stir in the ground almonds, almond extract and the saffron and its soaking milk.

Line a baking pan with parchment paper, spoon the warm *barfi* mixture onto the paper and pat it out to a ½ in (1 cm) thick rectangle. Cover the *barfi* with a second sheet of parchment paper, and with a rolling pin, gently roll it to a 6 x 7½ in (16 x 19 cm) rectangle, about ¼ in (5 mm) thick. Leave to set for 3-4 hours—if your kitchen is very warm, you can transfer the pan to the fridge.

Remove the top layer of paper. If you are feeling extravagant, gild the *barfi* with silver leaf sheets. To do this, put a sheet onto the sweetmeat, silver side facing downwards and gently rub the back of the paper; the silver leaf will transfer onto the *barfi*. Try not to touch the silver leaf as it will stick to your fingers. Cut the *barfi* into 1 x 1½ in (3 x 4 cm) diamond shapes and store at room temperature in an airtight box. They will stay fresh for 3-4 days.

SPICED PEAR & HONEY CAKE
Serves 8

We'd make this cake for afternoon tea when I worked at the Taj Mahal Hotel in New Delhi. The addition of yeast provides a soft, rich and bread-like crumb, which works well with the honey-caramelized pears. I've used conference, corncorde or bosc pears here because they hold their shape on cooking.

FOR THE PEARS

8 cardamom pods, seeds removed

1 tsp sugar

6 tbsp (80 g) unsalted butter

2 lb 3 oz (1 kg) conference, concorde or bosc pears, peeled, cored and diced

2½ tbsp honey

½ tsp ground ginger

½ tsp ground cinnamon

3 tbsp dark rum

FOR THE CAKE

2½ sticks (270 g) unsalted butter, softened

2¼ cups (250 g) confectioners' sugar, sifted, plus extra for dusting

4 eggs

½ tsp fast-action instant yeast

2 cups (250 g) self-rising flour

crème fraîche or whipped heavy cream, to serve

Oil and line the base of a round 8½ in (21 cm) diameter, deep cake pan with parchment paper.

In a mortar, using the pestle, grind the cardamom seeds with the sugar to a coarse powder. Leave to one side.

Melt the butter in a karahi or wok on medium-high heat and add the diced pears. Turn the heat to high and fry them for about 5 minutes, stirring often, until they start to soften.

Add the honey and continue cooking, stirring frequently, for around 10–15 minutes, until the pears caramelize. Stir in ground cardamom, add the ginger and cinnamon and, after a few seconds, add the rum and cook for another 2–3 minutes, or until the alcohol has evaporated. Turn off the heat and leave the pears to cool.

Preheat the oven to 350°F (180°C). For the cake, in a bowl beat the butter and confectioners' sugar until light and creamy, and gradually add the eggs, one at a time, beating well between each addition. If the mixture looks like it is splitting, add a tablespoon of the flour to bring it back together.

Whisk the dried yeast with the (remaining) flour and fold it into the cake mixture with the cooled pears. Scrape the cake mixture into the prepared pan and bake the cake for 40 minutes, or until it is golden and firm to the touch.

Remove the cake from the oven and leave it to cool in the pan for 10 minutes before turning it out onto a rack and peeling off the paper. Dust with confectioners' sugar and serve with crème fraîche or whipped heavy cream.

PHIRNI WITH HONEY, ORANGE & SAFFRON SYRUP
Serves 8

This creamy, ground rice pudding is spiced with sweet cardamom and scented with rose water and is best served very cold, straight from the fridge. It's often presented unadorned as a simple family dessert, but raisins, extra nuts and glistening silver leaf can be added for special occasions. The credit for the orange and saffron syrup here goes to my dear friend and cooking writer, Diana Henry—it's a beauty.

FOR THE PHIRNI

8 green cardamom pods, seeds removed

½ cup (90 g) sugar

4¼ cups (1 liter) whole milk

½ cup (75 g) ground rice

scant ½ cup (100 ml) heavy cream

1 tsp rose water, or to taste

FOR THE SYRUP

¼ cup (100 g) honey

juice of 1 orange

pinch of saffron strands, soaked in 1 tbsp of hot water for 1 hour, to taste

In a mortar, using the pestle, grind the cardamom seeds with 1 teaspoon of the sugar to a coarse powder. Leave to one side.

Heat the milk and ground cardamom seeds in a heavy-based pot on medium heat.

When the milk comes to a simmer, whisk in the ground rice and continue whisking until it returns to a boil and thickens.

Turn down the heat to low and simmer for 5 minutes, stirring often until the rice loses its raw taste. Add the remaining sugar and cook, still stirring, for about 10 minutes, until it has a coating consistency.

Stir in the cream and simmer for 3-4 minutes, then turn off the heat and add just enough rose water for a light and floral flavor.

Spoon the *phirni* equally into 8 ramekins and cover, while still hot, with a baking sheet, then leave to cool. Chill for 2-3 hours, or overnight if you have time.

For the syrup, heat the honey and orange juice in a small saucepan on medium-low heat for 10 minutes, until the honey thickens and the syrupy bubbles become bigger. Take the pan off the heat and stir in just enough saffron and its soaking water to lend a delicate flavor, then leave the syrup to cool.

The syrup should now be a coating consistency—if it's too thick, add a spoonful of hot water to let it down. Drizzle a little syrup over each ramekin before serving.

INDEX

A
almonds
    almond & saffron barfi 310
    spiced yogurt 46
amchoor see mango powder
apricots
    chicken with apricots & cinnamon 140-1
asafoetida 177

B
barfi, almond & saffron 310
beans
    black-eyed peas in garlic tomato masala 260
    roast portobello mushrooms with cannellini beans 102
beef
    Goan short ribs in tamarind masala 213
    pot roast beef with vegetables 210
beet, pickled onion & 70
Bene Israel fish curry 123
Bengal gram, split
    chana dal with spinach 245
Bengali-style butternut squash 227
bhajias, corn 28
Bhattacharyya, Monika 110
Bihari lamb broth with dumplings 192-3
biryani
    Mom's chicken biryani 161
    shrimp biryani 112-13
black-eyed peas in garlic tomato masala 260
bread
    chapatis 279
    cornmeal flatbreads 278
    layered mint parathas 280
    lentil puris 281
    luchis 282
broccoli
    charred broccoli with mushrooms in coconut sauce 98
broths
    lentil, ginger & tamarind broth 54
    spiced broth 77
butter
    ghee 18
buttermilk
    coconut, lime & buttermilk ice cream 298
butternut squash
    Bengali-style butternut squash 227
    butternut squash halwa 297

C
cabbage with mustard seeds & curry leaves 223
cake, spiced pear & honey 311
Canaga, Anita de 81-3, 87
cannellini beans, roast portobello mushrooms with 102
caramel
    lagan nu custard 305
cardamom pods
    garam masala 19
    Kashmiri lamb with saffron, cardamom & red chiles 177
    paneer, cardamom & rosewater sweetmeat 293
    pistachio & cardamom cookies 295

carrots
    carrot salad 289
    chicken & vegetable poriyal 87
    pot roast beef with vegetables 210
    roast baby carrots with raisin & lime relish 27
cauliflower
    cauliflower cheese with scallions & jalapeño chiles 108-9
    cauliflower with ginger, turmeric & orange 224
Central India 11, 269-71
chaat masala 19
Chadha, Shama 37-9, 43
chana dal with spinach 245
chapatis 279
    ground lamb & green chile wraps 74
Chatterji, Snigdha 129-31, 133
cheese
    cauliflower cheese with scallions & jalapeño chiles 108-9
    see also paneer
cherry & pistachio pudding 309
chicken
    chicken & red pepper skewers 88
    chicken & vegetable poriyal 87
    chicken curry with tomatoes & tamarind 138
    chicken in cumin & ground coriander yogurt 135
    chicken in roasted coconut masala 139
    chicken with apricots & cinnamon 140-1
    chicken with coconut cream & lemongrass 162
    grilled chicken kebabs in spinach & cilantro cream 78
    homestyle Punjabi chicken curry 136
    Keralan roast chicken with cinnamon & curry leaves 154
    Mangalorean chicken curry 151-2
    Mom's chicken biryani 161
    Parsi chicken curry with potatoes 157
    red chile & curry leaf chicken 90
    roast chicken thighs with pomegranate & walnut yogurt 158
    roast spatchcock chicken with turmeric 142
chickpeas
    brown chickpeas with ginger & mango powder 246
chiles
    cauliflower cheese with scallions & jalapeño chiles 108-9
    corn bhajias 28
    fresh red chile chutney 285
    ground lamb & green chile wraps 74
    ground lamb kebabs with green chiles, ginger & garlic 69
    Kashmiri lamb with saffron, cardamom & red chiles 177
    kohlrabi cooked in mustard oil with green chiles 235
    lamb shanks with Kashmiri chiles & garlic 196
    Mangalorean chicken curry 151-2
    mussels in ginger, coconut & red chile broth 114
    red chile & curry leaf chicken 90
    red chile & garlic lamb 189
    salmon with red chile & ground fennel 124
    sesame & green chile chutney 285
    sweet potatoes with mango powder & green chiles 43
    tomato-chile sauce 283
chocolate
    mango, white chocolate & passion fruit pots 306
Chophyhj, Kaholi 91

chorizo
  clams with chorizo & red chile masala 116
  Goan chorizo rolls 93
chutney
  coconut, cilantro & peanut chutney 286
  fresh red chile chutney 285
  sesame & green chile chutney 285
cider
  pork ribs with mango, chile & ginger glaze 200
cilantro
  coconut, cilantro & peanut chutney 286
  fresh cilantro & mint relish 284
  grilled chicken kebabs in spinach & cilantro cream 78
  pandi pork curry 209
  peas simmered in fresh cilantro & peanut masala 238
cinnamon
  chicken with apricots & cinnamon 140–1
  cinnamon-spiced duck breasts with orange & ginger sauce 174
  garam masala 19
  Keralan roast chicken with cinnamon & curry leaves 154
  lamb koftas in tomato & cinnamon masala 195
clams with chorizo & red chile masala 116
coconut
  baby peppers with coconut, tamarind & sesame seeds 236
  chicken in roasted coconut masala 139
  clams with chorizo & red chile masala 116
  coconut, cilantro & peanut chutney 286
  Konkan egg curry 106
  Mangalorean chicken curry 151–2
  peanut & coconut crumbs 283
coconut cream
  chicken with coconut cream & lemongrass 162
  coconut, lime & buttermilk ice cream 298
coconut milk
  charred broccoli with mushrooms in coconut sauce 98
  hake steaks with coconut & tamarind 127
  mussels in ginger, coconut & red chile broth 114
  shrimp in coconut masala 110
colocasia *see* taro root
condensed milk
  lagan nu custard 305
  paneer, cardamom & rosewater sweetmeat 293
cookies, pistachio & cardamom 295
corn
  corn bhajias 28
  corn-on-the-cob with brown butter, chile & mango powder 50
cornmeal flatbreads 278
crème fraîche, cumin 27
cucumber
  kachumber 288
cumin seeds
  chaat masala 19
  cumin crème fraîche 27
  cumin potatoes 220
  panch phoran 20
curry
  Bene Israel fish curry 123
  Bihari lamb broth with dumplings 192–3
  braised lamb with onion & almonds 179
  chicken curry with tomatoes & tamarind 138
  chicken in roasted coconut masala 139
  hake steaks with coconut & tamarind 127
  homestyle Punjabi chicken curry 136
  Kashmiri lamb with saffron, cardamom & red chiles 177
  Keralan roast duck 172–3
  Konkan egg curry 106
  lamb cooked in yogurt with ginger & orange 180
  Mangalorean chicken curry 151–2
  Mom's chicken biryani 161
  pandi pork curry 209
  Parsi chicken curry with potatoes 157
  popadum curry 275
  shrimp in coconut masala 110
  see also masala
curry leaves
  baby peppers with coconut, tamarind & sesame seeds 236
  cabbage with mustard seeds & curry leaves 223
  chicken & vegetable poriyal 87
  cinnamon-spiced duck breasts with orange & ginger sauce 174
  Keralan roast chicken with cinnamon & curry leaves 154
  Konkan-style shrimp with mango 62
  mixed lentil dal 257
  oyster mushrooms with ginger, black pepper & curry leaves 228
  potato dumplings 56–7
  shrimp biryani 112–13
  red chile & curry leaf chicken 90
  red lentil & tamarind dal 259
  tomato dal with mustard seeds & curry leaves 267
custard, lagan nu 305

D
dal
  chana dal with spinach 245
  dry-cooked moong dal with dill 263
  mixed lentil dal 257
  moong dal 258
  moong dal with green mangoes 264
  red lentil & tamarind dal 259
  tomato dal with mustard seeds & curry leaves 267
dates
  tamarind & date sauce 284
Delhi 37–9, 183–5, 301–3
Dhingra, Achi 91
dill, dry-cooked moong dal with 263
drinks
  hot rum punch 296
duck
  cinnamon-spiced duck breasts with orange & ginger sauce 174
  Keralan roast duck 172–3
dumplings
  Bihari lamb broth with dumplings 192–3
  potato dumplings with peanut-garlic crumbs 56–7

E
eggs
  Konkan egg curry 106
  stuffed eggs with tomato & popped mustard seeds 32
eggplants
  eggplant pakoras 35
  eggplant pickle 287
Elias, Sunil & Suja 165–70, 172

INDEX 315

F

fennel seeds
  panch phoran 20
fenugreek
  ginger-spiced greens 31
figs
  roast figs in spiced rum syrup 292
fish
  battered Amritsari haddock 65
  Bene Israel fish curry 123
  fish fry 61
  hake steaks with coconut & tamarind 127
  salmon & mustard seed fishcakes 66
  salmon with red chile & ground fennel 124
  steamed hake with mustard masala 133
flatbreads, cornmeal 278
fritters
  corn bhajias 28
  eggplant pakoras 35

G

Ganapathy, Suman 203-6, 209
garam masala 19
garlic
  lamb shanks with Kashmiri chiles & garlic 196
  potato dumplings with peanut-garlic crumbs 56-7
  red chile & garlic lamb 189
  spinach with garlic, chile & ginger 241
ghee 18
ginger
  brown chickpeas with ginger & mango powder 246
  cauliflower with ginger, turmeric & orange 224
  cinnamon-spiced duck breasts with orange & ginger sauce 174
  ginger-spiced greens 31
  lamb cooked in yogurt with ginger & orange 180
  lentil, ginger & tamarind broth 54
  oyster mushrooms with ginger, black pepper & curry leaves 228
  roast lamb shoulder with ginger & fresh turmeric 199
  spinach with garlic, chile & ginger 241
Goan chorizo rolls 93
Goan short ribs in tamarind masala 213
green beans
  chicken & vegetable poriyal 87
  pot roast beef with vegetables 210
Gujarat 249-52

H

haddock, battered Amritsari 65
hake
  fish fry 61
  hake steaks with coconut & tamarind 127
  steamed hake with mustard masala 133
halwa, butternut squash 297
Hammett, Justin 306
Haryana 129-31, 231-3
Himalayan belt 10, 231-3
homestyle Punjabi chicken curry 136

honey
  phirni with honey, orange & saffron syrup 312
  spiced pear & honey cake 311

I

ice cream
  coconut, lime & buttermilk ice cream 298

J

Jhirad, Yael 61, 119-21, 123

K

kachumber 288
kale
  ginger-spiced greens 31
Karnatka 203-6
Kashmiri lamb pulao 194
Kashmiri lamb with saffron, cardamom & red chiles 177
Kayasth community 101
kebabs
  chicken & red pepper skewers 88
  grilled chicken kebabs in spinach & cilantro cream 78
  grilled paneer 46
  ground lamb kebabs with green chiles, ginger & garlic 69
  peppery lamb kebabs 70
Kerala 165-70
Keralan roast chicken with cinnamon & curry leaves 154
Keralan roast duck 172-3
koftas
  lamb koftas in tomato & cinnamon masala 195
  lentil koftas in tomato, ginger & garlic masala 100-1
kohlrabi cooked in mustard oil with green chiles 235
kokum 116
Konkan egg curry 106
Konkan-style shrimp with mango 62
Kumar, Bridget White 210

L

lagan nu custard 305
lamb
  Bihari lamb broth with dumplings 192-3
  braised lamb with onion & almonds 179
  ground lamb & green chile wraps 74
  ground lamb kebabs with green chiles, ginger & garlic 69
  ground lamb with tomatoes & peas 190
  Kashmiri lamb pulao 194
  Kashmiri lamb with saffron, cardamom & red chiles 177
  lamb cooked in yogurt with ginger & orange 180
  lamb rib chops with mango powder, jaggery & tamarind 73
  lamb koftas in tomato & cinnamon masala 195
  lamb ribs simmered in fennel seed & ginger milk 77
  lamb shanks with Kashmiri chiles & garlic 196
  peppery lamb kebabs 70
  red chile & garlic lamb 189
  roast lamb shoulder with ginger & fresh turmeric 199
  slow-cooked lamb with lentils 176
lemongrass
  chicken with coconut cream & lemongrass 162

lentils
  lentil, ginger & tamarind broth 54
  lentil koftas in tomato, ginger & garlic masala 100–1
  lentil puris 281
  mixed lentil dal 257
  red lentil & tamarind dal 259
  slow-cooked lamb with lentils 176
limes
  coconut, lime & buttermilk ice cream 298
  raisin & lime relish 27
luchis 282

M
Maharashtra 119–21
Mangalorean chicken curry 151–2
mango powder (*amchoor*)
  brown chickpeas with ginger & mango powder 246
  corn-on-the-cob with brown butter, chile & mango powder 50
  lamb rib chops with mango powder, jaggery & tamarind 73
  potatoes with mango powder 45
  sweet potatoes with mango powder & green chiles 43
mangoes
  green mango salad 289
  Konkan-style shrimp with mango 62
  mango, white chocolate & passion fruit pots 306
  moong dal with green mangoes 264
  pork ribs with mango, chile & ginger glaze 200
Marker, Jasmine 301–3, 305
masala
  baby peppers with coconut, tamarind & sesame seeds 236
  baby zucchini in tomato sauce 217
  black-eyed peas in garlic tomato masala 260
  cauliflower with ginger, turmeric & orange 224
  charred broccoli with mushrooms in coconut sauce 98
  clams with chorizo & red chile masala 116
  eggplant pickle 287
  Goan short ribs in tamarind masala 213
  lamb koftas in tomato & cinnamon masala 195
  lentil koftas in tomato, ginger & garlic masala 100–1
  mixed vegetables with ground coriander & garam masala 218
  paneer in ginger & fennel seed masala 97
  peas simmered in fresh cilantro & peanut masala 238
  potato, onion & tomato masala 221
  shrimp biryani 112–13
  steamed hake with mustard masala 133
  see also curry
mascarpone
  mango, white chocolate & passion fruit pots 306
Mattoo, Anita & Umesh 231–3, 235
milk
  almond & saffron barfi 310
  butternut squash halwa 297
  lagan nu custard 305
  lamb ribs simmered in fennel seed & ginger milk 77
  paneer 20
  phirni with honey, orange & saffron syrup 312
  see also condensed milk

mint
  fresh cilantro & mint relish 284
  layered mint parathas 280
  tomato & mint raita 288
moong dal 258
  dry-cooked moong dal with dill 263
  moong dal with green mangoes 264
Mumbai 145–7
Mom's chicken biryani 161
mushrooms
  charred broccoli with mushrooms in coconut sauce 98
  oyster mushrooms with ginger, black pepper & curry leaves 228
  roast portobello mushrooms with cannellini beans 102
mussels in ginger, coconut & red chile broth 114
mustard oil 222
  kohlrabi cooked in mustard oil with green chiles 235
  steamed hake with mustard masala 133
mustard seeds
  cabbage with mustard seeds & curry leaves 223
  panch phoran 20
  stuffed eggs with tomato & popped mustard seeds 32
  tomato dal with mustard seeds & curry leaves 267

N
Northeast India 10
Northwest India 10, 183–5

O
onions
  braised lamb with onion & almonds 179
  ground lamb & green chile wraps 74
  onion & tamarind relish 35
  pickled onion & beet 70
  popadums with red onion, tomato & chaat masala 53
  potato, onion & tomato masala 221
oranges
  cauliflower with ginger, turmeric & orange 224
  cinnamon-spiced duck breasts with orange & ginger sauce 174
  hot rum punch 296
  lamb cooked in yogurt with ginger & orange 180
  phirni with honey, orange & saffron syrup 312
oyster mushrooms with ginger, black pepper & curry leaves 228

P
pakoras, eggplant 35
pancakes
  semolina pancakes with red pepper, tomato & red onion 49
panch phoran 20
  potatoes & pea shoots 222
pandi pork curry 209
paneer 20
  grilled paneer, marinated in saffron & almond yogurt 46
  paneer, cardamom & rosewater sweetmeat 293
  paneer in ginger & fennel seed masala 97
  paneer masala puffs 44
  paneer with green pepper & tomatoes 105
parathas, layered mint 280
Parsi chicken curry with potatoes 157

passion fruit
  mango, white chocolate & passion fruit pots 306
pastries
  paneer masala puffs 44
pea shoots, potatoes & 222
peanuts
  coconut, cilantro & peanut chutney 286
  peanut & coconut crumbs 283
  peas simmered in fresh cilantro & peanut masala 238
  potato dumplings with peanut-garlic crumbs 56-7
pears
  spiced pear & honey cake 311
peas
  ground lamb with tomatoes & peas 190
  peas simmered in fresh cilantro & peanut masala 238
peppercorns
  chaat masala 19
  garam masala 19
peppers
  baby peppers with coconut, tamarind & sesame seeds 236
  chicken & red pepper skewers 88
  paneer with green pepper & tomatoes 105
  semolina pancakes with red pepper, tomato & red onion 49
phirni with honey, orange & saffron syrup 312
pickles
  eggplant pickle 287
  pickled onion & beet 70
pigeon peas, split (toor dal)
  lentil, ginger & tamarind broth 54
  tomato dal with mustard seeds & curry leaves 267
pistachios
  cherry & pistachio pudding 309
  pistachio & cardamom cookies 295
pomegranate powder
  roast chicken thighs with pomegranate & walnut yogurt 158
pomfret
  Bene Israel fish curry 123
Pondicherry 81-3
popadums
  popadum curry 275
  popadums with red onion, tomato & chaat masala 53
pork
  pandi pork curry 209
  pork ribs with mango, chile & ginger glaze 200
  pork with Sichuan pepper 91
potatoes
  cabbage with mustard seeds & curry leaves 223
  cumin potatoes 220
  fried potatoes 173
  Goan short ribs in tamarind masala 213
  Parsi chicken curry with potatoes 157
  pot roast beef with vegetables 210
  potato dumplings with peanut-garlic crumbs 56-7
  potato, onion & tomato masala 221
  potatoes & pea shoots 222
  potatoes with mango powder 45
  salmon & mustard seed fishcakes 66
pulao, Kashmiri lamb 194
punch, hot rum 296
puris, lentil 281

R
raisin & lime relish 27
raita, tomato & mint 288
Rajasthan 269-71
relishes
  fresh cilantro & mint relish 284
  onion & tamarind relish 35
  raisin & lime relish 27
rice
  boiled basmati rice 18
  Kashmiri lamb pulao 194
  Mom's chicken biryani 161
  phirni with honey, orange & saffron syrup 312
  shrimp biryani 112-13
rolls, Goan chorizo 93
rosewater
  paneer, cardamom & rosewater sweetmeat 293
Royal Opera House, London 306
rum
  hot rum punch 296
  roast figs in spiced rum syrup 292

S
saffron
  almond & saffron barfi 310
  grilled paneer, marinated in saffron & almond yogurt 46
  Kashmiri lamb with saffron, cardamom & red chiles 177
  phirni with honey, orange & saffron syrup 312
salads
  carrot salad 289
  green mango salad 289
salmon
  salmon & mustard seed fishcakes 66
  salmon with red chile & ground fennel 124
sauces
  tamarind & date sauce 284
  tomato-chile sauce 283
semolina pancakes with red pepper, tomato & red onion 49
sesame & green chile chutney 285
Shafi, Naved 183-5, 189
Shah, Rasila 249-52, 257
Shetty, Anu 145-7, 151
scallions
  cauliflower cheese with scallions & jalapeño chiles 108-9
shrimp
  brown shrimp with ginger & mustard 58
  Konkan-style shrimp with mango 62
  shrimp biryani 112-13
  shrimp in coconut masala 110
Singh, Bhavna 269-71, 275
South India 11, 81-3, 165-70, 203-6
spice mixes
  chaat masala 19
  garam masala 19
  panch phoran 20
spinach
  chana dal with spinach 245
  ginger-spiced greens 31
  grilled chicken kebabs in spinach & cilantro cream 78
  spinach with garlic, chile & ginger 241

squash
  Bengali-style butternut squash 227
  butternut squash halwa 297
sweet potatoes with mango powder & green chiles 43

T
Taj Mahal Hotel, Delhi 7, 292, 311
tamarind pulp 21
  baby peppers with coconut, tamarind & sesame seeds 236
  chicken curry with tomatoes & tamarind 138
  crushed zucchini with tamarind & jaggery 239
  Goan short ribs in tamarind masala 213
  hake steaks with coconut & tamarind 127
  lentil, ginger & tamarind broth 54
  onion & tamarind relish 35
  red lentil & tamarind dal 259
  tamarind & date sauce 284
taro root with mango powder & green chiles 43
tomatoes
  baby zucchini in tomato sauce 217
  black-eyed peas in garlic tomato masala 260
  cabbage with mustard seeds & curry leaves 223
  chicken curry with tomatoes & tamarind 138
  chicken in roasted coconut masala 139
  chicken with apricots & cinnamon 140-1
  clams with chorizo & red chile masala 116
  Goan short ribs in tamarind masala 213
  homestyle Punjabi chicken curry 136
  kachumber 288
  lamb koftas in tomato & cinnamon masala 195
  lentil koftas in tomato, ginger & garlic masala 100-1
  ground lamb with tomatoes & peas 190
  paneer with green pepper & tomatoes 105
  popadums with red onion, tomato & chaat masala 53
  pork with Sichuan pepper 91
  potato, onion & tomato masala 221
  roast portobello mushrooms with cannellini beans 102
  semolina pancakes with red pepper, tomato & red onion 49
  shrimp biryani 112-13
  stuffed eggs with tomato & popped mustard seeds 32
  tomato & mint raita 288
  tomato-chile sauce 283
  tomato dal with mustard seeds & curry leaves 267
toor dal see pigeon peas, split
turmeric
  cauliflower with ginger, turmeric & orange 224
  roast lamb shoulder with ginger & fresh turmeric 199
  roast spatchcock chicken with turmeric 142

V
vegetables
  mixed vegetables with ground coriander & garam masala 218
  see also peppers, tomatoes *etc*
Vishal, Anoothi 101

W
walnuts
  roast chicken thighs with pomegranate & walnut yogurt 158
Wengers, Delhi 44
West Bengal 129-31
West India 11, 119-21, 145-7, 249-52, 301-3
wraps, ground lamb & green chile 74

Y
yogurt
  Bihari lamb broth with dumplings 192-3
  braised lamb with onion & almonds 179
  chicken in cumin & ground coriander yogurt 135
  Kashmiri lamb with saffron, cardamom & red chiles 177
  Keralan roast chicken with cinnamon & curry leaves 154
  lamb cooked in yogurt with ginger & orange 180
  lamb shanks with Kashmiri chiles & garlic 196
  red chile & garlic lamb 189
  roast chicken thighs with pomegranate & walnut yogurt 158
  slow-cooked lamb with lentils 176
  spiced yogurt 46
  tomato & mint raita 288

Z
zucchini
  baby zucchini in tomato sauce 217
  crushed zucchini with tamarind & jaggery 239

BIOGRAPHY

Brought up in Cumbria, England, Roopa Gulati lived in India for two decades, working as a chef at the Taj Mahal Hotel in New Delhi, and as a writer and broadcaster. On her return to the UK, she was Food Editor at UKTV's Good Food Channel and a restaurant reviewer with Time Out for 15 years. As a freelance journalist, she researches material for TV shows and contributes recipe features to national food magazines. Her previous book *India: The World Vegetarian* is published by Bloomsbury Absolute.

ACKNOWLEDGMENTS

This book owes so much to my brilliant publishing team, the steadfast support of friends and family, and the splendid home cooks across India and beyond.

Thank you, Rowan Yapp, Head of Lifestyle, for commissioning me to write *Indian Kitchens*. Emily North, this is the second project we've worked on together and I've enjoyed shaping stories and recipes under your editorial guidance. To my agent, Sabhbh Curran, your support and strength have kept me going throughout.

Dear Yuki Sugiura, I love your photography for these recipes, and thank you for the warm and generous welcome to your studio. Valerie Berry, your culinary skill is legendary—your homemade stock and grandma's cast iron pot did my curries proud. Jen Kay, I've really admired the way in which you've curated colors, textures and materials for dishes featured in this book. And, Alice Earll, it's been an honor to work alongside a first rate cook as well as a professional violinist. We are an outstanding photoshoot team.

A special mention to my copy editor, Jude Barratt, for her attention to detail, and to Sarah Greeno for the stunning design and page layout. I've been a friend of Susan Low for two decades and am especially appreciative of her honed scrutiny of this book in its final stages.

I traveled to India with my dear friend Ruth Spooner to meet twelve home cooks and their families. I remember us unfolding a huge map of India and making a list of potential destinations. Never has a felt-tip pen wielded so much power.

Sadly, both Ruth and my husband, Dan, fell ill in 2023. They have since been cared for by the wonderful medical team at University College Hospital, London. I thank the NHS for the gift of life.

Thank you, Diana Henry, for the lifeline calls at midnight and for your unwavering support. Our friendship is one that has been forged over many masalas and dals.

Ravinder Bhogal, you have been by my side during uncertain times, and we will have much to celebrate in the years ahead. Thank you for our shared suppers at your gorgeous restaurant, Jikoni.

Dear Madhu Colwill, you flew from the UK to India to introduce me to your extended family in rural Gujarat. I arrived as your pal and left feeling like a member of the Shah family.

Jane Mote and husband Jerry, thank you for showing me how to film and edit videos on my iPhone. I'm also grateful that you answered my cry for help when the microphone failed in Rajasthan.

Denise Wallin, when I needed it most, you took me out of the kitchen and into several cocktail bars—your thoughtfulness is nothing short of 24-carat gold.

Every Thursday at 6am, I walk around Pinner with my fitness coach, Andrew Kailou. He listens to a roll call of my real-life dramas as we stomp around our patch. Andrew, thank you for caring when I tell you that I have cremated the dal, and for supporting me through life's ups and downs.

To my family for keeping me on the straight and narrow—Bela, Rasagee, Anashri and daughters Malvika and Pallavi and their families. Thank you.

And most of all, to dearest Dan, for being there for me, and being here with me today, as I sign off on *Indian Kitchens*.